# CULTURE AS PRAXIS

# Theory, Culture & Society

*Theory, Culture & Society* caters for the resurgence of interest in culture within contemporary social science and the humanities. Building on the heritage of classical social theory, the book series examines ways in which this tradition has been reshaped by a new generation of theorists. It also publishes theoretically informed analyses of everyday life, popular culture, and new intellectual movements.

EDITOR: Mike Featherstone, *Nottingham Trent University*

SERIES EDITORIAL BOARD
Roy Boyne, *University of Durham*
Mike Hepworth, *University of Aberdeen*
Scott Lash, *Goldsmiths College, University of London*
Roland Robertson, *University of Pittsburgh*
Bryan S. Turner, *University of Cambridge*

THE TCS CENTRE
The Theory, Culture & Society book series, the journals *Theory, Culture & Society* and *Body & Society*, and related conference, seminar and postgraduate programmes operate from the TCS Centre at Nottingham Trent University. For further details of the TCS Centre's activities please contact:

Centre Administrator
The TCS Centre, Room 175
Faculty of Humanities
Nottingham Trent University
Clifton Lane, Nottingham, NG11 8NS, UK
e-mail: tcs@ntu.ac.uk

*Recent volumes include:*

**The Shopping Experience**
*edited by Pasi Falk and Colin Campbell*

**Undoing Aesthetics**
*Wolfgang Welsch*

**Simmel on Culture: Selected Writings**
*edited by David Frisby and Mike Featherstone*

**Nation Formation**
Toward a Theory of Abstract Community
*Paul James*

**Contested Natures**
*Phil Macnaghten and John Urry*

**The Consumer Society**
Myths and Structures
*Jean Baudrillard*

**Georges Bataille – Essential Writings**
*edited by Michael Richardson*

**Digital Aesthetics**
*Sean Cubitt*

**Facing Modernity**
Ambivalence, Reflexivity and Morality
*Barry Smart*

# CULTURE AS PRAXIS

## New Edition

ZYGMUNT BAUMAN

SAGE Publications
London • Thousand Oaks • New Delhi

© Zygmunt Bauman 1999

This edition published 1999

First edition published by Routledge & Kegan Paul Ltd 1973

SAGE Publications Ltd
6 Bonhill Street
London EC2A 4PU

SAGE Publications Inc
2455 Teller Road
Thousand Oaks, California 91320

SAGE Publications India Pvt Ltd
32, M-Block Market
Greater Kailash – I
New Delhi 110 048

Published in association with *Theory, Culture & Society*,
Nottingham Trent University

**British Library Cataloguing in Publication data**
A catalogue record for this book is available
from the British Library

ISBN 0 7619 5988 2
ISBN 0 7619 5989 0 (pbk)

**Library of Congress catalog card number   98–75101**

Typeset by M Rules
Printed in Great Britain by The Cromwell Press Ltd,
Trowbridge, Wiltshire

# CONTENTS

# INTRODUCTION

Reprinting a book born almost three decades earlier calls for an explanation. If the author happens to be still alive, the job of explaining falls upon him.

The first part of the job is to find out what in the book is still, after all these years, topical and fresh enough to justify offering it once more to readers – to different readers, a generation or two younger than those who might have read the book when it was first published. The second task is opposite, but also complementary to the first: it is to ponder what the author would have changed in the text were he writing it anew or for the first time.

The first is not an easy task by any standard, given the mind-boggling speed with which all ideas vanish and fall into oblivion before given the chance of maturing and ageing properly in our era of thoughts and things calculated, as George Steiner put it, 'for maximal impact and instant obsolescence'; an era in which, as another writer reputedly observed, the shelf-life of a bestselling book is somewhere between milk and yoghourt. At first sight, a daunting, perhaps altogether impossible task . . .

Some consolation may be drawn, though, from the not at all fanciful suspicion that given the speed with which fashionable 'talks of the town' are replaced and forgotten, one cannot be really sure that the bygone ideas have truly aged, outlived their use and been abandoned by reason of their obsolescence. Do topics stop being talked about because they have lost their topicality, or do they cease to be topical because people have become tired of talking about them? About us, social scientists, Gordon Allport once said that we never solve any problems, we only get bored by them. But since then it has become a trade-mark of our society as a whole that we no longer move, nor believe to be moving, 'forward', but sideways and often from back to front and back again. On the other hand, we live in an era of re-cycling; nothing seems to die once for all, and nothing – even eternal life – seems to be destined to last forever.

And so ideas may be buried alive – well before they are 'quite dead' – their apparent death being just the artefact of their disappearance from view; it is the act of burial, rather than any clinical test, that warrants the death certificate. If dug up from the collective amnesia to which they have been consigned to hibernate, they may – who knows? – earn (again not for long, to be sure) another lease of life. And not just because they have not been squeezed really dry at the time of their first visit, but because, as the dynamics of discourses go, ideas prod the debate and set it moving 'by impact', hardly ever following that initial effect with full assimilation. There is in principle no limit to the number of repeated entries; each time the impact has a novel effect – as if the entry had happened for the first time. If it is true that one cannot enter 'the same' river twice, it is also true that the river of thoughts cannot be entered twice by 'the same' idea. We proceed nowadays not so much by continuous and cumulative learning, as through a mixture of forgetting and recalling.

This seems to be in itself a good enough reason to republish a book; all the more so for the fact that it would not return alone. It was written in active dialogue with other books, then in the forefront of the intellectual debate, but now also gathering dust on library shelves; recalling the problems they jointly struggled with and tried to resolve will not be amiss for all immersed and engrossed in present-day concerns.

The second of the two tasks is, on the face of it at least, simpler; it is also, for the author, more gratifying. It calls for something which authors have seldom time to do in their day-to-day thinking and writing: looking back at the road they passed – or rather arranging the scattered footprints into a simile of a road. While answering that call, authors have a rare chance to imagine (discover? invent?) a logical progression in what they lived through as a succession of 'one at a time' problems and one-off themes: the task normally left to the students charged with dissertations about their work. And confronting once more their own early thoughts, authors may bring in sharper relief their present ideas. All identities, after all – including the identities of ideas – are made of differences and continuities.

The aim of this introduction is an attempt to fulfil both tasks.

To anticipate the direction this attempt is about to take: when read thirty years after it was written, the book seems to pass well the test of 'truth'. It fares somewhat less well in the test of 'nothing but the truth'. And it fails rather abominably the test of 'the whole truth'. I believe that most of what is wrong with it is what is missing – but should be present, as I see it now, in any account of culture that aims to be comprehensive and sustained. Were I to write this book again, I would perhaps delete little of the old text, but would in all probability add quite a few topics and most certainly would reshuffle the emphases. The rest of the introduction, therefore, will contain some revisions, but will focus mainly on filling the blank spots which the original text unwittingly entailed.

One more observation is in order, particularly in view of the notoriously short span of our collective memory. A book on culture written thirty years ago was bound to confront readers very different from those likely to be present at its second incarnation. Few allowances on the readers' entrenched ideas could be made at that time, while today the same book may count on readers well seasoned in the 'problematics of culture', with basic cognitive frames and essential concepts firmly in place. Certain ideas which had to be laboriously explained thirty years ago would seem now self-evident to the point of triviality.

The most conspicuous case in point is the very notion of culture: in Britain that notion was almost completely absent from the public, and particularly the social-scientific, discourse of the 1960s – and that notwithstanding early

Matthew Arnold's pioneering effort to insert it into the vocabulary of the British learned classes and the later valiant struggle for its legitimacy waged by Raymond Williams and Stuart Hall. I readily admit that – fortunately for British learned opinion – it is difficult to believe today that such was the state of affairs a mere thirty years ago; but quite a few years after the first edition of this book had appeared I went through the agony of explaining to the illustrious scholars sitting on the university planning committee what the word 'culture' stands for; the occasion was the proposal to institute an inter-departmental Centre for Cultural Studies – then an exceedingly rare species in the British Isles. Neither was the idea of structure as a diachronic rather than synchronic phenomenon easy to convey and be grasped and digested by prospective readers before Anthony Giddens' 'structuration' made it into the canon of first-year sociology courses.

It seems to be a general rule that what was once a daring intellectual adventure turns into the thoughtless repetitiveness of routine; it is in the nature of ideas that they are born as off-putting heresies and die as boring orthodoxies. It takes a lot of imaginative power to resurrect, let alone to relive, their once potent emancipatory, thought-provoking impact: for instance the excitement caused by Claude Lévi-Strauss' view of culture as an endless series of permutations. After all, the function of all routine is to make reflection, scrutiny, testing, vigilance and other costly and time-consuming efforts into luxuries one can do without.

And so, in addition to the two tasks previously mentioned, it is incumbent on the author to resharpen some of the by now 'routine' ideas with the hope to restore, if at all possible, their cutting power; or, if you wish, to resurrect in a lullaby its past of the clarion call. . .

## Culture as self-consciousness of modern society

In tune with the prevalent sociological vision of three decades ago, I viewed culture as a feature of social reality; one of the many 'social facts' to be adequately grasped, described and represented. The main concern of the now republished book was how to do this properly. I assumed that there was an objective phenomenon called 'culture' which – because of the notorious 'knowledge lag' – might have been discovered belatedly, but since discovered could be deployed as an objective reference point against which the propriety of any cognitive model could be measured and assessed. There might have been three different discourses in which the same term was turned around, causing a degree of semantic confusion; one therefore needed to separate them carefully, so that the meaning in which the term 'culture' is used in each case would be clear and uncontaminated by other uses, but the presence, cohabitation and mutual interference of the three discourses seemed to me then, by itself, unproblematic. Another 'social fact', not a puzzle calling for the effort of an archaeological dig or needing to be 'deconstructed'. There was as yet no Foucault nor Derrida around to help . . .

It is a paradox of sorts that the deconstruction of the concept of culture came eventually in the wake of 'culturalization' of social sciences. Originally, in the second half of the eighteenth century, the idea of culture was coined to separate human accomplishments from the 'hard and fast' facts of nature. 'Culture' stood for what humans can do; 'nature' for what humans must obey. The overall trend of social thought through the nineteenth century, culminating in Émile Durkheim's concept of 'social facts', was, however, to 'naturalize' culture: cultural facts might be human products, but once produced they confront their erstwhile authors with all the unyielding and indomitable obstinacy of nature – and the efforts of social thinkers focused on the task of showing that this is so and explaining the whys and hows of it being so. It is only in the second part of the twentieth century that the trend began gradually yet resolutely to reverse: the time of 'culturalization' of nature has arrived.

What possibly could be the reason for such a turnabout? One can only surmise that after an era dominated by the frantic search for solid and unshakable foundations of human order conscious of its fragility and lacking in confidence came a time when the thick layer of human artifices made nature all but invisible – and its boundaries, particularly the yet impassable ones among them, ever more distant and exotic. Man-made foundations of human existence reached deep enough to make all care of other, better foundations redundant. The era of counter-attack could start: the weapons, the will and the self-confidence were all in place by now. No longer did 'culture' have to mask its own human fragility and apologize for the contingency of its choices. Naturalization of culture was part and parcel of the modern disenchantment of the world. Its deconstruction, which followed the culturalization of nature, was made possible – perhaps inevitable – by the world's postmodern re-enchantment.

Reinhart Koselleck baptized the eighteenth century 'the age of mountain-passes' ('Sattelzeit').[1] It deserves that name since before that century ended a steep philosophical watershed of sorts was negotiated and left behind, simultaneously in several points; for the story of human thinking the consequences of that event were not a bit less seminal than those of Caesar's crossing the Rubicon were for political history. In 1765, the concept of 'philosophy of history' appeared in Voltaire's *Essai sur les moeurs*, spawning a spate of *geschichtsphilosophische* tracts. In 1719, Gottfried Müller began to teach a course in philosophical anthropology, in which the Carthesian cognitive subject was expanded to the life-size model of the 'whole man'. And in 1750 Alexander Gottlieb Baumgarten published his *Aesthetica*, which expanded the idea of the 'humanity' of human beings yet further, adding to rational faculties those of sensibility and the creative urge. All in all, a vision of 'man' emerged which for the next two hundred years or so was to serve as the hub around which the imagery of the world rotated.

That was a new vision, a collective product of a new philosophy; one that viewed the world as an essentially human creation and a testing ground for human faculties. From now on, the world was to be understood primarily as the setting for human pursuits, choices, triumphs and blunders. In an attempt to explain the abrupt appearance of a new *Weltanschauung*, Odo Marquard quotes Joachim Ritter: suddenly, the future was 'uncoupled' from the past – the realization had dawned that a future which has its starting point in human society is not continuous with the past. Koselleck himself points to the new experience of a gap between reality and expectation; one could no more remain a creature of habit, one could no more deduce the future state of affairs from their present and past stages. With the pace of change accelerating by the year, the world appeared ever less God-like – that is, ever less eternal, impervious and intractable. It assumed instead an ever more human form, becoming more in 'man's image' – protean, fickle and flickering, whimsical and full of surprise.

There was more to it though: the fast pace of change revealed the temporality of all wordly arrangements, and temporality is a feature of human, not divine, existence. What seemed a few generations ago a divine creation, a verdict against which appeals could not be lodged with any of the earthly courts, looked now suspiciously to be the stubborn trace of human – right or wrong, but mortal and revocable – undertakings. And if the impression was not misleading, then the world and the way people lived in it was a task, rather than something given and unalterable. Depending on how people went about it, this task could be fulfilled in a more or less satisfactory fashion. It could be botched, but it could be also performed well, to the benefit of human happiness, the safety and meaningfulness of human life. To secure success and avoid failure, it was necessary to start with a careful inventory of human resources: what people can do, if they stretch their cognitive faculties, logical capacity and determination to the utmost.

This was, in a nutshell, the premise of the new *Weltanschauung*: of modern humanism, of which John Carroll wrote that[2]

> it attempted to replace God by man, to put man in the centre of the universe. . . . Its ambition was to found a human order on earth, in which freedom and happiness prevailed, without any transcendental or supernatural supports – an entirely human order. . . . But if the human individual were to become the still-point of the universe he had to have somewhere to stand that would not move from under his feet. Humanism had to build a rock. It had to create out of nothing something as strong as the faith of the New Testament that could move mountains.

In *Legislators and Interpreters* (Polity Press 1987) I traced the common roots and the mutual resonance, the 'elective affinity' between the new challenge confronting the managers of social life – the task to replace the crumbling divine or natural order of things with a man-made, artificial, legislatively-grounded one – and the philosophers' concern with replacing revelation with rationally-grounded truth. The two essentially modern and closely intertwined concerns converged on the third – the pragmatics of order-making, entailing the technology of behavioural control and education: the technique of mind- and will-shaping. All three newly-aroused, yet acute and overwhelming interests were to come together and blend in the idea of 'culture' –, that fourth alongside *Geschichtsphilosophie*, anthropology and

aesthetics, and perhaps the most salient among them, markers of the eigh-
teenth-century 'mountain pass'.

What brought seventeenth-century thought to the mountain pass was the
gnawing doubt in the reliability of the Divine guarantees of human conditions. Non-negotiable verdicts of the Supreme Power looked suddenly to be
sediments of sometimes human wisdom, sometimes human ignorance or stupidity; indomitable fate, pre-determined at the moment of Creation, began to
appear more like a moment in history – a human accomplishment and a
challenge to human wits and will; not an open-and-shut case, but an unfinished chapter waiting to be completed by the characters of the plot. In other
words, beneath the meanders of fate human self-determination had been
adumbrated.

Freedom of self-determination is a blessing – and a curse. Exhilarating for
the bold and resourceful, frightening for the weak-in-spirit, weak-in-arms or
weak-in-resolve. But there is more. Freedom is a social relation: for some to
be free to achieve their purpose, others must be unfree to resist. One's own
freedom may be off-putting, given that it is pregnant with the risk of error;
but the freedom of others looks at first sight to be a noxious obstacle to
one's own liberty of action. Even if one's own freedom may be contemplated
as unpolluted bliss, the prospect of the unbound freedom of all the others is
seldom relished. For even the most ardent enthusiasts of human self-determination the thought of 'necessary constraints' was hardly ever totally alien.
In its most radical manifestation, embodied in the idea of emancipation and
transcendence, the apotheosis of human freedom was as a rule complemented
by worry about the limits which need to be imposed upon the actions of pro-
tagonists. What was proudly named an exercise of free will in one's own case
tended to be dubbed freakishness, irresponsibility, prejudice or just an ill-
intended whim when contemplated as a universally available possibility. The
heralds of double standards did not always dare to go as far as did the
allegedly proto-fascist Nietzsche ('the great majority of men have no right to
existence, but are a misfortune to higher men'[3]) or the socialist H. G. Wells
('swarms of black, and brown, and dirty-white, and yellow people', who do
not meet the high criteria set for human self-assertiveness, 'have to go'[4]), but
none would entertain any doubt as to the need to tie the hands that could not
be trusted.

The idea of culture which came into common use towards the end of the
eighteenth century faithfully reflected that attitudinal ambivalence. The dou-
ble-edged – simultaneously 'enabling' and 'constraining' – character of
culture, much written about in recent years, was in fact present in the vision
of culture since its inception. In one 'universally human' model of culture two
sharply different human predicaments were to be merged into the joint condition, and so there was a paradox endemic to that concept of culture from
the start.

The concept was coined to set apart and bring into focus a growing area of
human condition deemed to be 'under-determined', or such as could not be
fully determined without the mediation of human choices: an area which for

that reason opened up a space for freedom and self-assertion. But the concept was meant to stand simultaneously for the mechanism which allowed the use of that very freedom to limit its scope, to enclose potentially infinite choices in a finite, comprehensible and manageable pattern. The idea of 'culture' served the reconciliation of a whole series of oppositions unnerving due to their ostensible incompatibility: those of freedom and necessity, of the voluntary and the constrained, of teleological and causal, chosen and determined, random and patterned, contingent and law-abiding, creative and routine, novel and repetitive; in short, of self-assertion and normative regulation. The concept of culture was designed to respond to the concerns and anxieties of the 'mountain-passes era' – and the response was bound to be as ambiguous as the longings born of those anxieties were ambivalent.

Writers on culture tried in earnest to efface the ambiguity; they could not succeed, though, since the idea of culture as 'self-determined determination' owes its intellectual attraction precisely to the resonance of its inner ambivalence with the endemic ambivalences of the modern condition; it makes little sense unless it attempts to 'ground' simultaneously freedom and unfreedom. In this respect it is bound to share the quality of 'undecidability' with the Derridean *pharmacon* (drug), simultaneously poison and cure, or *hymen*, simultaneously virginity and its loss. . .

The discourse of culture has been notorious for blending themes and perspectives which scarcely fit together in one cohesive, non-contradictory narrative. The volume of 'anomalies' and logical incongruities would have long exploded the most enduring of Kuhnian 'paradigms'. It is difficult to conceive of a discourse which would better illustrate Foucault's point about the capacity of discursive formations for generating mutually contradictory propositions without falling apart.

Thirty years ago I tried to disentangle the incoherences evident in the usages of 'culture' through separating three distinct discursive contexts in which the concept was entangled, while drawing different meanings from each of the contexts. In that attempt, I assumed that the incoherences in question were in principle rectifiable; I was guided by the belief that they have arisen from mainly analytical faults, and by the hope that with due care the confusion of distinct categories hiding behind one term might be avoided and prevented. I still think that keeping apart the three discourses which offer three related, yet different, meanings to the idea of culture remains a preliminary condition of any attempt to clarify the subject of disagreement, but I no longer believe that this operation will eventually remove the ambivalence which the discourse of culture necessarily contains. More importantly, I do not think that the elimination of such ambivalence, were it at all conceivable, would be a good thing, enhancing as it were the cognitive usefulness of the term. Above all, I no longer accept that the ambivalence which truly matters – one which prompted me to dissect the complex meaning of culture in the first place but stayed unaffected by the operation and remained an elusive target – was an accidental effect of methodological neglect or error. I believe, on the contrary, that the inherent ambivalence of the idea of culture which faithfully reflected the ambiguity of the historical condition it was meant to capture and narrate was exactly what made that idea such a fruitful and enduring tool of perception and thought.

The ambiguity which truly matters, the sense-giving ambivalence, the genuine foundation on which the cognitive usefulness of conceiving human habitat as the 'world of culture' rests, is the ambivalence between 'creativity' and 'normative regulation'. The two ideas could not be further apart, yet both are – and must remain – present in the composite idea of culture. 'Culture' is as much about inventing as it is about preserving; about discontinuity as much as about continuation; about novelty as much as about tradition; about routine as much as about pattern-breaking; about norm-following as much as about the transcendence of norm; about the unique as much as about the regular; about change as much as about monotony of reproduction; about the unexpected as much as about the predictable.

The core ambivalence of the concept of 'culture' reflects the ambivalence of the idea of order-making, that hub of all modern existence. Man-made order is unthinkable without human freedom to choose, human capacity to rise imaginatively above reality, to withstand and push back its pressures. But inseparable from the idea of man-made order is the postulate that freedom is to result in the end in establishing a reality which cannot be so resisted; that freedom is to be deployed in the service of its own cancellation.

That *logical* contradiction in the *idea* of order-making is in its turn a reflection of the genuine *social* contradiction constituted through the order-making *practice*.

'Order' is the opposite of randomness. It stands for the trimming down of the range of possibilities. A temporal sequence is 'ordered' and not random in as far as not everything may happen or at least not everything is equally likely to happen. To 'make order' means, in other words, to manipulate the probabilities of events. If it is a set of human beings that is to be ordered, the task consists in increasing the probability of certain patterns of behaviour while diminishing, or eliminating altogether, the likelihood of other kinds of conduct. That task entails two requisites: first, an optimal distribution of probabilities has to be designed; second, obedience to the designed preferences has to be secured. The first requisite calls for freedom of choice; the second spells out the limitation or total elimination of choice.

Both requisites had been projected upon the image of culture. The genuine opposition between the conditions of legislating and being legislated about, managing and being managed, setting the rules and rule-following (the opposition sedimented in equally genuine social divisions of roles and potentials for actions), had to be subsumed, reconciled, overcome and obliterated in one concept: a project unlikely ever to be successfully completed.

The idea of culture was a historical invention, prompted by the urge to assimilate intellectually an undoubtedly historical experience. And yet the idea itself could not grasp that experience otherwise than in supra-historical terms, in terms of the human condition as such. Complexities revealed in the course of grappling with a historically determined task of order-making (no determination imposes itself, Gadamer pointed out, unless it is recognized as such) were, through the idea of culture as the universal property of all human forms of life, elevated to the rank of the existential paradox of humanity.

As Paul Ricoeur reminds us, 'paradox' shares with 'antinomy' the traits of unresolvability: in both cases 'two adversary propositions equally strongly resist refutation and so can be only accepted jointly or jointly rejected'; but paradox differs from antinomy in that in its case the two theses in question are grounded in the same 'discursive universe'. In this sense, one may speak of the incurable *paradoxicality* of the idea of culture as formed at the threshold of modern era, yet projected upon the human condition of all times, since irreconcilable ideas assimilated in that concept arose from the same historical experience.

The paradox arising within the universe of cultural discourse is that of *autonomy* and *vulnerability* – or, as Ricoeur prefers, *fragility*. The autonomous human being cannot but be fragile; there can be no autonomy without fragility (i.e. without the absence of a solid foundation, without under-determination and contingency); 'autonomy is a feature of the fragile, vulnerable being'. Let us observe that the intimate link between autonomy and fragility becomes a 'paradox' only when conceived as a problem for philosophy, which is bound, by its nature, to seek *Eindeutigkeit*, logic, coherence and clarity in the world which possesses none of these traits, and treat all ambivalence as a challenge to reason. When seen as a problem of philosophy, the kinship of autonomy and vulnerability presents indeed a vexing problem: figures of vulnerability and fragility[5]

> carry particular marks, proper for our modernity, which makes philosophical discourse difficult, condemning it to mix considerations of modern and even extremely contemporary condition with features which can be treated as if not universal then at least as of long or even very long duration.

We may add that what makes the philosophical treatment accorded to the issue of autonomy/fragility particularly prospectless is its refusal to take history seriously (as the *cause* of the 'human condition', rather than its exemplifying *case*); the refusal which brings in its wake the tendency to gloss over sociological contradictions which are mirrored in logical paradoxes. Sociologically speaking, the pair autonomy/fragility reflects the polarization of capacity and incapacity, resourcefulness and the lack of resources, power and powerlessness of self-assertion. Essentially modern is the condition under which the place between the two poles which mark the continuum along which all human individuals are plotted is never fully 'grounded', being forever subject to continuous negotiation and struggle. It is the fate of modern – unbound and thus under-determined – individuals, under-constituted and thus doomed to self-constitution, to veer between the extremes of might and powerlessness and so to perceive of their freedom as a 'mixed blessing', a modality saturated with ambivalence.

When translated as a philosophical problem, the real ambivalence of life becomes a logical paradox. No more is there a problem of coping with ambivalence which structures the flow of real life; instead there is a problem of refuting a paradox which offends logic. As Ricoeur puts it:[6]

> numerous contemporary thinkers, and particularly the politologists, view the era of democracy as starting from the loss of transcendental guarantees, which left to contractual and procedural arrangements the task of filling the 'foundational void'. . . . [However, they] cannot avoid situating themselves in a certain sense after the foundations, after a moral Big Bang, and assuming the phenomenon of authority with its three limbs of antecedence, superiority and externality.

The philosophers' urge to ablate in thought the contradictoriness of life is overwhelming and unlikely ever to lose much of its power. Contradictions rebound as paradoxes: painful thorns in the flesh of philosophy – that Herculean project of remaking the messy world of human experience after the pattern of elegance and harmony to be found solely in the serene orderliness of thought.

The concept of culture bears all the marks of that philosophical urge. It incorporates the vision of the modern human condition already recycled as a logical paradox. It is aimed at overcoming the opposition between autonomy and vulnerability conceived as *propositions* – while glossing over the 'real life' contradiction between the autonomous and the vulnerable: between the task of self-constitution and the fact of being constituted.

With the effort to resolve the paradox bringing no convincing results, no wonder that another tendency is born to set the two awkwardly embraced propositions apart; to forget or play down the common origin and commonality of fate, to shift the unresolvable *paradox* of two incompatible qualities blossoming from the same root to the status of *antinomy* between two mutually alien and unrelated forces – of a war waged between separate armies, and thus a war capable in principle of being won or lost, of ending in the ultimate defeat or attrition of one of the antagonists. Ideas which cannot be easily blended within one concept tend to exert a centrifugal pressure and sooner or later explode the fragile totality.

No wonder two different and not easily reconcilable discourses ramified from the common stem, shifting ever further apart. To put it in a nutshell: one discourse generated the idea of culture as the activity of the free roaming spirit, the site of creativity, invention, self-critique and self-transcendence; another discourse posited culture as a tool of routinization and continuity – a handmaiden of social order.

The product of the first discourse was the notion of culture as the capacity to resist the norm and rise above the ordinary – *poïesis*, arts, God-like creation *ab nihilo*. It stood for what the most daring, the least compliant and conformist spirits were assumed to be distinguished by: irreverence to tradition, the courage to break well-drawn horizons, to step beyond closely-guarded boundaries and blaze new trails. Culture so understood could be possessed or not; it was the property of a minority and bound to remain so. To the rest of humanity it came at best in the form of a gift: it sedimented 'works of art', tangible objects which could be appropriated or at least learned to be appreciated by others – non-creative beings. Their efforts to learn how to appreciate the products of high culture would not make them creative; they would remain, as before, more or less passive recipients (viewers, listeners, readers). But gaining obliquely an insight into the arcane world of high spirit, the non-creative majority will nevertheless become 'better beings' – undergo a process of spiritual uplifting, enhancement and ennoblement.

The product of the second discourse was the notion of culture formed and applied in orthodox anthropology. There, 'culture' stood for regularity and pattern – with freedom cast under the rubric of 'norm-breaking' and 'deviation'. Culture was an aggregate, or better still a coherent system of sanction-supported pressures, interiorized values and norms, and habits which assured repetitiveness (and thus also predictability) of conduct at the individual level and the monotony of reproduction, continuity over time, 'preservation of tradition', Ricoeur's *mêmeté*, at the level of collectivity. 'Culture' in this sense stood, in other words, for 'filling the gap' left by the disappearance of the pre-ordained order (either in factual experience or as an explanatory device). It conveyed an image of volatile, indeterminate choices solidifying into foundations. It implied the 'naturalization' of artificial, man-made order; it told the story of the fashion in which a species doomed to freedom used that freedom to conjure up necessities no less overwhelming and resilient than those of blind, purposeless 'nature'. The orthodox anthropological narrative of 'culture' emerged in the early-modern times of 'order panic' as simultaneously a theory of social coherence and a moral tale.

The two notions of culture stood in stark opposition to each other. One denied what the other proclaimed; one focused on the aspects of human reality which the other presented as impossible or, at best, as abnormality. 'Artistic culture' explained why human ways and means do not last; the culture of orthodox anthropology, on the contrary, explained why they are durable, obstinate and tremendously difficult to change. The first was the story of human freedom, of the randomness and contingency of all man-made forms of life; the second assigned to freedom and contingency a role akin to aetiological myths, concentrating instead on the ways in which their order-disrupting potency is defused and devoid of consequence.

It is the second story that prevailed in social sciences for a century or so. It reached its fullest rendition (expectedly, just when it was about to collapse and lose authority) in the monumental theoretical system of Talcott Parsons, in which culture was allotted the role of a 'de-randomizing' factor.

Parsons rewrote the story of social science as a succession of failed attempts to answer the Hobbesian query: how is it that human voluntary agents, endowed with free will and pursuing their ostensibly individual and freely chosen objectives, behave nevertheless in a remarkably uniform and regular fashion so that their conduct 'follows a pattern'? In the sought-after proper answer to that vexing question, Parsons asserted, culture is called to play a decisive role of the medium assuring the 'fit' between 'social' and 'personality' systems; 'Without culture neither human personalities nor human social systems would be possible'; both are possible only in their mutual coordination, and culture is precisely the system of ideas or beliefs, of expressive symbols and value-orientations, which secures that coordination in perpetuity.[7]

> Selections [of value-orientations] are of course always actions of individuals, but these selections *cannot be* inter-individually random in a social system. Indeed, one of the most important functional imperatives of the maintenance of social systems is that the value-orientations of different actors in the same social system *must be* integrated in some measure in a *common* system. . . . The sharing of value-orientations is especially crucial. . . . The regulation of all these allocative processes and the performance of the functions which keep the system or the subsystem going in a sufficiently integrated manner *is impossible* without a system of definitions of roles and sanctions for conformity or deviation.

'Cannot be', 'must be', 'is impossible' . . . If not for the coordinative function performed by the shared and consensually accepted values, precepts and role-ascribed norms (i.e. by culture) no orderly life (i.e. no self-equilibrating and self-perpetuating, durable, identity-retaining system) is thinkable. Culture is the social system's service station; through penetrating the 'personality systems' in the course of pattern-maintenance efforts (i.e. through being 'internalized' in the process of 'socialization'), it secures the system's 'identity with itself' over time – it 'keeps society going' in its distinctly recognizable form.

Parsons' culture, in other words, is what makes the departure from an established pattern impossible, or at least highly improbable. Culture is an immobilizing, 'stabilizing' factor; indeed, it stabilizes so well that unless culture 'malfunctions' all change of pattern is incredible and the actual occurrence of change is a puzzle which cannot be solved within the frame of the same theory which accounts for the system's inertia. In the ideal-typical description of culture in terms of the 'must's and 'cannot but's, there was no room for the alteration of entrenched patterns. Explaining change was the notorious Achilles' heel of the Parsonian (and the most authoritative) version of the orthodox view of culture, but one that only brought into sharper relief what had been the essential weakness of the extant cultural-anthropology approach.

It was that weakness which eventually dashed all hope of escaping the paradox of culture by cutting the coin in half and handling each of its two faces separately. The current state of cultural theorizing reflects the new determination (or resigned consent) to face the paradox in all its complexity, in all the ambivalence of enabling/disabling, of freedom/constraint.

As in the case of so many 'new' ideas in social theory, it was Georg Simmel who – long before Parsons' abortive and self-defeating attempt to by-pass the paradox by reducing the image of culture to just one of its two inseparable faces – anticipated the ultimate futility of all such trials, and the need of a theorization of culture such as would embrace the endemic ambivalence of the cultural existential mode and would try neither to theorize it away nor to play it down as a mere error of method.

Simmel preferred to speak of the tragedy, rather than the paradox, of culture. In his view, the simile most fitting to cope with the mysteries of culture was to be drawn from the universe of Greek drama rather than from that of logical embarrassment. Indeed, in the human existential mode two formidable forces stood against each other in radical contrast: 'subjective life, which is restless but finite in time, and its contents, which, once they are created, are fixed but timelessly valid. . . . Culture comes into being by a meeting of the two elements, neither of which contain culture by itself.'[8] What makes the drama into real tragedy is the fact that the two adversaries are close relatives. The 'fixed and timelessly valid' is the offspring of the 'restless and finite' – nothing but the solidified, 'reified' trace of the latter's past self-expressive labours; but it confronts its parent, Electra-style, as an alien, hostile force. The emancipatory drive gave birth to constraint, restlessness rebounds in fixity: the unruly and intractable spirit creates its own shackles.

> We speak of culture whenever life produces certain forms in which it expresses and realises itself – works of art, religions, sciences, technologies, laws and innumerable others. These forms encompass the flow of life and provide it with content and form, freedom and order. But although these forms arise out of the life process, because of their unique constellation they do not share the restless rhythm of life. . . . They acquire fixed identities, a logic and lawfulness of their own; this new rigidity inevitably places them at a distance from the spiritual dynamic which created them and which makes them independent. . . .
>	Herein lies the ultimate reason why culture has a history. . . . Each cultural form, once it is created, is gnawed at varying rates by the force of life. . . .

The battle never stops; it is all cultures' proper mode of life. Sedimentation of forms and their erosion go hand in hand, though they proceed 'at varying rates', and so the balance between the two aspects of the cultural process changes from one time to another. Our own – modern – times are, according to Simmel, marked by a particular restlessness of life forces: 'The basic impulse behind contemporary culture is a negative one, and this is why, unlike men in all these earlier epochs, we have been for some time now living without any shared ideal, even perhaps without any ideals at all.'[9]

One wonders why this might be the case. It may be that the modern quest for order – the bold, self-conscious leap from temporality to timelessness, from restiveness to fixity – is self-defeating. If no 'fixed form' can claim foundation other than that of that human creative force which gave it birth, then no form is likely ever to achieve the status of *an* 'ideal' – in the sense of a 'final state', or 'ultimate objective' which, once reached, would make criticism of forms grind to a halt and induce the 'subjective life' and 'its contents' to live in peace. The more self-conscious, determined and resourceful is the order-making urge, the more visible is the birth-mark of fragility carried by its products; the weaker appears the products' authority, the less 'timeless' proves their fixity.

Simmel's tragedy of culture, like all tragedies, lacks a happy ending. Like all tragedies, it tells the story of actors buffeted by forces ever more wild the more they try to tame them, driven by a fate they do not control. In more mundane, though no less dramatic terms, the seminal ideas of Simmel are now rehearsed throughout the realm of social sciences – most notably in Ulrich Beck's model of *risk society* and Anthony Giddens' idea of *manufactured uncertainty*. Or, for that matter, in Cornelius Castoriadis' vision of modern democracy as a 'regime of reflexivity and autolimitation', as a society which knows, ought to know, that it has no guaranteed signification, that it lives upon chaos, that it itself is the chaos which needs to give itself a form, never fixed once for all.[10]

To sum it all up: culture, as it tends to be seen now, is as much an agent of disorder as it is the tool of order; a factor of ageing and obsolence as much as of timelessness. The work of culture does not consist so much in its self-perpetuation as in securing the conditions for further experimentation and change. Or, rather, culture 'self-perpetuates' in as far as not the pattern, but the urge to modify it, to alter and to replace it with another pattern, stays viable and potent over time. The paradox of culture may be thus reformulated: whatever serves the preservation of a pattern undermines its grip.

The quest of order renders all order pliable and less-than-timeless; culture may produce nothing but constant change, though it cannot produce change otherwise than through the ordering effort. It was the passion for order born of the fear of chaos, and the discovery of culture, the realization that the fate of order is in human hands – which ushered the modern world into the era of unstoppable and accelerated dynamism of forms and patterns. In the quest for order and *Eindeutigkeit*, the ambivalence of freedom has found the patented method of its own self-preservation. . .

### System or matrix?

The image of culture as a workshop in which the steady pattern of society is repaired and kept in shape chimed together with the perception of all things cultural – values, behavioural norms, artefacts – forming a *system*.

Speaking of an aggregate of items as a 'system', what we have in mind is that all items are 'interconnected'; that is, the state of each item depends on the states assumed by all other items. The range of possible variations in the state of any item is thereby kept within certain limits imposed by the network of dependencies in which it is entangled. As long as such limits are observed, the system is 'in equilibrium': it retains the capacity for returning to its proper shape, for preserving its identity despite local and temporal disturbances; it stops all and every unit from reaching the point of no return. As long as they remain within the system, all items (units, ingredients, variables) are bound together in the web of reciprocal determination and kept in line lest they should transgress the allowed limit and throw the whole out of balance. Or, to rephrase the same requirement in a negative way, no item which is not kept in line, or cannot be brought in line when need be, is or may remain a part of the system. In its essence, systemness is the way to subordinate the freedom of the elements to the 'pattern maintenance' of the totality.

It follows from what has been said before that in order to meet the criteria of systemness the set of items needs to be circumscribed – must have boundaries. One cannot speak of system unless it is always possible to decide which item belongs to the system and which is outside. Systems resent grey areas and no-man's lands. Borders need to be guarded, movement across the borders to be limited and above all controlled; uncontrolled border passages are equal to the collapse of the system. Outside elements may be let into the system on certain conditions: they must undergo the process of *adaptation* or *accommodation* – a modification which would make them 'fit' the system and so allow the system to *assimilate* them. Assimilation is a one-way street: it is the system which sets the rules of admission, designs the procedure of assimilation and evaluates the results of adaptation – and it continues to be a system as long as it is capable of doing so. For the newcomers, assimilation means transformation, while for the system it means reassertion of self-identity.

Presumably, there was a mixture of heterogeneous experiences which combined into such an image of culture as a self-enclosed, system-style totality. One may suppose that an uneasy marriage of the insider's and outsider's view was needed to conjure up the systemic vision.

The latter view was the product of the cultural-anthropologists' practice, originated by Bronisław Malinowski, of visiting 'native populations' with a way of life evidently distinct from their own, immersing oneself in their daily pursuits, recording the native ways and means and then attempting to 'make sense' of them by dovetailing each of the observed, or reported by 'informers', habits or rites into a comprehensive totality of routines assumed to make the investigated way of life viable and capable of self-perpetuation.

The first view rested on the experience of one's own society's selectiveness, its inclusive/exclusive practices, its assimilatory pressures exerted upon 'foreign elements' inside the nation-state boundaries and its struggle for its own distinctive identity.

Both views were naturally available at the time the orthodox model of culture took hold. There were yet numerous areas of the globe with little or no communication with neighbours; populations which without too much fact-twisting could be talked about as self-contained wholes. And there were nation-states explicitly and forcefully promoting unified national languages, calendars, standards of education, versions of history and legally supported ethical codes; states concerned with homogenizing the loose ensemble of local dialects, customs and collective memories into one, common, national set of beliefs and style of life.

Just as it came naturally to the cultural explorers of the day to assume matter-of-factly that all populations must have been concerned with the problems known from the explorers' own home-ground practices, so it comes naturally to us now to doubt the credibility of the system-like 'totalities' conjured up by orthodox cultural anthropology. It is difficult to be sure whether the casting of explored cultures as systems was an optical illusion prompted by a historically framed and transient point of view, or an adequate perception of now bygone reality. Whatever might have been the case, that image jars stridently with our current experience of free-floating cultural tokens, of the porosity of boundaries which some people wish, but no one is able, to tighten up, and of the state governments which actively promote 'multiculturalism', are no more interested in privileging any particular model of national culture, but careful not to infringe any of the numberless 'cultural choices' made individually or severally. Of present-day France – the land particularly famous in the past for its governments equating statehood and citizenship with national culture – Marc Fumaroli has commented acidly that[11]

> one speaks still of a French society, of a French cultural policy, but this adjective is but a term of convenience serving to denote the immediate present, and aggregate flow of fashions and opinions recorded by the polls. . . . It is neither a place nor an environment – just a zone. Instead of France one speaks of culture – even if that term is but a milder substitute for the more vulgar 'Babel'. . . .
>
> The word 'culture' has become an enormous conglomerate composed of 'cultures', each one on equal footing with all the others. . . . The 'cultural state', while wishing to be a national one, wants as well to be everything for everybody, a puppet- and even chameleon-like, following of the flows and reflows of fashions and generations.

In the light of by now common experience, it seems plausible that whether or not there was ever a truly 'system-like' culture, the possibility (and the likelihood) of perceiving cultural phenomena as forming a cohesive and self-enclosed totality (a 'system' in a sense spelled out before) was a historical contingency. We have now the opportunity to understand better than before the true meaning of an otherwise banal observation, that spatial phenomena are socially produced, and that therefore their role in setting apart and bringing together social entities is likely to change together with the change in productive techniques and procedures.

Looking backward in history, one can ask to what extent geo-physical factors, natural as well as artificial borders of territorial units, separate identities of populations and *cultures*, as well as the distinction between the 'inside' and 'outside' of any socio-cultural entity, were in their essence but the conceptual derivatives of the material sediments/artifices of 'speed limits' – or, more generally, of the time-and-cost constraints imposed on freedom of movement in space.

Paul Virilio suggested recently that while Francis Fukuyama's declaration of the 'end of history' sounds grossly premature, one can with growing confidence speak presently of the 'end of geography.'[12] Distances do not matter as much as they used to, while the idea of a geo-physical border is increasingly difficult to sustain in the 'real world'. It seems suddenly clear that the divisions of continents and of the globe as a whole into more or less self-enclosed, or even self-sustained, enclaves were the function of distances – made imposingly real thanks mainly to the primitivity of transport and the hardships and exorbitant costs of travel.

Indeed, far from being an objective, impersonal, physical 'given', 'distance' is a social product; its length varies depending on the speed with which it may be traversed and thus for all practical intents and purposes overcome (though in a monetary economy also on the cost involved in the attainment of that speed). All other socially produced factors of constitution, separation and maintenance of collective identities – like state borders or cultural barriers – seem in retrospect but secondary effects of that speed.

The 'here' versus 'out there', 'near' versus 'far away' oppositions, and so also the opposition between 'inside' and 'outside', recorded the degree of taming, domestication and familiarity of various (human as much as non-human) fragments of the surrounding world.

'Inside' is an extrapolation of 'being at home', treading familiar ground, known to the point of self-evidence or even invisibility. 'Inside' entails humans and things seen, met, dealt or interacted with daily, intertwined with habitual routine and day-to-day activities. 'Inside' is a space where one seldom, if at all, finds oneself at a loss, feels lost for words or uncertain how to act. 'Outside' – 'out there' – is, on the other hand, a space which one enters only occasionally or not at all, in which things tend to happen which one cannot anticipate or comprehend, and would not know how to react to once they occurred; a space that contains things one knows little about, one from which one does not expect much and for which one does not feel obliged to care. Compared with the cosy security of home, finding oneself in such space is an unnerving experience; venturing 'out there' means being beyond one's ken, out of place and out of one's element, inviting trouble and fearing harm.

To put it in a nutshell, the crucial dimension of the 'inside – outside' opposition is that between certainty and uncertainty, self-confidence and hesitation. Being 'outside' means inviting and fearing trouble – and so it demands cleverness, cunning, slyness or courage, learning foreign rules one can do without elsewhere, and mastering them through risky trials and often costly errors. The idea of the 'inside', on the other hand, stands for the unproblematic; painlessly acquired and half-consciously possessed habits, skills needing little reflection, will suffice – and since they are such they feel weightless and call for no choice, certainly not agonizing choices, giving no occasion to anxiety-prone hesitation. Whatever has come to be retrospectively dubbed as 'community' used to be brought into being by this opposition between 'right here' and 'out there', 'inside' and 'outside'.

Modern history has been marked by the constant progress of the means of transportation, and so the volume of mobility. Transport and travel was the field of particularly radical and rapid change; progress here, as Schumpeter pointed out a long time ago, was the result not of multiplying the number of stagecoaches, but of the invention and mass production of totally new means of travel – trains, motor cars, and aeroplanes. It was primarily the availability of fast means of travel that triggered the typically modern process of eroding and undermining all locally entrenched social and cultural 'totalities'; the process first captured (and romanticized) by Tönnies' famous formula of modernity as the passage from *Gemeinschaft* to *Gesellschaft*.

Among all technical factors of mobility, a particularly great role was played by the transport of information – the kind of communication which does not involve movement of physical bodies or involves it only secondarily and marginally. Technical means were developed which allowed information to travel *independently* from its bodily carriers, but also from the objects about which the information informed: such means set 'signifiers' free from the hold of 'signifieds'. The separation of the movement of information from the shifting in space of its carriers and its objects in its turn allowed the differentiation of the speed of two mobilities; the movement of information gathered speed on a pace far exceeding that which the travel of bodies, or the change of the situations about which information informed, was able to reach. In the end, the appearance of the computer-served World-Wide Web put paid – as far as information is concerned – to the very notion of 'travel' (and of 'distance' to be travelled) and has rendered information instantaneously available throughout the globe. The overall results of this latest development are enormous. Its impact on the interplay of social association/dissociation has been widely noted and described in great detail.

One consequence, though, is particularly important for our argument. Martin Heidegger pointed out that the 'essence of hammer' comes to our attention, and so becomes an object of cognition, only when the hammer has been broken. For reasons similar to those suggested by Heidegger, we now see clearer than ever before the role played by time, space and the means of saddling them in formation, instability or flexibility, and in the eventual demise of socio/cultural and political totalities. The so-called 'closely-knit communities' of yore were, as we can see it now, brought into being and kept alive by the gap between the nearly instantaneous communication *inside* the small-scale community (the size of which was determined by the innate qualities of 'wetware', and thus confined to the natural limits of human sight, hearing and memorizing capacity) and the enormity of time and expense needed to pass information *between* localities. On the other hand, the present-day fragility and short life-span of communities and the unclarity and permeability of their boundaries appear to be primarily the result of that gap shrinking or altogether disappearing: the inner-community communication loses its advantage over the inter-communal exchange if *both* are instantaneous. 'Inside' and 'outside' have lost much of their once so clear meaning.

Michael Benedikt thus summarizes our retrospective discovery and the new understanding of the intimate connection between the speed of travel and social cohesion:[13]

> The kind of unity made possible in small communities by the near-simultaneity and near-zero cost of natural voice communications, posters and leaflets, collapses at the larger scale. Social cohesion at any scale is a function of consensus, of shared knowledge, and without constant updating and interaction, such cohesion depends crucially on early, and strict, education in – and memory of – culture. Social flexibility, conversely, depends on forgetting and cheap communication.

Let us add that the 'and' in the last quoted sentence is superfluous. The facility to forget and cheapness (as well as high velocity) of communication are but two aspects of the same condition and can hardly be conceived of in separation. Cheap communication means quick overflooding, stifling or elbowing away of the information acquired as much as it means speedy arrival of news. With the capacities of 'wetware' remaining largely unchanged since at least the paleolithic times, cheap communication floods and smothers memory instead of feeding it and stabilizing. Capacity of retention is no match for the volume of information vying for attention. New information has hardly the time to sink, to be memorized, to harden into a solid floor on which successive layers of knowledge can be laid. To a large extent, instead of being added to the 'memory bank', perceptions start from a 'clean slate'. Fast communication services the activity of site-clearing and forgetting rather than learning and accumulation of knowledge.

Arguably the most seminal of recent developments is the dwindling difference between the costs of transmitting information on a local and supra-local or global scale (however 'geographically far' you send your message through the Internet, you pay by the tariff of the 'local call'; the circumstance as important culturally as it is economically); this, in turn, means that the information eventually arriving and clamouring for attention, for entry to and (however short-lived) stay in one's memory, tends to originate in the most diverse and mutually independent sites. It is therefore unlikely to possess any paraphernalia of 'systemness' – coherence and sequentiality above all. It is instead likely to convey mutually incompatible or mutually cancelling messages – in sharp contradiction to the messages which used to float inside communities devoid of hardware and software and relying on 'wetware' only; that is, to the messages which tended to reiterate and reinforce each other and so assisted the process of (selective) memorizing. There are now no advantages attached to the spatial closeness of the source of information. In this crucial respect, the distinction between 'inside' and 'outside' has lost its sense.

As Timothy W. Luke[14] puts it – 'the spatiality of traditional societies is organized around the mostly unmediated capacities of ordinary human bodies':

> Traditional visions of action often resort to organic metaphors for their allusions: conflict was chin-to-chin. Combat was hand-to-hand. Justice was an-eye-for-an-eye, a-tooth-for-a-tooth. Debate was heart-to-heart. Solidarity was shoulder-to-shoulder. Community was face-to-face. Friendship was arm-in-arm. And, change was step-by-step.

This situation had changed beyond recognition with the advent of means which allowed to stretch conflicts, solidarities, combats, debates or administration of justice far beyond the reach of human eyes and arms. Space had become then, in Luke's words, 'processed/centered/organized/normalized' – and above all emancipated from the natural constraints of the human body. It was therefore the capacity of technics, the speed of its action and the cost of its use, which from then on 'organized space'.

> The space projected by such technics is radically different: engineered, not God-given; artificial, not natural; mediated by hardware, not immediate to wetware; rationalized, not communalized; national, not local.

To put it bluntly: that space – the modern space – was the object of *administration*, of management. Space was the playground of authority charged with the task of 'principal coordination', of legislating the rules which made the 'inside' uniform while at the same time setting it apart from the 'outside', of smoothing up the rough edges and frictions between extant norms and behavioural patterns, of homogenizing the heterogeneous and unifying the differentiated: in short, of re-shaping an incoherent aggregate into the coherent system. Global space was sliced into sovereign realms – separate territories with separate, sovereign agencies – to perform those tasks of modern authority. Things which this arrangement had no room for were a 'no-man's land', 'master-less people', unpatterned conduct and ambivalent messages. The image of culture as 'system' after the pattern of a managerial chart was the projection of that space-management task/ambition.

Engineered, modern space was to be tough, solid, permanent and non-negotiable. Concrete and steel were to be its flesh, the web of rail-tracks and highways its blood vessels. Writers of modern utopias did not distinguish between social and architectural order or between social and territorial units and divisions; for them – like for their contemporaries in charge of social order – the key to an orderly society was to be found in the organization of space. Social totality was to be a hierarchy of ever larger and inclusive localities, with the supra-local authority of the state perched on the top and surveilling the whole, while itself protected by the shroud of official secrecy from day-to-day interference.

This picture, however, is itself receding in the past. Over the territorial/urbanistic/architectural, engineered space, a third – *cybernetic* – spacing of human world has been imposed with the advent of the global web of information. Elements of this space, according to Paul Virilio,[15] are

> devoid of spatial dimensions, but inscribed in the singular temporality of an instantaneous diffusion. From here on, people can't be separated by physical obstacles or by temporal distances. With the interfacing of computer terminals and video-monitors, distinctions of *here* and *there* no longer mean anything.

Cyberspace is territorially un-anchored; it stays in a different dimension, unreachable, let alone controllable, from the dimensions in which earthly 'sovereign powers' operate. The flow of information and the chart of control are, one may say, 'principally *un*coordinated'. If the idea of culture as a system was organically tied to the practice of the 'managed' or 'administered' space in general, and to its nation-state rendition in particular, it has no more hold on the realities of life. The global web of information does not have, nor may have, 'pattern-maintenance' agencies, neither does it have authorities capable of setting apart the norm from abnormality, the regular from the deviant. Any 'order' that may conceivably appear in cyberspace is emergent, not contrived; and even so it could be but a momentary order, an 'until further notice' order, and an order which in no way binds the shape of future orders nor determines their occurrence.

The first insight into the futility of the 'systemic' conception of culture was the formidable achievement of Claude Lévi-Strauss, whose work inspired most of this book's arguments. Rather than as an inventory of a finite number of values overseeing the whole field of interaction or a stable code of closely related and complementary behavioural precepts, Lévi-Strauss portrayed culture as a structure of choices – a matrix of possible, finite in number yet practically uncountable permutations. Let us note in passing that though he denied his kinship with his strategy, Michel Foucault's idea of discursive formation, able to generate mutually contradictory propositions while retaining its own identity, was hardly conceivable without the decisive shift of cultural discourse accomplished with great persuasive power by Lévi-Strauss.

The ordering passion of social scientists extends to their own playground, and so Lévi-Strauss was promptly dubbed a structuralist (just like the revolutionary edge of Georg Simmel's sociology was blunted, tamed and defused for years by classifying him as a 'formalist'); but this strange 'structuralist' did more than any other thinker to explode the orthodox idea of structure as a vehicle of monotonous reproduction, repetitiveness and sameness. In Lévi-Strauss's vision, structure has turned from a cage into a catapult; from a trimming/truncating/cramping/fettering device into the determinant of freedom; from a weapon of uniformity into the tool of variety; from a protective shield of stability into the engine of never-ending and forever incomplete change. Moreover, Lévi-Strauss hotly denied the existence of anything like *the* structure of a 'society' or 'culture': while it is true that all human activities – from myth-telling through the selection of marriage partners to pet-naming and cooking – are *structured*, the idea of '*structure* as such' is but an abstraction from this non-randomness of the infinitely varied kinds of human interactions.

This proved, in retrospect, to have been a decisive step – and at the time it felt like a liberating event. It put paid to many a barren issue which preoccupied the minds and practices of the students of culture and closed many a blind alley. Personally, I found the end to the one-sided assignment of culture to the 'continuity side' of the continuity–discontinuity dilemma the most attractive feature of the Lévi-Strauss revolution. No more was culture to be seen as a constraint upon human invention, as a tool of monotonous self-reproduction of life-forms, resistant to change unless pushed or pulled by extraneous forces; Lévi-Strauss's culture was itself a dynamic force (only one small step remained from there to Jacques Derrida's *iteration* – the novelty ingrained in every act of repetition), and the very opposition between continuity and discontinuity seemed to lose much of its nuisance power. The former adversaries appeared now more like loyal allies in one unending process of cultural creativity – continuity being thinkable now in no other form but the endless chain of permutations and innovations.

I suppose now that Lévi-Strauss's message was somewhat weakened by the attention he paid, to the detriment of other aspects, to another misleading dilemma – that of synchrony versus diachrony. It was perhaps Lévi-Strauss's bad luck to be maneouvred by Jean-Paul Sartre into the famous debate on history and historicity, during which the issue was diverted to what from the point of view of cultural theory could be only seen as a sidetrack, and kept there much too long by sensation-greedy yet half-informed academic opinion. This unhappy coincidence does not, however, absolve Lévi-Strauss from at least partial responsibility for the wrong uses to which the commentators could, and did, put his unduly stubborn insistence on the opposition between synchronic and diachronic views of culture. The synchronic approach, gleaned from Ferdinand de Saussure's 'war of liberation' waged against etymology then dominating the study of linguistics, was a welcome remedy against the more gruesome inanities of evolutionist or diffusionist visions beclouding the realm of cultural studies. A good starting point to the much needed site-clearing operation, the synchronic strategy could, however, easily be converted into another false recipe if only applied to the construction of the new and improved version of cultural theory; particularly if the polemically justified sharpening of the opposition between synchrony and diachrony was carried over from the field of methodology to that of the 'ontology' of culture.

I believe that the synchrony–diachrony dilemma is but a methodological reflection of the opposition between continuity and discontinuity in the life of culture. The great merit of Lévi-Strauss's renewal of cultural theory was to show the way to unmasking the futility of that latter opposition. The ensuing revolution in the understanding of how culture works, how continuity and discontinuity intertwine and condition each other in the life of culture, was not, however, matched by a closer look at the dialectics of synchronic and diachronic approaches and little had been done to alert the students of culture to the truth that the two methodological principles are not just alternatives – certainly not in the strong, disjunctive sense.

I am inclined today to read Lévi-Strauss's message together with Cornelius Castoriadis' rejoinder – a right and proper critique of the 'synchronic radicalism' and timely reminder of the subtle, yet vital, interaction of diachronic and synchronic networks of connections in the cultural production of meaning as well as in understanding. What one can learn from Castoriadis' critique, is that however pragmatically fruitful the emphasis on the diachronic/synchronic opposition and on the heretofore neglected merits of the synchronic perspective could be, the understanding of culture can gain little from a theoretical model constructed at a flat, horizontal level of the 'now'. What Castoriadis wrote on language in the passage which follows, can be easily extended to culture as a whole:[16]

> the 'synchronic state' of the French language, that is this language itself, changes, for example, between 1905 and 1922, every time that Proust completes a sentence. Since at the same time Saint-John Perse, Apollinaire, Gide, Bergson, Valéry and so many others are also writing – each of whom would not be a writer if he did not imprint on a good number of the 'signifieds' entering into his text an alteration that is his own but that henceforth belongs to the significations of the words in the language – *what* is then the 'synchronic state' of French as a language, as it refers to significations, during this period? . . .
>
> It is obviously an essential property of language as well, as history . . . to be able to alter itself while continuing to function efficiently, constantly to transform the uncommon into the common, the original into the established, to be continual acquisition or elimination, and, in this, to perpetuate its capacity to be itself. Language, in its relation to significations, shows us how instituting society is

constantly at work and also . . . how this work, which exists only as instituted, does not hamper the continued instituting activity of society.

Society and culture, like language, retain their distinctiveness – their 'identity' – but this distinctiveness is never 'the same' for long. It lasts *through change*. Moreover, there is no 'now' in culture, not in the sense postulated by the precept of synchrony, in the sense of a point in time cut from its own past and self-sustained when its openings into the future are ignored. To resort once more to Paul Ricoeur's distinction between *l'ipséité* and *la mêmeté*, the two ingredients of identity, one may say, following Castoriadis, that the second – durability of identity – consists in the preservation of the first – distinctiveness; but that the first is inconceivable outside or independently of its duration, which brings together successive – different – forms of distinctiveness as belonging *to the same* identity, and thus conjures up identity out of mere difference.

To quote Castoriadis again:

There would be no language, no society, no history, nothing if an ordinary Frenchman of today were not able to understand *Le Rouge et le Noir*, or even Saint-Simon's *Mémoires*, as well as an innovative text of an original writer.

To put it in a nutshell: to 'master a culture' means to master a matrix of possible permutations, a set never fully implemented and always far from completion – not a finite collection of significations and the art to recognize their carriers. What collects cultural phenomena into a 'culture' is the presence of such a matrix, a constant invitation to change, not their 'systemness' – that is, not the mixture of petrification of some ('normal') choices and elimination of some other ('deviant') ones.

Which leads us to another theme insufficiently attended to in the now reprinted book, yet currently very much in the centre of cultural debate: that of culture as – simultaneously – the factory of identity and its shelter.

## Culture and identity

The notoriously intense attention paid nowadays to the issue of identity is itself a cultural fact of great importance and, potentially at least, of great enlightening power.

Aspects of experience come into focus and begin to be debated in earnest when they can no longer be taken for granted; when they cease to be self-evident, or likely to survive if left alone, unpropped by vigilant reflection. The more feeble they seem, the stronger is the urge to discover or invent, but above all to demonstrate the solidity of, their foundations.

'Identity' is no exception; it has become a matter of acute reflection once the likelihood of its survival without reflection began to dwindle – when instead of something obvious and *given* it began to look like something problematic and a *task*. That happened with the advent of modern times, with the passage from 'ascription' to 'achievement': letting human individuals loose so that they may – need, must – determine their own place in society.

No thoughts are given to identity when 'belonging' comes naturally, when it does not need to be fought for, earned, claimed and defended; when one 'belongs' just by going through the motions which seem obvious thanks simply to the absence of competitors. Such belonging which renders all concern with identity redundant is possible, as we have seen before, only in a world *locally confined*: only if the 'totalities' to which one belongs before thinking of it and before really trying are for all practical purposes clearly defined by the capacity of the 'wetware'. In such 'mini-worlds', being 'in here' feels evidently different from being 'out there', and the passage from here to there seldom, if ever, occurs. Such belonging, however, is not feasible if the totality in question transcends the capacity of the 'wetware' – when it becomes, for that reason, an abstract, 'imagined' community. To the assembly of people not larger than the network of face-to-face, personal interactions entailed in the daily routine or the annual cycle of encounters, one *belongs*; with the 'imagined' totality one must *identify*. The latter is a task which takes some special effort, set aside from daily business and so conceived of as a separated activity of learning. It involves passing certain tests and requires a certain form of confirmation that the test has been indeed successfully passed.

The mark of modernity is increased volume and range of mobility and so, inevitably, the weakening of the hold of locality and the local networks of interaction. For much the same reason, modernity is also an era of supra-local totalities, of power-assisted or aspiring 'imagined communities', of nation-building – and of 'made-up', postulated and constructed, cultural identities.

With his usual insightfulness, Friedrich Nietzsche saw through the rising tide of modern nationalism: 'That which is at present called a "nation" in Europe is rather a *res facta* than *nata* (indeed, sometimes confusingly similar to a *res ficta et picta*).'[17] And Ernest Gellner explained why this had to be the case: 'Nations as a natural, God-given way of classifying men, as an inherent though long-delayed political destiny, are a myth; nationalism, which sometimes takes pre-existing cultures and turns them into nations, sometimes invents them, and often obliterates pre-existing cultures; *that* is a reality, for better or worse, and in general an inescapable one.'[18]

As Frederick Barth pointed out emphatically, 'ethnic categories provide an organizational vessel that may be given varying contents and forms in different socio-cultural systems. They may be of great relevance to behaviour, but they need not be; they may pervade all social life, or they may be relevant only in limited sectors of activity.' Whichever option becomes reality is an open question. It was the task of the modern state to see that the option to 'pervade all social life' be given preference over the marginality or partiality of ethnic membership. After all, the continuous existence of an 'ethnic category' depends solely on the *maintenance of a boundary*, however changeable are the cultural factors selected as the border posts. Thanks to its monopoly of the means of coercion the modern state had the might needed to claim and to defend boundries.

It is in the end 'the ethnic *boundary* that defines the group, not the cultural stuff that it encloses', Barth insists.[19] All having been said and done, the very identity of that cultural stuff (its 'unity', 'totality' and 'distinctiveness') is an artefact of a firmly drawn and well-guarded boundary, though the designers and the guardians of borders would as a rule insist on the opposite order of causality. The orthodox cultural theorists sided, as a rule, with those in charge of the borders – allegedly natural and genuine borders, but in fact artificial and all too often merely postulated.

'Having an identity' seems to be one of the most universal human needs (though, let me repeat, its recognition as a need is far from universal – indeed, a historically coincidental evidence of its fragility). We all seem to share in the pursuit of what Michel Morineau aptly dubbed *la douceur d'être inclu*:[20]

> By itself, in some sense this expression says it all; it corresponds to a primary desire – that of belonging, of belonging to a group, of being received by another, by others, of being accepted, of being retained, of being sure of support, of having allies. . . . More important still than all those specific satisfactions received one by one, separately, is that underlying and all-embracing feeling, on top of having one's personal identity endorsed, confirmed, accepted by the many – the feeling that one has obtained a second identity, this time a social one.

*Personal* identity gives meaning to the 'I'. *Social* identity guarantees that meaning, and in addition allows one to speak of the 'we', in which the otherwise precarious and insecure 'I' may be lodged, rest safely and even wash out its own anxieties.

The 'we' made of inclusion, acceptance and confirmation is the realm of gratifying safety cut out (though seldom as securely as one would desire) from the frightening wilderness of an *outside* populated by 'them'. The safety would not be obtained unless the 'we' were trusted to have the power of acceptance, and the strength to protect those who have already been accepted. Identity is felt to be secure if the powers that have certified it seem to prevail over 'them' – the strangers, the adversaries, the hostile others – construed simultaneously with the 'we' in the process of self-assertion. 'We' must be powerful, or social identity won't be gratifying. There is little pleasure in being included if – as Heinrich Heine once remarked on one of the less effective protective walls, those of the ethnic ghetto – 'cowardice guards the gates from inside, and stupidity stands on guard outside'.

The strength required will not come by itself. It must be created. It also needs its creators and authorities. It needs *culture* – educating, training and teaching. Reflecting on the intellectual and moral reform that nineteenth-century France needed, Ernest Renan bewailed the 'state of the masses', but most of all the incapacity of the 'masses' to extricate themselves from that state by their own will and force: 'the masses are onerous, crude, dominated by a most superficial view of their interest'. 'Imbeciles or ignorants may well unite, but nothing good would follow from their union.' 'The spectacle of the physical suffering of the poor is no doubt lamentable. I admit, however, that it causes me infinitely less pain than the sight of the great majority doomed to intellectual parochialism.'[21] The obvious moral and practical lesson to draw was that 'the masses' had to become, and for a foreseeable future to remain, an *object* of tender care aimed at their spiritual elevation: prevented from becoming *subjects* of autonomous action, since unlikely to become makers of the choices *one would be ready to accept*. It is the presence of the masses that founded the necessity of spiritual leadership, and thus offered the wardenship of the spiritual elite its *raison d'être*. At the time Renan wrote these words, this was the generally accepted opinion, shortly to be further elaborated by LeBon, Tarde or Sorel among many others. That opinion summed up a century or more of *estrangement* and *reconquest*.

'The masses' belong to the populous family of categories born together with modernity – all reflecting the modern ambition to dissolve many and different local identities in a new, supra-local and homogeneous assignment – to unify the heterogeneous aggregate of people through instruction and control, drilling and teaching, and if need be coercion. The intellectual corollary of that political process – heaping together the variety of regional, legal and occupational identities of *le petit peuple* into an indiscriminate 'mass', or a *mobile vulgus* ('mob') – started in earnest in the seventeenth century, and reached its conceptual maturity only in the thought of the Enlightenment. According to Robert Muchembled,[22]

> All social groups of the fifteenth and sixteenth centuries moved at the same level in that universe, enormously distant from ours. Real cleavages caused by birth or wealth did not result in profound differences in sensibility and common conduct between the dominant and the dominated. . . .
> Beginning with the eighteenth century, the break between two separate mental planets intensifies. The civilized people can no longer feel the people, in the proper sense of the word. They reject everything which appears to them savage, dirty, lecherous – in order to better conquer similar temptations in themselves. . . . Odour became a criterion of social distinction.

There were many divisions and sub-divisions, big or minute, in that *divine chain of being* that the pre-modern mind of Christian Europe forged to piece together its life-world; too many in fact for a single, all-embracing, all-defining 'division of divisions', like that *modern* division between the 'cultivated' and the 'uncultivated' – raw, coarse, vulgar, unrefined, in need of uplifting – to emerge.

In a truly revolutionary way, the 'civilizing process' which took off in the seventeenth century was first and foremost a drive to the self-separation of the elites from 'the rest' – now forcefully blended, despite all internal variety, into a homogenic mass: a process of a sharp *cultural de-synchronization*. On one, active end (that of the elites) it produced a growing preoccupation with the task of self-formation, self-drill and self-improvement. On the other, receiving end it sedimented a tendency to biologize, medicalize, criminalize and increasingly to police 'the masses' – 'judged brutal, filthy and totally incapable of constraining their passions in order to accommodate to the civilized mould'.

To sum up: at the threshold of modernity one finds the process of the *self-*

formation of the learned or enlightened elite (now set apart by its 'civilized mode', with its two faces of spiritual refinement and bodily drill) which at the same time was a process of the power-assisted formation of the *masses* as the potential field of the elite's supervising function, action and responsibility. *Responsibility* was for leading the masses into humanity; the *action* might take the form of persuasion or enforcement. It was that responsibility and the associated propulsion to act that defined 'the masses' – in their two co-existing and mutually complementary, even if ostensibly opposed, incarnations: 'the mob' (coming to the fore whenever force was the order of the day) and 'the people' (invoked when education was hoped to make the enforcement redundant).

What applied to the grand separation applied as well to the grand re-assembly which was bound to follow. The reintegration of divided society was to be led by the new civilized elite of the educated, now firmly in the saddle. To quote Gellner again,[23]

> at the base of the modern social order stands not the executioner but the professor. Not the guillotine, but the (aptly named) *doctorat d'état* is the main tool and symbol of state power. The monopoly of legitimate education is now more important, more central than is the monopoly of legitimate violence.

The task of integration and reproduction of society could no longer be left to the spontaneous, unreflexively operating forces of sociability set in motion by the multitude of compact localities, in each one separately and drawing on local resources. More correctly, modern elites had consciously and resolutely broken with what they now viewed, in retrospect and with horror, as such a de-centred, diffuse, chaotic, and thus dangerous and always pregnant with catastrophe, *irrational* state of affairs.

Processes of integration and reproduction of social order had become the domain of specialization, expertise – and of a legally defined authority. They reaffirmed and reinforced what the processes of separation which preceded them had accomplished. The 'project of enlightenment' simultaneously constituted the learned, 'cultivated' elite at the helm and the rest of society as a natural object of the elite's teaching, 'cultivating' action, and thereby reproduced the structure of domination in its new, modern form: one that stretched beyond the pre-modern tasks of re-distributing the surplus product and entailed now, as its major concern, the intention to shape the spirits and the bodies of the subjects, to penetrate deeply into their daily conduct and the construction of their life-worlds. The call for the education of the masses was simultaneously a declaration of the masses' own social incompetence and a bid for the dictatorship of the *professoriat* (or, to use the educated elite's own vocabulary, for the 'enlightened despotism' of the guardians of reason, humane manners and good taste).

Nation-building was, essentially, such a bid. It was, therefore, as modern as the structure of domination around which and through which the new integration of society was perpetrated, or as the social strata elevated to managerial positions in the process. In the course of modern history, nationalism played the role of the hinge fastening together state and society (the latter conceptualized as – identified with – the nation). State and nation emerged as natural allies at the horizon of the nationalist vision, at the finishing line of the re-integrating spurt. The state supplied the resources of nation-building, while the postulated unity of the nation and shared national destiny offered legitimacy to the ambition of the state authority to command obedience.

There was a close, though elective, affinity between the modern effort to secure supra-local integration through state-managed legal order and the entrenchment of supra-local, national culture. One may say that, consciously or instinctively, the rising state sought legitimizing support through siding with an already existing nationalism or fomenting a new one; while nationalist projects sought the instruments and assurances of their effectiveness in the powers of the extant or yet-to-be-built states. Indeed the elite-promoted alliance between nationhood and statehood had become so close that by the end of the nineteenth century Maurice Barrès could look back on the link between the state and the nation as on a result of an utterly *natural* and unprompted process, a product of the law of nature of sorts: 'Peoples emancipated from historical constraints by natural rights, by the Revolution, organized themselves into nationalities. . . . They decided spontaneously to form groups resting on shared legends and on life in togetherness.'[24] To become national, culture had to deny first its being a project: culture had to masquerade as nature.

'What is *la patrie*?' asked Barrès, and answered: '*La Terre et les Morts.*' The two named constituents of *la patrie* have one thing in common: they are not a matter of choice. They cannot be *chosen freely*. Before any choice can be as much as contemplated, one has been already born and grown on this soil here and now and into this succession of ancestors and their posterity. One can move places, but one cannot take one's soil with one, and one cannot make another soil one's own. One may change company, but not one's dead – the dead ancestors who are one's own and not the others'; nor may one transform other people's dead into one's own ancestors. Commenting on the conflict between Creon and Antigone, Barrès made it clear just what the limits of the choice are:[25]

> Creon is a master who arrived from abroad. He said: 'I know the laws of the country and I'll apply them.' This was the judgement of his intelligence. Intelligence – what a trifling thing at the very surface of our selves! Antigone, on the contrary. . . . engages her profound heredity, she is inspired by those subconscious parts where respect, love, fear no more differentiated form the magnificent might of veneration.

Antigone had what Creon, armed solely with his wit and an appropriated – learned – knowledge, would never acquire: *l'épine dorsale*, the backbone on which and around which everything else in the human creature rests and is shaped (the backbone, Barrès insists, is not a metaphor, 'but a most powerful analogy'). By comparison with the solidity of the backbone, intelligence is no more than 'a trifling thing on the surface'. The backbone is a fixed point which defines everything else's place. It determines which motions of the whole body and any single part of the body are feasible or permitted and which are not (i.e. threaten to break the backbone). Truth is also a fixed point, like the backbone: not a point of arrival (not the *end point* of the learning process), but the *starting* point of all knowledge, a point that cannot be created but only found, recovered if missed – or lost; 'a unique point, this one here, none other, the point from which everything appears to us in its right proportions'.

> I ought to situate myself exactly at the point which my eyes demand, such eyes as have been formed by centuries: the point from which all things offer themselves in the measure of a Frenchman. The totality of right and true relations between given objects and the determined man, the Frenchman, this is the French truth and the French justice. Pure nationalism is nothing else than the knowledge that such a point exists, the search to find it, and – once it has been reached – cleaving to it in order to derive from it our arts, our politics, all our activities.

In other words: the point was fixed before I was born, I myself was 'fixed' by it before I began to think of points or of anything else – yet finding this point is still my task, something I must do through exercising my reason. I must seek that point actively, and then choose what is not a matter of choice: to embrace *voluntarily* the *inevitable*, to submit *by choice*, in full *consciousness*, to that which has been present all along in my *subconscious*. The outcome of free choice is given in advance: while exercising my will, I am not really free to will, as there is but one thing that in my case may be willed effectively: for me to be determined by *la terre et les morts*, to relish my stern and demanding masters – to say to myself, 'I wish to live with these masters, and – through making them the objects of my cult – to fully partake of their force.'

But there are other things as well that I may happen to will, or think (mistakenly) that I am free to will them: for instance, disowning my own masters or appropriating masters that are not mine. In both cases I may really come to believe that I am free and that my reason-dictated choice, like reason itself, knows no bounds. In both cases the result is the same: *déracinement*, rootlessness – limp flesh without a backbone, wandering and blundering thought with no fixed point on which to rest.

What unites certain human creatures (and sets them apart from others) is not *solidarity* – something they can forge or disavow at will, negotiate, agree or reject – but *kinship*: liens they have not chosen and are not at liberty to trade off. 'The fact of being of the same race, of the same family, forms a psychological determinism; it is in this sense that I take the word kinship.' The status of kinship is precarious: strong enough to inspire faith in the final victory of the unity drive but not strong enough to breed complacency and legitimize quietism. True nationalism (certainly a nationalist Barrès-style) would shun the exceptionless, impersonal, overpowering determinism of *race*: 'it is incorrect to say that there is a French race in the exact meaning of the word. We are not a race, but a nation: a nation which goes on creating itself daily, and to avoid being diminished, annihilated, we – the individuals who make it – must protect it'.[26]

If group membership depends on race, everything was said and done before anything had time to be thought or spoken, and everything of importance would remain unaltered whatever might be yet thought or spoken. If, on the other hand, togetherness of the group hangs on the *willing* acceptance of fate (if the nation is Renan's 'daily plebiscite'), it also (and most importantly) hangs on what is being spoken, how often and with what force of conviction, and on those who speak it. Unlike the race, the nation is incomplete without its 'conscience-arousing' spokespersons; unlike the race, the nation includes consciousness among its defining attributes; it must yet turn from *en soi* into *pour soi* by its own effort – but first and foremost through the strenuous effort of *cultivation* made daily by the guardians of national culture.

A most pronounced feature of the nationalist project was always the overwhelming urge to *make sure* that Barrès 'I must' means what it says, that the 'discovery of backbone' is made by everybody, and that everyone 'clings' to what has been discovered in 'all activities'. And there was but one way of making sure: using the state prerogative of legislated coercion to render 'missing the point' as unlikely as possible, and 'finding the point' virtually inescapable. The nation unpropped by the power of state would be just one 'reference group' among many – like them uncertain of its survival, buffeted by cross-waves of changing fashions, obliged to appeal daily to flickering loyalties, to lean over backwards to deliver proof of the advantage of its benefits over competitors' offers. The nation-state (the idea of a nation made into the state's flesh) could, on the other hand, *legislate* loyalty and determine in advance the results of free choice. The postulated roots could be legislated into existence and taken care of by the state agencies of law and order, the state-defined canon of cultural heritage and the state-authorized curriculum of history teaching.

Let us recall that the purpose of all that was to loosen or break the grip in which 'communities' (*local* traditions, customs, dialects, calendars, loyalties) held the would-be patriots of the one and indivisible nation. The idea guiding all the efforts of the modern nation-state was to superimpose one kind of allegiance over the mosaic of communitarian, local 'particularisms'. In terms of practical politics, this meant the dismantling, or legal disempowering, of all *pouvoirs intermèdiaires*; the end to the autonomy of any unit less than the nation-state but claiming to be more than the executor of the nation-state's will and assuming more than the delegated power.

As Charles Taylor points out, after two centuries or so of all these (in the end inconclusive) efforts of national unification, 'minority communities' are 'struggling to maintain themselves'. They struggle to maintain themselves, that is, *as communities*. And this means in turn that 'these people' (Taylor does not specify who 'these people' are, tacitly accepting the postulate of unity of interests and destiny voiced by the shepherds and the flock) 'are striving for more than their rights as individuals'. If there is indeed something *more than the 'rights as individuals'* (i.e. there is something so important that it justifies the suspension of the rights of individuals *qua* individuals), then, of course, struggle is inevitable and any benevolent person, owes the fighters sympathy and assistance. But what is that 'something more'?

'Something more' (that "something" which makes the restrictions of the individual right to choose palatable and even welcome) is the 'goal of *survivance*'; and this means in turn 'the continuance of the community through future generations'. Put in simpler, and above all *practical*, terms, the pursuit of the 'goal of survivance' calls for the right of the community to *limit or pre-empt* the choices of younger and not-yet-born generations, to decide for them what their choices should be like. In other words, what is demanded here is the power of enforcement; to make sure that people would act in these rather than other ways, to taper the range of their options, to manipulate the probabilities; to make the individuals *do what they otherwise would not do, to make them less free* than they otherwise would be. Why is it important to do so? Taylor points out that this is to be done (not a new argument, as the history of intellectuals goes) in people's own well-understood interest, since 'human beings can only make meaningful choices of their way of life against a background of alternatives which can only come to them through the language and cultural tradition of their society'.[27]

A similar idea was expressed over and over again by the generations of prophets and court poets of the *nation-state*, and it is not immediately obvious why under Taylor's pen it should be an argument in favour of the 'struggling minorities' cause. For the change of address to become understandable, one needs first to spy out the hidden corollary: namely, the realization that the nation-state has not delivered on its promise, that for one reason or another it is now bankrupt as a fount of 'meaningful choice of the way of life', that nationalism devoid of its state foundation has lost the authority without which the overriding of individual choosing rights is neither feasible nor felt acceptable, and that in the resulting void it is the 'struggling minorities' which are now believed to be the second line of trenches, where 'meaningful choice' can be protected from extinction; it is now hoped that they will succeed in the task which the nation-state has definitely failed to perform.

The striking similarity (indeed, identity – bar the change of address) between the nationalist and the communitarian hopes and paradoxes is not at all accidental. Both 'future perfect' visions are, after all, philosophers' reactions to the widespread experience of acute and abrupt 'disembedment' of identities, caused by the present-day accelerated collapse of the frames in which identities were habitually inscribed. Nationalism was the response to the wholesale destruction of the 'cottage industry' of identities, and the ensuing devaluation of the locally (and matter-of-factly, unreflexively) produced and endorsed patterns of life.

The nationalist vision arose from the desperate hope that the clarity and security of existence which ostensibly marked pre-modern life can be rebuilt at a higher, supra-local level of social organization, around national membership and state citizenship blended into one. For reasons too vast and numerous to be listed here, that hope failed to come true. The nation-state proved to be the incubator of a modern society ruled not so much by the unity of feelings as by the diversity of unemotional market interests. Its thorough job of uprooting local loyalties looks in retrospect to be not so much a production of higher-level identities as a site-clearing operation for the market-led confidence-game of quickly-assembled and fast-dismantled modes of self-description.

And so once more 'meaningful identities' ('meaningful' in the sense once postulated by nationalists, now by the communitarians) are hard to come by. Keeping them in place and intact, for however brief a moment, taxes the taught/learned juggling skills of individuals far beyond their capacity. Since the idea that the society institutionalized in the state will lend a helping hand does not now hold much water, no wonder that our eyes are shifting in a different direction; by an irony of history, however, they are drifting towards entities whose radical destruction used to be seen, since the beginning of modernity, as the condition *sine qua non* of 'meaningful choice': it is now the much-maligned natural communities of origin, 'local' and necessarily *lesser than the nation-state*, once described by modernizing propaganda as parochial, backwater, prejudice-ridden, oppressive and stultifying and made the targets of cultural crusades waged in the name of 'meaningful choices', which are looked to hopefully as the trusty executors of that streamlining, de-randomizing, meaning-saturating of human choices which the nation-state, and national culture, abominably failed to bring forth.

Admittedly, old-fashioned state-oriented nationalism is far from having run its course – particularly in the post-colonial world, in Africa or in Eastern Europe, among the debris left by the collapsing capitalist or communist empires alike. There, the idea of a nation providing a home for the lost and the confused is still fresh and above all untried. It is lodged securely in the future (even if nationalism, just as communitarianism, deployed with gusto the language of heritage, roots and a shared past), and the future is the natural place in which to invest one's hopes and cravings. For Europe (with the exception of its Eastern-most, post-colonial part), on the other hand, nationalism together with its crowning achievement, the nation-state, has lost much of its former lustre. It failed to resolve in the past what once more is to be resolved now, and it would be foolish to expect that the second time round it will perform much better. Europe knows as well that the post-colonial world does not know or does not care much about: that the closer the nation-state's works come to the ideal of solid foundations and a secure home, the less there is freedom to move around the house, and the more rank and foul becomes the air inside. For these as well as for other reasons, nothing which present-day nation-states are used, able or willing to do seems adequate to meet the anguish of uncertainty which devours the psychic resources of the late-modern or postmodern individual.

Under the circumstances, what makes the vision or 'natural community' conjured up in communitarian writings so attractive is above all the fact that they have been imagined independently from, and even in opposition to, the state and the homogeneous 'national culture' the state once actively promoted. It looks as if the state, in resonance with popular feelings, has been abandoned by the communitarian philosophers to the 'risk-producing' side of human existence: it takes care of individual freedom, but by the same token it abandons individuals to their patently inadequate resources in their pursuit of 'meaningful choice'. Like the nation once did, so now the 'natural community' stands for the dream of meaning – and so of identity. Paradoxically, however eager are the communitarians to 'root' new shelters of meaningful choices in the genuine or invented, but always pre-modern past, it is the modern spirit of adventure, of exploring the unexplored, of trying the untried, which makes them attractive to philosophers and to their readers alike.

Politically, the communitarian vision of culture (in the primal sense of 'culture' as the *activity* – of cultivating, enlightening, proselytizing, converting, waging cultural crusades) stands in opposition to the homoegenizing ambition of 'national culture' as embodied in the practices of its self-proclaimed guardian and manager, the nation-state. Sociologically speaking, though, the opposition does not seem all that evident.

The state promotion of the 'national culture' was, as we have seen above, a bid for culture as a 'system' – a self-enclosed totality. It proceeded by the elimination of all residues of custom and habit which did not fit the unified model, meant to become obligatory in the area under the state's sovereignty, now identified as national territory. That model was organically opposed to 'multi-culturalism' – a condition which from the perspective of national culture could be conceived of only negatively, as the failure of the state-administered project: as the persistence of many separate and autonomous sets of values and behavioural norms and so the absence of one dominant and uncontested cultural authority. Communitarianism does not, in principle, break with that perception. The communitarian postulate of multi-culturalism tacitly assumes, just like the project of national culture did, the systemic, 'totalistic' character of culture. It only reverses the evaluation of the co-presence of many such 'totalities' in one political realm and postulates its forceful continuation where the project of national culture postulated their power-assisted dissolution in one, national, cultural system.

Suspicion towards nation-state cultural ambitions and the loss of faith in the state's promises of meaningful, well-founded identity have not been without reason. State-promoted national culture proved to be a weak protection against the commercialization of cultural goods and the erosion of all values except those of seductive power, profitability and competitiveness. And so there are holes in the ground where road-signs and milestones seemed once to be firmly dug in. And there is widespread fear and resentment of the experience of 'disembedded', 'unencumbered', free-floating, unanchored, fragile and vulnerable identity – the experience gestated on a massive scale in a situation where the task of construction and preservation of identity is left to the individual, 'deregulated' and 'privatized', initiative and to mostly inadequate individual resources. The self-assertion which such a modern condition made into the individual's fate and duty requires considerable resources, yet the prospect of supplying them to all members of society alike never materialized and looks increasingly nebulous. With the gap between the range of publicly brandished choices and the limited individual capacity to choose widening, nostalgia for the 'sweetness of belonging' could only grow. State-promoted national culture was meant to provide a counter-weight for the despair of helplessness, to cut down the psychological damage and to draw limits to the atomization, mutual estrangement and loneliness fed by the unleashed forces of market competition; but it failed to do so – or rather the hopes that it would ever deliver on its promise faded, as the market-prodded atomization proceeded unabated and the feeling of uncertainty gathered force.

Communitarianism takes over the banner falling (dropped?) from the nation-state's hands. It promises to deliver what the state promised but failed to deliver: the sweetness of belonging. In the war declared against 'disembedding', 'dis-encumbering', de-personalizing forces of free-for-all competition, communitarianism follows the same strategy as the state did at the times of cultural crusades: to heal the psychological wounds by spiritual unity, while resigning itself to the invincibility of divisive pressures which caused the wounds in the first place. Shared culture is posited in both cases as the compensation for the market-caused uprooting. The promise of compensation is addressed particularly to those many who for lack of strength tend to sink and drown rather than swim in the turbulent waters of competition. Notably, the project of national culture and the communitarian projects are unanimous as to the non-feasibility of the alternative solution: that of rendering freedom of self-assertion truly universal, by providing to every individual the resources needed and the self-confidence which goes with them, and thus rendering compensation redundant.

In a recent study under the apt title 'False and Real Problems',[28] Alain Touraine demanded that we distinguish two phenomena (or two programmes) which are all too often confused, to the detriment of public debate: 'multi-culturalism' and 'multi-communitarianism':

> cultural pluralism cannot be achieved otherwise than by breaking down the communities defined by their relationship to a society, an authority and a culture. *It is necessary to reject the idea of a multi-communitarian society in order to defend the idea of a multi-cultural one.*

Far from being two faces of the same coin, multi-culturalism and the communitarian idea stand in stark opposition to each other: 'Creation of societies and political authorities on the basis of cultural identity and common tradition is contrary to the idea of multiculturalism.' Its genuine result would be, rather,

> fragmentation of the cultural space into a plurality of communitarian fortresses, that is, politically organized groups whose leaders derive their legitimacy, their influence and the power of their appeal from cultural tradition.

Appeals to the rights of communities to preserve their cultural distinctiveness more often than not 'hide brutality of dictatorial power under a thin crust of culturalism'. There is a lot of political capital in the despair of the dispossessed and insecurity of many more who fear dispossession as a possible prospect – and there are many would-be community leaders eager to draw on it with the help of culturalist nets.

We have traced so far the similarity between state nationalism and the communitarian project; that similarity boiled down in the last account to the vested interests of both programmes in the 'systemness' of culture, in smothering of difference and effacing ambivalence of cultural choices in order to create an imagined totality capable of resolving the thorny issue of social identity. But let us note that there are differences between the two projects as well – and seminal ones, to be sure.

First, the national-culture project was conceived as a necessary supplement to another modern departure: the universality of citizenship. National community was to be another face of the republic of equal rights and duties – indifferent, for the sake of citizens' equality, to the cultural choices citizens might have made. The republic of citizens is also a republic of risk-taking individuals; as Iosif Brodski once remarked, the free person is a person who does not complain in case of defeat, and being a free citizen entails the constant possibility of defeat and willingness to assume responsibility for its consequences. The national-culture supplement was indeed necessary to integrate what the impersonality of citizenship set apart; in principle, though not always in practice, it enabled the republic of equal citizens to function smoothly, as it collectively insured citizens against the most unwholesome consequences of their individually-made choices, promising to stretch the safety-net of communal solidarity under individual tightrope-walking. The safety-net service was, as a matter of fact, mutual: the republic offered security of citizen rights, and protected against the extremities of cultural crusades. The relationship between the national culture and the republican projects was not free from friction; but it was precisely thanks to the tension between the two projects that the modern condition could emerge and develop.

In this sense the communitarian project betrays quite a pronounced anti-modern streak. It is not bound and kept within limits by the nation-state's commitment to the republic and to citizen freedom. Cultural community is but what is says – a *cultural* community, existing solely courtesy of the shared tradition (or its assumption). It is all about foreclosure of free choice, about the promotion of preference for one cultural choice and staving off all other choices – about strict surveillance and censorship. Its pressure to conform is not mitigated by the need to promote legal universalism which would stop the penalty for unapproved cultural choices short of extradiction. There is therefore every reason to expect communities to push their cultural intolerance to the limits which even the least tolerant nation-states seldom reached. Indeed, the cultural community of communitarians is cast in a 'conform or perish' situation.

The second difference follows from the first. The cultural community of the communitarian project – necessarily a self-conscious, self-proclaimed community, a postulated community – has nothing but the unswerving loyalty of its members to hold it together. In this respect it is sharply different from the pre-modern community which it allegedly resuscitates or imitates – a genuine 'totality', in which the aspects of life now analytically prised apart from the rest of life and synthesized as 'culture' were intertwined or blended with other aspects, and never codified as a set of rules to be learned and followed, let alone posited as a task. It differs sharply also from the modern project of 'national community', which – realistically or not – aimed at the re-creation of such totality at the supra-local level. For that reason, 'culture' is in the idea of *postulated* cultural community burdened with integrative functions it has no strength to carry on its own. Such community must be vulnerable from the start, and conscious of its fragility – which makes all tolerance and compromise regarding the beliefs to be believed and ways of life to be followed a luxury it cannot afford. Cultural norms turn into the hottest of political issues; little in the conduct of the community's members is indifferent to the 'survivance' of the whole and can be left to the members' own discretion and responsibility. In accordance with Frederick Barth's rule, all genuine distinctive marks must be blown up in importance and new distinctions vehemently sought or invented to set the community apart from its neighbours – particularly physically (economically, politically) close neighbours, the partners of dialogue and exchange. A 'no-alternative' condition must be enforced upon a world in which all other aspects of life promote and offer a variety of alternatives; cultural homogeneity must be forced, by conscious effort, upon inherently pluralist reality.

Cultural community must therefore be a site of cultural coercion – all the more painful for being *experienced*, lived through, as coercion. It may survive solely at the expense of its members' freedom of choice. It cannot perpetuate itself without close surveillance, disciplining drill and severe penalties for all deviation from its norms. It is, therefore, not so much 'postmodern', as 'anti-modern': it proposes to reproduce all the more sinister and odious excesses of modern ambivalence-busting nation-building cultural crusades in a yet more stringent and merciless form, while militating against self-assertion and individual responsibility, also the products of modern revolution, which used to counterbalance and mollify the impact of homogenizing pressures. In a postmodern or late-modern world of free-flowing information and a global communicative network, the 'cultural community', so to speak, swims against the stream.

The third distinctive mark of the communitarians' 'cultural community' follows from this contradiction: preachers and defenders of cultural communities almost inevitably develop the mentality of a 'besieged fortress'. Indeed, virtually every characteristic of the surrounding world seems to conspire against the project. The feeling of fragility does not feed confidence, while lack of confidence feeds suspicion verging on paranoia. For its own spiritual security, cultural communities need many enemies – the more evil and scheming the better. Preachers and would-be leaders of cultural communities feel best in the role of border patrols. Cross-border movement and dialogue is to them an anathema; the physical closeness of people of different forms of life an abomination; free exchange of ideas with such people the most terminal of dangers.

This is perhaps what Touraine had in mind when speaking of cultural communities advocated by the communitarians as thinly-veiled dictatorships. If 'multi-culturalism', at least in some of its versions, may be a unifying and integrating, 'inclusive' force, no such chance is given to 'multi-communitarianism'. The latter is a divisive factor, 'exclusivist' by nature, with vested interest in the breakdown of communication. It cannot but generate intolerance and social and cultural separation.

If multi-culturalism, while lifting cultural diversification to the rank of supreme value, credits all cultural variation with potentially universal validity, multi-communitarianism thrives on peculiarity and non-translatability of cultural forms. For the first, cultural diversity is universally enriching; for the second, universal values are identity-impoverishing. The two programmes are not in dialogue; they talk past each other.

One wonders to what extent the debate is a cul-de-sac to which the 'totalistic', systemic view of culture must have sooner or later led the protagonist in a pluralist, diversified society of the late-modern or postmodern type. One wonders as well how much progress can be made in resolving the differences while clinging to that view, on which both programmes, explicitly or tacitly, agree.

The multi-cultural and multi-communitarian programmes are two different strategies meant to deal with a similarly diagnosed situation: the co-presence of *many cultures within the same society*. It seems, however, that the diagnosis is false to start with. The most prominent feature of contemporary life is cultural variety of societies, rather than *variety of cultures* in society: acceptance or rejection of a cultural form is no more (if it ever was) a package deal; it does not require the acceptance or rejection of the whole inventory nor does it mean a 'cultural conversion'. Even if cultures were once complete systems in which all units were crucial and indispensable for the survival of all the others, they most certainly have ceased to be such. Fragmentation has affected all fields of life, and culture is not an exception.

In the essay under the symptomatic title 'Who Needs Identity', Stuart Hall[29] proposes to distinguish between 'naturalistic' and 'discursive' understandings of identificatory processes. According to the first, 'identification is constructed on the back of a recognition of some common origin or shared characteristics with another person or group, or with an ideal, and with the natural closure of solidarity and allegiance established on this foundation'. According to the second 'identification is a construction, a process never completed – always "in process". It is not determined in the sense that it can always be "won" or "lost", sustained or abandoned.' It is the second understanding which grasps the true character of contemporary identificatory processes.

> [The concept] of identity does *not* signal that stable core of the self, unfolding from the beginning to end through all the vicissitudes of history without change. . . . Nor . . . is it that collective or true self hiding inside the many other, more superficial or artificially imposed 'selves' which a people with a shared history and ancestry hold in common.
>
> Identities are never unified and, in late modern times, increasingly fragmented and fractured; never singular but multiple, constructed across different, often intersecting and antagonistic, discourses, practices and positions.

Stuart Hall's observations are crucial and deserve close attention. If taken seriously, they require a thorough rethinking and revision of the concepts deployed and generated in the ongoing 'cultural identity' debate.

Take, for instance, the concept of cross-cultural exchange, or better still cultural diffusion. Diffusion, once a disturbing event in the daily life of cultures, has now become the culture's mode of day-to-day existence. One may go a step further, though, and conclude that the term itself has lost its usefulness. The concept of diffusion makes sense only when it is seen as a traffic between wholesome, well-defined entities; when, in other words, the treating of cultures as separate wholes itself makes sense. It is doubtful, however, whether it (still) does. If there are no rules, there are no exceptions; if there are no comprehensive and self-enclosed totalities, there is no diffusion. The idea of diffusion or cross-cultural exchange does not help understanding of contemporary culture. Neither do other traditional concepts of cultural analysis, like, for instance, assimilation or accommodation – in a similar way closely associated with the 'systemic' reality or systemic view of culture.

The idea of 'multi-culturalism' does not venture as far as 'multi-communitarianism' in suggesting self-enclosure of cultures and their overlap with similarly (though for spiritual reasons alone) self-enclosed populations. And yet it goes too far in this direction to be able to account for the dynamics of contemporary culture. After all, it is also amenable to the charge of implying that distinctiveness of cultures remains the primary reality, and that all movements and mixing of values, symbols, meanings, artefacts, patterns of behaviour and other things cultural are in consequence secondary – more or less a disturbing factor, an abnormality, even if not a reprehensible nor objectionable one. The same is implied by the currently fashionable terms like cultural hybridity, metisization or grafting: they all imply a cultural space divided more or less neatly into separate plots, each marked by more or less clearly defined difference between 'inside' and 'outside', with limited and controlled across-the-border traffic. Mixed marriages are allowed in this scheme, with 'hybrid' offspring, however, immediately claiming its own sovereign territory. Whether deliberately or against the will of their users, terms like 'multi-culturalism', 'hybridization' etc. do arouse such an image (they, after all, rely on it for their sense); an image convenient perhaps as a front for political ambitions, but fast losing touch with cultural reality. It had better be abandoned – together with the terminology of cultural debate which it evokes and resuscitates.

The most prominent feature of today's cultural stage is that the production and the distribution of cultural products has by now acquired, or is in the process of acquiring, a great deal of independence from *institutionalized* communities, and particularly the territorial *politically* institutionalized communities. Most cultural patterns reach the realm of daily life from outside the community, and most of them carry persuasive power much in excess of anything the locally-born patterns may dream of mustering and sustaining. They also travel with speed inaccessible to bodily movement, which sets them at a safe distance from agora-type face-to-face negotiation; their arrival, as a rule, takes the addressees unprepared, and the time-span of the visit is too short to allow for dialogical test. Cultural products travel free, negligent of state and provincial frontiers. Short of the Khmer Rouge or Taliban style of censorship, or prohibition of electronics, their ubiquitous presence cannot be averted. If linguistic barriers are still capable of diverting or slowing down their movement, their capacity to do so shrinks with every successive step in the development of the electronic technology.

This does not mean the ultimate demise of cultural identities. But it does mean that cultural identities and the diffusion of cultural patterns and products has changed place – at least if compared with their rendition in the orthodox imagery of culture. Motility, non-rootedness and global availability/accessibility of cultural patterns and products is now the 'primary reality' of culture, while distinct cultural identities can only emerge as outcomes of a long chain of 'secondary processes' of choice, selective retention and recombination (which, most importantly, do not grind to a halt once the identity in question does emerge).

I suggest that the image more likely to grasp the nature of cultural identities is one of the *eddy* rather than the *island*. Identities retain their distinct shape only in as far as they go on ingesting and divesting cultural matter seldom of their own making. Identities do not rest on the uniqueness of their traits, but consist increasingly in distinct ways of selecting/recycling/rearranging the cultural matter which is common to all, or at least potentially available to all. It is the movement and capacity for change, not the ability to cling to once-established form and contents, that secures their continuity.

## Relativity of culture and universality of humanity

As long as *cultural plurality* is theorized as *plurality of cultures*, students of culture cannot but see cross-cultural communication and cross-cultural comparison as one of their central problems. Indeed, since each culture divides the cultural universe into an 'inside' and 'outside', then there are at least two, and in all probability infinitely more, ways of interpreting the meaning of cultural products. There may be many 'outsider' interpretations; yet they all distort in one way or another the 'insider's' understanding. If a tacit assumption is added that the insider's interpretation is privileged over all the others, parallel to the privilege enjoyed by truth over errors, then the ideal target set for 'outside' readings is to approach as close as possible the meaning which a given cultural product has for its native producers/users. The snag is how to come close enough to that insider's understanding while not losing touch with one's own universe of meaning. This seems to be the main difficulty haunting 'cross-cultural translation'.

Historians, who explore lands not visited by ordinary folks due to their distance in time, and ethnologists, who examine lands equally unseen for reason of their distance in space, supply paradigmatical cases for the plight of experts-in-translation. Their predicament has been succintly summarized by Cornelius Castoriadis:[30]

The historian or the ethnologist is obliged to try to understand the universe of the Babylonians or Bororos . . . as they lived it and . . . to refrain from introducing into it determinations that did not exist for this culture. . . . But one cannot stop here. The ethnologist who has so thoroughly assimilated the Bororos' view of the world that he or she can no longer see the world any other way, is no longer an ethnologist but a Bororo, and the Bororos are not ethnologists. The ethnologist's *raison d'être* is not to be assimilated to the Bororos but to explain to the Parisians, the Londoners and the New Yorkers in 1965 the other humanity represented by the Bororos. And thus he can do so only through *language*. . . .

Castoriadis points out immediately that the language translated and the language through which the translation is made available to the Parisians or the New Yorkers are not 'equivalent codes' – they are structured by different 'imaginary significations'. To do her job properly the translator must come as close as possible to those significations, but when that end seems about to be reached, when she comes quite close, she might, literally, fall inside and her locutions would be as illegible to the readers back home as the experiences she set out to translate.

Aspiring anthropologists used to be forewarned by the sad story of Frank Cushing, once the top expert in Zuni culture. The better Cushing understood Zunis, the stronger he felt that his reports, gratefully received and praised by fellow anthropologists, distorted rather than conveyed Zuni reality. He came to suspect that all translation was a deformation. He wouldn't be satisfied with any depth of his own understanding; he sensed another bottom beneath each bottom he reached. In the search of perfect translation Cushing resolved to experience the Zuni's universe 'from inside'. He succeeded; the Zuni accepted him as one of their own and bestowed on him the highest accolade a Zuni may earn: the office of the Archpriest of the Rainbow. Since then, though, Cushing has not written a single sentence of anthropology.

There is a paradigmatical description of the ethnologist's situation in the marvellous story 'Averroes' Search' by the great Latin American writer Jorge Luis Borges[31] – the thinker equally at home in all the traditions converging on the world of modern learned classes. Puzzled by the words 'tragedia' and 'comedia' found in Aristotle's text, the Averroes of Jorge Luis Borges' story struggled for days on end to find its adequate rendition in Arabic. His trouble was not, however, merely of the dictionary, linguistic kind. It went deeper: Averroes never in his life went to the theatre, an invention unknown and alien to the world of Islam in which he was born and lived. He had no experience to which the unfamiliar words could be referred. In the end, Averroes wrote the following lines: 'Aristu gives the name of tragedy to panegyrics and that of comedy to satires and anathemas. Admirable tragedies and comedies abound in the pages of the Koran and in the *mohalacas* of the sanctuary.' With an unsurpassed clarity Borges reveals the sense of what has happened here:

> In the foregoing story, I tried to narrate the process of a defeat, I first thought of the archbishop of Canterbury, who took it upon himself to prove there is a God; then, of the alchemists who sought the philosopher's stone; then, of the vain trisectors of the angle and squarers of the circle. Later I reflected that it would be more poetic

to tell the case of a man who sets himself a goal which is not forbidden to others, but is to him. I remembered Averroes who, closed within the orb of Islam, could never know the meaning of the terms *tragedy* and *comedy*.

Then comes the main point, a report of remarkable self-discovery, anticipating by quite a few years the tormented soul-searching and dazzling revelations of cultural anthropologists:

> I related his case; as I went along, I felt what that god mentioned by Burton must have felt when he tried to create a bull and created a buffalo instead. I felt that the work was mocking me. I felt that Averroes, wanting to imagine what a drama is without ever having suspected what a theatre is, was no more absurd than I, wanting to imagine Averroes with no other sources than a few fragments from Renan, Lane and Asín Palacios. I felt, on the last page, that my narration was a symbol of the man I was as I wrote it and that, in order to compose that narration, I had to be that man and, in order to be that man, I had to compose that narration, and so on to infinity. (The moment I cease to believe in him, 'Averroes' disappears.)

The difficult wisdom obtained by Western readers of foreign cultures after a couple of centuries of unwarranted, yet no less for that reason arrogant, self-confidence is all here already – in the musings of the great mind thinking his thoughts inside the world cast by the centre as peripheral – yet for that very reason kept forcefully on the top of the 'translation barricade'. Translation is a process of self-creation and of mutual creation; far from exercising the translator's authority to put the translated in his right place, the translator must first rise herself to the level of the translated; but if translation creates the translated text, it also creates the translator. Without the story of Averroes' search, the searching Averroes disappears; both the translator and the translated come into being and vanish in the process of translation – each being an imaginary screen on which the same ongoing labour of communication is projected. We are often worried by what is 'lost in translation'. Perhaps we worry unduly, or we worry about the wrong thing: what is truly lost we will never *know*, anyway, and if we come to know, we won't be able to *share* our knowledge with those for whom we wished to translate. Let us count the gains instead. There are things which can be gained only in translation.

For a longer part of its history the theory of hermeneutics – of the understanding of what is not immediately understandable or carries the danger of misunderstanding – was a narration of the truth-seeker's exploits in the land of prejudice, ignorance and self-ignorance; the story of bringing light to darkness, fighting superstition, correcting the error – and otherwise cleaning up the stains left by accidents of history, always local and most often far-away, on the pure face of the objective meaning and the universally valid. In that narrative, the interpreter was a mask of the legislator; the interpreter construed through that narrative was expected to reveal the truth of what the experiencers of the interpreted experience, due to their own pristine and unenlightened naivety, were unable to penetrate. Like Joseph Conrad's Marlow and Kurtz, the explorer of other cultures was pushed by the urge to bring light into what has been therefore 'the heart of darkness'. In the last account, translation was not an exchange between two different languages, let alone an equal exchange between two equal languages; it was an act of lifting the contingent to the level of the objective through the act of meaning-legislation, to which only the translator, not the translated, was entitled.

In the famous 1983 lecture which introduced into the present-day social-scientific discourse the concept of 'anti-anti-relativism'[32] and in numerous studies subsequently published, Clifford Geertz popularized the idea that in the work of the explorer of 'another culture', 'natives', immersed in their similarly contingent worlds, meet on *both sides* of the encounter. There is no supra-cultural and supra-historical (and so free from all contingency) observation point from which the true and universal meaning can be sighted and subsequently portrayed; none of the partners in the encounter occupies such a point. Translation is an ongoing, unfinished and inconclusive *dialogue* which is bound to remain such. The meeting of two contingencies is itself a contingency, and no effort will ever stop it from being such. The act of translation is not a one-off event which will put paid to the need of further translating effort. The meeting ground, the frontierland, of cultures is the territory in which boundaries are constantly obsessively drawn only to be continually violated and re-drawn again and again – not the least for the fact that both partners emerge changed from every successive attempt at translation.

Cross-cultural translation is a continuous process which *serves* as much as *constitutes* the cohabitation of people who can afford neither occupying the same space nor mapping that common space in their own, separate ways. No act of translation leaves either of the partners intact. Both emerge from their encounter changed, different at the end of act from what they were at its beginning – and so with the translation left behind the moment it has been completed, in need of 'another go' – and that reciprocal change is the work of translation.

In a recent book[33] Anthony Giddens comments profusely on Nigel Bailey's anthropological trip to Indonesia, which in his view set the pattern for the approach the students of 'other cultures' may and should follow. 'Anthropology', Giddens observes approvingly, 'discovered what might be called the essential *intelligence* of other cultures and traditions.' It has done it, however, belatedly. For a long time, following the canons of orthodox methodology meant to observe in anthropological reports the principle of the 'absence of the author'. That pretended absence was, however, a disguise for the assumption of the author's superiority, of his omniscience: as if the author dissolved, and disappeared with all his socially contrived or private failings and follies – in the objective knowledge for which he acted as the spokesman ('the anatomy of man', Karl Marx explained, is the key to the anatomy of ape; by that view, 'higher forms' of human evolution reveal what the 'lower forms' were about: they were groping in the dark to reach the truth which only opens to their 'more advanced' successors). In Giddens' view, the putative 'absence of the author' had the effect that the studies so produced were 'not full dialogical engagements with "other cultures"'. On his trip to Indonesia Bailey behaved differently, and admirably: '*He* is the *ingénu*, rather than those whom he goes to investigate. He is like a Lucky Jim of the anthropological world.'

Giddens grasps here the essence of the new anthropology, one made to the measure of the post-colonial world, where most frontiers are encounters between strangers of whom none come to the meeting with the permission to set the agenda in their pockets. All residents of the frontierland face now a similar task. To understand, not to censure; to interpret, not to legislate; to abandon soliloquy for the sake of the dialogue – this seems to be the precept for a new, humbler, yet for this reason more potent humanities, promising bewildered men and women inhabiting our times some insight and a modicum of orientation in the mass of increasingly uncoordinated and often contradictory experiences – and, for once, capable of delivering on its promise. But there is more to be said.

The above seems also to be the precept for humanities made to the measure of our times of global exchange and communication, of time flattened and space shrunk or abolished altogether. In this kind of a world, inter-cultural boundaries can be drawn only tentatively and live but a tenuous, adventurous and precarious life. They are mostly imagined – and the imagination which sustains them faces overwhelming odds: virtually all the material and spiritual forces of our times must count amongst its adversaries. Borders, real or putative, are crossed so often that rather than to speak of boundary lines which maybe alternatively guarded or breached it is more to the point to describe our plight as life carried in the *frontierland*. Whatever the borders are meant to keep apart is in fact mixed and randomly dispersed, and dividing lines are never anything more than unfinished projects which are bound to and indeed tend to be abandoned before coming anywhere near completion. Lines are drawn in the moving sands only to be effaced and redrawn the day after.

Wojciech Burszta, a distinguished member of the brilliant generation of young Polish anthropologists who did a lot to take stock of that new state of affairs, points out that 'the traditional theory of culture, so well tested in case of stable, isolated, relatively small populations, economically simple and self-contained etc., is hopeless in the face of 'cultures on the move'.[34]

> Cultures become inter-dependent, they penetrate each other, none is a 'world in its own right', each one has a hybrid and heterogeneous status, none is monolithic and all are intrinsically diversified; there is, simultaneously, a cultural *mélange* and globality of culture. . . .
>
> The time of intellectual travels to the 'silent peripheries' is over; the latter speak in their own voices, or travelled themselves to the centre, often uninvited. . . .

One looks suspiciously, concludes Burszta, at the very notion of 'culture' as a self-enclosed entity, self-consistent and neatly circumscribed. One would rather abandon the supposition of separate cultures altogether, and instead speak of 'otherness' – a mode of existence and co-existence as universal as it is unsystemic and often random. The difference is the shape of the world around; diversity is the shape of the world inside each of us. We are all translators now, whenever we speak to each other – but also whenever we ponder what we justly, but to a large extent putatively, perceive as our own thoughts.

I mentioned before Geertz's anti-anti-relativism stance. There is a parallel, yet somewhat different, idea in the work of Richard Rorty: the programme of anti-anti-ethnocentrism. Quite a few critics of orthodox cultural anthropology which considered otherness as symptom of parochialism and local particularism as well as of ignorance, immaturity or another manifestation of inferiority, while mistaking its own similarly local and contingent perspective for the objective and universal point of view, proclaimed for a change the *equality* of all cultural choices and thus denied the possibility of cross-cultural comparisons and evaluations. In their well-justified resentment of orthodox extremism these critics went straight to the opposite extreme, thus making themselves an easy target for criticism, coming this time from the quarters rightly worried by the dire ethical consequences of the radically relativist stance. Rorty's anti-anti-relativism purports to steer clear of both extreme stances; but it refers to the contemporary cultural stage to demonstrate that the extremist stand is unnecessary in the first place. What Rorty's anti-anti-relativism implies is, roughly, the following:

It is not true that all cultural values and precepts are equal just because the fact that all of them have been chosen somewhere and at some stage of history. Some cultural solutions are indeed 'more equal than others' – though not in the once upheld sense of being endemically superior answers to the universal problems of the human condition, but solely in the sense that unlike other cultures they are ready to consider their own historicity and contingency, and so also the possibility of comparison on equal terms. A culture may claim superiority in as far as it is ready to look seriously at cultural alternatives, treat them as partners for dialogue rather than passive recipients of monological homilies, and as the source of enrichment rather than collections of curios waiting to be censured, buried or confined to a museum. The superiority of such cultural solutions consists precisely in not taking its own substantive superiority for granted and acknowledging itself as a contingent presence, which like all contingent beings needs yet to justify itself in substantive terms – also in terms of its ethical value.[35]

Now all this is precisely the characteristic of our own – liberal, democratic, and above all *tolerant* – 'cultural frontierland'. That is, in as far as this land remains liberal, democratic and tolerant; which, being a *frontier*land, it has some, even a considerable, chance to be. Being liberal and democratic means to be 'in a dialogical mood' – invitingly open and hospitable, thinking of the borders as places of encounter and friendly conversation rather than places of passport and visa control and custom checks. It means to be inclusive, not exclusive – treating others as speaking subjects, assuming their right and ability to speak at least until proven otherwise, and hoping for a new light to come from exercising that right.

All this the living in a frontierland which we – by choice or by necessity – inhabit *may be*. But there is no guarantee – no 'historical inevitability' – for it to be such. Poly-vocality may be resented as much as it may be enjoyed. Confusion, ambivalence and uncertainty which accompany it show that the frontierland life is not all beer and skittles and may inspire indignation, vexation and anger. The frontierland is a territory of intense exchange; a breeding ground for tolerance and even for mutual understanding, but also a site of perpetual squabbles and skirmishes and a fertile soil for tribal sentiments and xenophobia. The frontierland-type cultural condition is notorious for being torn apart by opposite and mutually hostile tendencies, all the more difficult to be reconciled for the fact of arising from the same condition.

Which tendency will eventually prevail is an open question; let us beware of theories which boast to preempt historical choices. Equally strong arguments may be gathered to support a bleak prospect of communal self-entrenchment and inter-communal silent or vociferous hostility as may be advanced for the likelihood of further effacement of cultural boundaries. Whatever turn the events may take, one would be well advised to heed Michel Foucault's warning:[36]

> What is good, is something that comes through innovation. The good does not exist, like that, in an atemporal sky, with people who would be like the Astrologers of the Good, whose job is to determine what is the favourable nature of the stars. The good is defined by us, it is practiced, it is invented. And this is a collective work.

No astrologers, no people with a direct telephone line to the preordained order of creation – however numerous are the applicants for such jobs. 'Better' and 'worse' are not pre-selected in advance and no way of making the selection can be vouched to be foolproof. The good cannot be guaranteed – but it can be given the chance to appear: the collective work going on, the negotiation continuing and successfully resisting all premature closure (a pleonasm, to be sure: in the question of values, no closure can be well timed – all closure cannot but be premature).

Our time, the time of cultural pluralism as distinct from plurality of cultures, is not the time of nihilism. It is not the absence of values nor the loss of their authority which makes the human situation confusing and choices difficult, but the multitude of values, poorly coordinated and linked (but weakly) to a variety of different, often discordant, authorities. No longer is the assertion of one set of values accompanied with the detraction of all the others; a constant trade-off situation is the result – an unnerving experience, which makes the promises of a 'great simplification' alluring. The safety of Foucault's 'collective work' is in no way guaranteed – the will to negotiation and dialogue is buffeted and frayed by the contrary dream of an ultimate choice which would make all further choices redundant and irrelevant. The real dilemma is one not of living with values, versus living without, but of readiness to recognize validity, the 'good reasons' of many values and the temptation to denigrate and condemn the values other than the ones currently chosen. As Jeffrey Weeks has put it recently.[37]

> The problem does not lie in the absence of values, but in our inability to recognize that there are many different ways of being human, and in articulating the common strands which often unite them.

This problem, though, is itself a source of problems. Strands presented as 'common' may themselves be the instruments of value-erosion. It seems that the present-day astonishing popularity of 'economic values' – like effective-ness, efficiency, competitiveness – stems to a considerable extent precisely from their indifference to the quality of values which they propose to serve as a 'common denominator'. The said economic values offer allegedly foolproof guidance to choice just by glossing over, playing down or effacing everything that made the choice necessary and 'collective work' indispensable in the first place: the genuine difference between various ways of being human, the good which each way promotes, the impossibility of value-choice without value-sacrifice. As Simmel pointed out a long time ago, what makes values valuable is the price we must pay for choosing them – in terms of forfeiting or surrendering something else, no less precious and worth defending. In this sense, the promotion of economic calculation to the rank of the supreme, indeed the sole, value is, alongside other varieties of contemporary funda-mentalism, a most important source of the nihilist threat.

Again, Jeffrey Weeks puts the present dilemma in the right perspective when he says in the case of 'humanity' understood as 'the unity of the species'

> the challenge is to construct that unity in a way which achieves ('invents' or 'imag-ines') a sense of 'universal human value' while representing human variety and difference. . .
>
> Humanity is not an essence to be realised, but a pragmatic construction, a per-spective, to be developed through the articulation of the variety of individual projects, of differences, which constitute our humanity in the broadest sense. . . .

And finally, a warning: 'The danger lies not in the commitments to com-munity and difference, but in their exclusive nature.' There is no necessary link between value-preference and denial of other values. Neither inclusive-ness nor exclusion, neither openness nor closure, neither readiness to learn nor the impulse to teach, neither readiness to listen nor the urge to command, neither sympathetic curiosity nor the posture of hostile negligence towards ways of being human different from one's own are works of historical inevitability or attitudes rooted in human nature. None of the alternatives is more likely to be fulfilled than another – and in each case the passage from possibility to reality is mediated by the polity, that is, by the forum of think-ing and talking people.

For more than a century, cultures were posited primarily as technologies of discrimination and separation, factories of differences and oppositions. Yet dialogue and negotiation are also cultural phenomena – and such as are given in our times of plurality an ever-rising, perhaps decisive, importance. The pragmatic construction called 'humanity' is also a cultural project, and a project not at all outside the reach of human cultural capacity. That this is so, one can find ample confirmation in our shared experience of daily life. After all, living together, talking to each other and successfully negotiating mutually satisfactory solutions to joint problems are in that experience the norm, not an exception. One can express about cultural plurality the same opinion Gadamer expressed about the plurality of cognitive horizons: if understanding is a miracle, it is a daily miracle and one accomplished by ordinary people, not professional miracle-makers.

## Notes

1 See Reinhart Koselleck, 'Richtlinien für das Lexikon politisch-sozialer Begriffe der Neuzeit', *Archiv für Begriffsgeschichte*, vol. 9. Also Odo Marquard, *Abschied von Prinzipiellen: Philosophische Studien*, Stuttgart, Philipp Reckam jun, 1991.

2 John Carroll, *Humanism: The Wreck of Western Culture*, London, Fontana Press, 1983, p. 2.

3 Friedrich Nietzsche, *The Will to Power*, trans. by Walter Kaufmann and R. J. Hollingdale, London, Weidenfeld & Nicholson, 1968, p. 476.

4 H. G. Wells, *Anticipations of the Reactions of Mechanical and Scientific Progress upon Human Life and Thought*, London, Chapman & Hall, 1901, p. 317. See John Carey's discussion of the above in *The Intellectuals and the Masses: Pride and Prejudice among the Literary Intelligentsia 1880–1939*, London, Faber & Faber 1992, chapter 'H. G. Wells getting rid of people'.

5 See Paul Ricoeur, 'Autonomie et vulnérabilite', in *La justice et le mal*, ed. Antoine Garapon & Denis Salas, Paris, Odile Jacob 1997, pp. 166–7.

6 Ibid, p. 178.

7 See *Towards a General Theory of Social Action: Theoretical Foundations for the Social Sciences*, ed. Talcott Parsons and Edward A. Shils, New York, Harper & Row 1951, pp. 16, 24 (italics added).

8 Georg Simmel, 'On the concept and the tragedy of culture', in *Conflict in Modern Culture and other Essays*, trans. by K. Peter Etzkorn, New York, Teachers college Press, 1968, pp. 29, 30.

9 Georg Simmel, 'The conflict in modern culture', ibid., pp. 11, 15.

10 Cornelius Castoriadis, 'Le délabrement de l'Occident', in *La Montée d'insignifiance*, Paris, Seuil, 1996, pp. 67, 65.

11 Marc Fumaroli, *L'état culturel: Essai sur la religion moderne*, Paris, Fallois, 1991, pp. 42, 171–2.

12 Cf. Paul Virilio, 'Un monde surexposé: Fin de l'histoire, ou fin de la géographie?', *Le Monde Diplomatique*, August 1997, p. 17. The idea of the 'end of geography' was first advanced, to my knowledge, by Richard O'Brien (cf. his *Global Financial Integration: The End of Geography*, London, Chatham House/Pinter, 1992).

13 Michael Benedikt, 'On cyberspace and virtual reality', in *Man and Information Technology* (lectures from an international symposium arranged by the Committee on Man, Technology and Society at the Royal Swedish Academy of Engineering Sciences [IVA] in 1994), Stockholm, 1995, p. 41.

14 Timothy W. Luke, 'Identity, meaning and globalization: Detraditionalization in postmodern space-time compression', in *Detraditionalization*, ed. Paul Heelas, Scott Lash and Paul Morris, Oxford, Blackwell, 1996, pp. 123, 125.

15 Paul Virilio, *The Lost Dimension*, New York, Semiotext(e), 1991, p. 13.

16 Cornelius Castoriadis, *L'institution imaginaire de la société*, Paris, Seuil, 1975. Here quoted in English translation by Kathleen Blamey, Cambridge, Polity, 1987, pp. 218–19.

17 Friedrich Nietzsche, *Beyond Good and Evil*, trans. by Helen Zimmern, Quoted after *The Philosophy of Nietzsche*, ed. Geoffrey Clive, New York, Mentor Books, 1965, p. 211.

18 Ernest Gellner, *Nations and Nationalism*, Oxford, Blackwell, 1983, pp. 48–9.

19 Frederick Barth, *Ethnic Groups and Boundaries: The Social Organization of Cultural Difference*, ed. Frederick Barth, Bergen, Universitets Forlaget, 1969, pp. 14–15. This is what Elias Canetti had to say on the role, the folly, and the costs of borders: 'The heroes who died for them, and their posterity, who pull the borders away from under the graves. Walls in wrong places, and where they actually ought to be put up if they didn't have to stand in other places long since. The uniforms of dead border officials, and the mischief in difficult passes, eternal transgressions, dislocations, and unreliable detritus. The arrogant ocean; uncontrollable worms; birds from country to country, a proposal for exterminating them.' *The Human Province*, trans. Joachim Neugroschel, London, Deutsch, 1985, p. 20.

20 'La douceur d'être inclu', in *Sociabilité, Pouvoirs et Société*, Actes du colloque de Rouen, Novembre 1983, textes réunis par F. Thelamon, University of Rouen Press, 1987, p. 19. The

alternative to the 'doucer d'être inclu' is 'la cruauté d'être exclu' (p. 31), One may guess that it is precisely the fear of the cruelty of exclusion which makes the prospect of belonging so sweet; the experience of exclusion (arising sometimes from eviction, other times from the disappearance or wilting of frames that made belonging secure and thus unreflexive) precedes the conscious embracement of inclusion as an end and a task; it creates the thirst for identity and triggers off the active search for the sweet nectar of belonging; that is, of the authoritative confirmation of identity, stamping the identity with an entry visa.

21 Ernest Renan, from 'L'avenir de la science', in *Pages Choisis*, Paris, Calman Levy, 1896, pp. 27, 31.

22 Robert Muchembled, *L'invention de l'homme moderne: Sociabilité, moeurs et comportements collectives dans l'Ancien Régime*, Paris, Fayard, 1988, pp. 12, 13, 150. The idea of the two-pronged, sharply differentiated effects of the 'civilizing process' (aimed polemically against the 'trickling down' model popularized by Norbert Elias) has been systematically pursued by Muchembled also in his other works (see particularly *La violence en village: Sociabilité et comportements en Artois du XVᵉ au XVIIᵉ siècle*, Paris, Bregnols, 1989). According to Muchembled, the most profound mutations in sensibility and behavioural standards of quotidianity were limited to a narrow elite; they functioned simultaneously as a vehicle of self-distancing and as a vantage point for a new perspective from which the rest of the population was scanned as uniformly vulgar and, for the initial period at least, *uncivilizable*. Self-polishing as the strategy of the elite was juxtaposed to confinement, policing and universal surveillance as the strategy to be deployed in dealing with 'the masses'. The civilizing process is best understood as the 'recomposition' of the new structure of control and domination once the pre-modern institutions of social integration had proven inadequate and had gradually decomposed (I have argued this point more fully in my *Legislators and Interpreters: On Modernity, Postmodernity and the Intellectuals*, Cambridge, Polity Press, 1987).

23 Gellner, op. cit., p. 34. Let us recall that Renan (though his views on the subject are remembered mostly for the constantly quoted description of the nation as 'un plébiscite de tous les jours') would never accept that *le peuple* (it was not for nothing that he saw them, and feared them, as ' la masse lourde et grossiére' . . .) can vote in that plebiscite as of right. He considered freedom of education an absurdity; what the objects of educational action needed was *authority*, not freedom of choice, which they would not know how to exercise anyway. Until education achieves its purpose and the trainees are shaped and trimmed in the right way, 'to preach freedom is to preach destruction; it is as if, of respect for the laws of bears and lions, one would open the cages of the zoo' (cf. Renan, op. cit., pp. 28–34). Almost a century before Renan (in 1806), Fichte postulated that new education must consist in this, 'that it completely destroys freedom of will in the soil which it undertakes to cultivate, and produces, on the contrary, strict necessity in the decision of the will. . . . If you want to influence him [the object of the educating effort] at all, you must do more than merely talk to him; you must fashion him, and fashion him, and fashion him in such a way that he simply cannot will otherwise than you wish him to will.' Quoted after Elie Kedourie, *Nationalism*, London, Hutchinson, 1960, p. 83.

24 Maurice Barrès *Scènes et doctrines du nationalisme*, Paris, Émile Paul, 1902, p. 443.

25 Ibid., pp. 8–13.

26 Ibid., pp. 16, 20.

27 See Charles Taylor, 'Can liberalism be communitarian?', *Critical Review*, vol. 8 no. 2, 1994, pp. 257–62.

28 Alain Touraine, 'Faux et vrais problèmes', in *Une société fragmentée? – Le multiculturalisme en debat*, sous la direction de Michel Wiewiorka, Paris, La Découverte, 1997, pp. 312, 306, 310.

29 Stuart Hall, 'Who needs identity?', in *Questions of Cultural Identity*, ed. Stuart Hall and Paul du Gay, London, Sage 1996, pp. 3–4.

30 Cornelius Castoriadis, *Imaginary Institution of Society*, trans. by Kathleen Blamey, Cambridge, Polity Press, 1987, p. 163.

31 Jorge Luis Borges, 'Averroes' search', in *Labyrinths*, Harmondsworth, Penguin, 1970, pp. 187–8.

32 Clifford Geertz, 'Distinguished lecture: Anti-anti-relativism', *American Anthropologist*, no. 2, 1984, p. 263. Summing up the long and still ongoing debate about the linguistic limits of

all beliefs, Leszek Kołakowski points out that 'legitimacy is always relative to a certain game, culture, collective or individual purpose. . . . We have no tools which would enable us to force open the gate leading beyond language, beyond contingent cultural norms, beyond practical imperatives that form our thought'. *Horror Metaphysicus*, Warsaw, PWN 1990, p. 9.

33 Anthony Giddens, 'The future of anthropology', in *In Defence of Sociology: Essays, Interpretations, and Rejoinders*, Cambridge, Polity Press, 1996, pp. 121–6.

34 Wojciech J. Burszta, *Czytanie Kultury*, Łódź, 1996, pp. 73, 68, 70.

35 Cf. Richard Rorty, 'On ethnocentrism: A reply to Clifford Geertz', in *Objectivity, Relativism and Truth*, Cambridge, Cambridge University Press, 1991, pp. 202–4.

36 See Michael Bess' interview with Michel Foucault, in *History of the Present*, Spring 1988, p. 13.

37 Jeffrey Weeks, 'Rediscovering values', in *Principal Positions*, ed. Judith Squares, London, Lawrence & Wishart, 1993, pp. 192–200.

# 1

# CULTURE AS CONCEPT

The unyielding ambiguity of the concept of culture is notorious. Much less so is the idea that this ambiguity follows not so much from the way people define culture, as from the incompatibility of numerous lines of thought, which have come together historically in the same term. Scholars are usually sophisticated enough to realize that similarity of terms is a poor guide when identity or diversity of concepts is to be established. Still, methodological self-consciousness is one thing, the magic of words is another. Only too many people too often find themselves misled by a rash though commonsensical inclination into imposing a frail conceptual unity on similar terms. The effort, which can be of some profit in the case of the artificial languages of science, would hardly have borne fruit if the terms at stake, like the term of culture, had had a long pre-scientific and cosmopolitan history of their own. Terms of this kind would almost certainly have been adopted by different scholarly communities to answer diverse problems rooted in divergent interests. As a rule, the inherent qualities of the term do not constrain too tightly its eventual conceptual usage. Neither is there a 'natural' necessity for a free-floating term to be adopted each time a particular conceptual demand is felt.

Few people know this last rule better than Anglo-Saxon anthropologists on opposite sides of the Atlantic. Though driven by the same overpowering urge 'to put on record' the alien ways of life on the verge of extinction, they faced two very different situations. As W. J. M. Mackenzie has recently pointed out, 'the Americans had to work principally with languages, artefacts, individual survivors; the British could sit and watch quietly, in the midst of social systems which were superficially untouched by British rule'.[1] By dint of their own (though not voluntarily chosen) procedure, what they extracted orally from isolated survivors of the débâcle appeared to the Americans as a cobweb of mental 'oughts'. They called what they saw (or, more exactly, what they imagined they saw), 'culture'. At the same time, their British counterparts – since the oral information they obtained seemed to be backed by the reality of living communities – were inclined to organize basically similar data into a network of 'ises'. They called it 'social structure'. In the last analysis, both sides were after the same thing: to what extent and in what respect the behaviour of people X differs from the behaviour of peoples Y and Z. More than that: both sides did realize that to achieve this aim they should discover and/or reconstruct repeatable patterns of human behaviour in which communities differ from each other. Both sides, therefore, pursued the same aim and sought the same kinds of primary data. The theoretical concepts they riveted onto their explanatory and ordering models were, however, different. The whole, into which individual conduct was expected to fit, meant to the British a group of interlocking individuals; for the Americans it meant a system of interlocking norms. The British wanted to know in the first instance why and how people integrate; the Americans were curious how norms and principles collaborate or clash. Both groups were fond of the concept of role, and both considered it the indispensable and crucial analytical tool in making the dispersed empirical data intelligible. Still the British would see the role as the intermediate link integrating individual behaviour with the exigencies of the social structure, while the Americans would have chosen rather to put it in the position intermediate between individual conduct and the intricate web of norms and moral imperatives. Of much greater importance still was the fact that the two divergent theoretical inclinations had been eventually crowned with two contrasting names. Long after both sides had accepted the legitimacy of each other's approach and had ceased to comprehend the fury of their past methodological crusades, the belief that one can deal with 'social relations *rather* than culture'[2] remained the main, if not the only, relic of the otherwise forgotten controversies.

The above is a conspicuous example of a situation in which acceptance of the term by some and rejection of it by others can inspire both sides to exaggerate whatever conceptual peculiarities happen to separate them. Conversely, much deeper conceptual rifts tend to be overlooked or underestimated if they happen to be concealed behind kindred terms.

Symptomatic of this tendency is the fact that the majority of scholars who try to introduce some order into the vast spectrum of contexts in which the term 'culture' appears approach their task as, in the first instance, the need 'to classify the accepted definitions'. In most cases the overlapping, if not identity, of semantic fields is tacitly, if not explicitly, assumed. What is allegedly left to be reconciled are divergent preoccupations of schools or single authors with one or another aspect of the field. Thus A. Kroeber and C. Kluckhohn,[3] having divided carefully collected *definitions* of culture into six groups, remained convinced that what made each group different from the others was the diversity of aspects the authors had chosen as the defining features of an otherwise common semantic field (the terminological essence of acknowledged divergences was appropriately stressed by the choice of classificatory entries; there were descriptive, historical, normative, psychological, structural and genetical definitions in Kroeber and Kluckhohn's taxonomy). A decade later Albert Carl Cafagna[4] set out on the same exploratory trip to produce divisions only nominally different (definitions stressing social heritage, or learned behaviour, or ideas, or standardized behaviour). It did not occur to him either that domains having the fullest phenomenal resemblance may still acquire quite contradictory meanings if placed in disparate semantic frameworks.

Closest to this discovery were those sociologists and anthropologists who pushed forward the famed distinction between the value-bound and the value-neutral understandings of culture, though the belief that the most important dividing line between social theories runs along the value-com-mitted–value-free axis seems to have appeared, fortunately, to be a passing fad. The distinction sanctioned, even if only implicitly, the inevitable con-tention that the concepts opposed to a term in a particular context have more to say on its meaning than the most meticulously phrased definition derived analytically from the same term taken in isolation. In Sapir's famous distinction between a culture which embodies 'any socially inherited element in the life of man' and one which 'refers to a rather conventional ideal of indi-vidual refinement'[5] the same term appears in two obviously distinct semantic fields: in the first case it is opposed to a 'state of nature', e.g. lack of a socially inheritable lore, while in the second it is contrasted with a roughness deter-mined by slackness or failure of the refining (educational) processes. It is not that the concept has been defined in two different ways in turn; the same term stands, as a matter of fact, for two different theoretical concepts. It would be a vain effort to try to bridge the semantic gap between them and to encom-pass both concepts by a single definition.

In fact the conceptually institutionalized cognitive interests lurking behind the single term of 'culture' are more numerous than one can learn from Sapir's dichotomy. Each is located in a substantially different semantic field, surrounded by a specific set of paradigmatically and syntagmatically linked notions and deriving/manifesting its meaning in a distinct series of cognitive contexts. This circumstance seems to be decisive for the choice of taxonomi-cal strategy in the domain of theoretical concepts. The alternative strategy, the one applied in fact in most popular classifications, would consist in sorting out the attributes used by various authors to describe an 'objectively' sepa-rated class of substantial phenomena. We would have to assume that there is some objective way of defining a peculiar class of cultural phenomena; that the task of a scholar wishing to define it consists in picking up or discovering a number of features which are present in each member of the class; and that the task of a scholar wishing to classify the proposed definitions consists in splitting them in the most convenient and parsimonious way into a limited number of divisions, each of them possessing its own common denominator. The philosophy behind this strategy assumes an unquestionable priority of the phenomenal universe, objectively and in itself determined and ordered, and a merely subordinate, derivative role for human discourse.

This brings us into the midst of a controversial philosophical problem of the nature of meaning – something however we cannot elaborate here at any length proportionate to its significance and the sophistication granted to it by the experts. However important the problem is in itself, it plays a mere auxil-iary role in our consideration. I hope I may simply declare that from among many current theories of meaning I opt for the use theory, i.e. the one which tries to elucidate the meaning of semantically-loaded linguistic elements through study of the locations in which they appear in both paradigmatical and syntagmatical dimensions.[6] As J. N. Findlay says,[7]

What is implicit in the slogan 'Don't ask for the meaning: ask for the use' is not that use covers much *more* than the connotative and denotative functions of language,

but that it somehow resumes and completely explains the latter, that we can completely see around and see through talk about the reference and connotation of
expressions by taking note of the way people operate with such expressions, how
they combine them with other expressions to form sentences, and the varying *circumstances* in which producing such sentences is reckoned appropriate or fully
justifiable.

I would not certainly go all the way with the most pragmatically-minded
spokesmen for the use theory, who deny the significance of 'pre-existent
meanings', i.e. pre-existent in relation to the actual utterance.[8] But I shall
insist on the intimate connexion and *inter*-dependence (in opposition to a
one-way dependence only) between the contextual plane and the plane of
meaning. The two planes are inseparable and constitute each other by the
force of 'a correlation between the contextual variation on the one hand and
the variations of content on the other'.[9] Each term usable in meaningful communication is an index in the semiological sense of the word, to wit, it reduces
the previous incertitude of the perceived universe, brings some order into the
hitherto amorphous domain. But this index is related not only to the class of
phenomena it 'names'; the index-term organizes the whole universe and so is
related to the universe as a whole and can be understood in its total framework only. The act of indication (the activity which constitutes the index)
'inevitably presents a negative aspect beside its positive one'. The class indicated by the index 'is not an absolute entity; what it is, it is only due to its
relationship to another, complementary class. . . . To determine a class, one
has to start from "un univers du discours"; the complement of the class may
be defined as a class formed by the objects belonging to the "univers du discours" but not embraced by the class in question'.[10] Now neither the index
and the class positively denoted by it, nor the *univers du discours* in which
alone it is meaningful, leads an independent existence. A more or less constant bond between a particular index-term and a particular class of objects
may be, and indeed quite often is, established in a given community, to the
extent of foisting itself, with the force of an external inevitability, on each particular    member    of    the    community    and    on    each    particular
communication-event. Viewed historically, however, it obviously exists no
longer, but not less long either, than the *univers du discours* it not only orders
but also brings into existence.

Because of historical circumstances not exceedingly relevant to our subject,
the term 'culture' has been incorporated into three separate *univers du discours*. In each of the three contexts the term orders a different semantic field,
singles out and denotes different classes of objects, brings into relief different
aspects of the members of these classes, suggests different sets of cognitive
questions and research strategies. Which means that in each case the term,
though keeping its form intact, connotes a different concept. There is one
term, but three separate concepts. One can obviously point to numerous tan-
gential points common to the three fields. One can perhaps try to belittle the
most protruding and apparently irremovable discrepancies as marginal and
temporary controversies which would have been better eliminated for the

sake of 'conceptual clarity' or 'terminological unambiguity'. But before doing this, one should be sure that the game is indeed worth the candle. In fact it most probably is not.

One of the assumptions of the present study is that what is different between three co-existing concepts of culture (and what is determined by the by no means contingent and secondary divergencies between their respective semantic fields) is exactly the most cognitively rich, fruitful, and thus academically exciting part of their content. Three questions which shape their subordinate *univers du discours* are equally legitimate and significant. We had better exploit the immense cognitive opportunities seminal in their specificity than strain ourselves in a much less rewarding effort to achieve a one-to-one symmetry between a single concept and a single term. I will try to show in this study that the price would have been too high to be easily justified by a predominantly aesthetic satisfaction. The decisive point is not so much whether the three notions can or cannot be reduced to a common denominator, but whether this reduction is indeed desirable.


## Culture as hierarchical concept

This usage of the term 'culture' is so deeply ingrained in the common pre-scientific layer of the Western mentality, that everybody knows it well, though sometimes unreflectively, from his own everyday experience. We admonish a person, who has failed to live up to the group standards, for his 'lack of culture'. We repeatedly stress the 'transmitting of culture' as the leading function of educational institutions. We are prone to grade the persons with whom we come in touch according to the *level* of their culture. If we mark somebody as a 'cultured person', we mean usually that he is well-educated, polished, urbane, enriched above his 'natural' state, ennobled. We tacitly assume that there are others who do not possess any of these attributes. The 'cultured person' is an antonym of an 'uncultured' one.

Several assumptions were necessary to make sense of the hierarchical notion of culture.

(1) Whether inherited or acquired, culture is a detachable part of a human being, a possession. It is a very peculiar kind of possession, to be sure: it shares with the personality the unique quality of being simultaneously the defining 'essence' and the descriptive 'existential feature' of the human creature. Since the lyric poets of seventh-century Greece discovered the discord between desire and duty, between duty and necessity, Western man has been condemned to the agonizing precariousness of a dual, Janus-faced identity: he is a personality, but he also has a personality, he is an actor, but also an object of his own action, created and creating at the same time. What he is, is determined by his essence; but he is insistently made responsible for this essence and required to shape it through his existential performance. Culture in its hierarchical meaning leads the same frustrating and awesome life of an object being its own subject. 'What Socrates tried to get the Athenians to

understand was the duty of "caring for their souls". . . . To an Athenian of the
fifth century BC . . . it must have seemed very strange indeed.'[11] To an
Athenian of the fifth century the soul (Ψυχή) was the seed and the bearer of
life which disappears together with the conscious existence of the human
being. An idea that one can – much more, should – try to act on something
which was the fountainhead of all action was at the time revolutionary
enough to make a genius of Aristophanes' stature ridicule its prophet. Still
the culture, the peculiarity of its existence notwithstanding, is a possession.
And all possessions can be acquired or squandered, manipulated and transformed, shaped and framed.

(2) Indeed, the quality of a human being can be shaped and framed; but it
can be also left unattended, raw and coarse, like fallow land, abandoned and
growing wild. The Τέχνη is the medium through which the wilderness of
Nature is forced to fit human needs. Plutarch's immortal metaphor of *cultura
animi* was comprehensible to his contemporaries only because it was buttressed by Cicero's codification of the stance behind agricultural practice:
the soil bears ripe and sweet fruits only when attended by an apt and skilful
farmer who assiduously and painstakingly selects the seed of best quality.
After eighteen centuries the primary source of inspiration was still alive – and
the *Dictionnaire de l'Académie Française* supplemented its discussion of 'culture' by a Plutarchian remark: 'se dit aussi au figuré, du soin quon prend des
arts et de l'esprit.'[12] To Aristotle the analogy between soul-perfection and
*techne* must have seemed self-imposing; the soul was to him like 'the capacity
of a tool'.[13] A very odd tool, to be sure once again, with its edge pressed
against itself. Faithful in this respect to Socratic adage, Aristotle wanted men
to be moulders of their own souls. It remains, alas, an unexplored question to
what extent the ancient Greeks' intense preoccupation with the mystery of
soul-formation, revealed in their well-nigh religious treatment of everything
related to educational processes, was stimulated by the ambiguous existential
status of the human personality. Against the background of, say, Gorgias'
rigid distinction between 'acting' and 'acted upon', the first alone pretending
to the kind of perfection available only to eternal, never-originated existence,
the second always transitional, imperfect, degraded, the elusive human personality loomed dangerously over the critical boundaries of the world order.
It was only natural in the circumstances for Plato to bestow on the human
soul the sacred status of immortality: 'Only that which moves itself, since it
does not leave itself, never ceases to move. . . . Every soul is immortal. For
what is ever moving is immortal.'[14] To a logical Greek mind this solution-by-
taboo would have easily revealed its nature as a desperate subterfuge, had
Plato been less consistent in drawing necessary conclusions from the fateful
decision. But he was not. Re-shaping according to an extrinsic project – the
very heart of Τέχνη – was replaced by a self-revealing cultivation of intrinsic
qualities; the soul-formation lays bare its essence which always was there
even if inconspicuous and invisible to the sensory experience. Which leads us
directly to the absolute nature of the educational ideal, the inexorable
attribute of the hierarchical concept of culture. Before we turn to it, let us

note that even the absolutistic system of Plato allowed for the hiatus between the potential and the actual, thus leaving plenty of room for the creative activity of *techne*.

(3) The hierarchical notion of culture is value-saturated. The above phrase indicates however (to everybody trained in the descriptive preoccupations of post-Boasian anthropology) merely taking a partisan stance in the notorious argument over the comparability and/or relativity of cultural solutions. For fear of understatement of what constitutes the pith and marrow of the hier-archical concept, we had better re-phrase the initial idiom. The real issue is not the admission or denial of the existence of an objective criterion for the comparative evaluation of cultures. The term 'cultures', if understood hier-archically, can hardly be used in the plural. The concept makes sense only if denoted straightforwardly as *the culture*; there is an ideal nature of the human being, and *the culture* means the conscious, strenuous and prolonged effort to attain this ideal, to bring the actual life-process into line with the highest potential of the human vocation.

The hierarchical notion of culture is unshaken not only by our otherwise meticulous distinction between description and evaluation. It remains immune to another distinction which haunts modern culturological thinking, the one between culture and nature. Culture *is* attaining, reaching, nature; cultural is what *in actu* became identical with its natural *potentia*. Robert A. Nisbet rightly blames the Romans for engendering many of our notorious methodological and conceptual troubles by reckless translation of the Greek *physis* as the Latin *natura*. Violating our own well-established linguistic divi-sions, we must admit that *physis* conveys a concept which long ago disappeared from our own vocabulary: it denotes, taking it for what it is worth, our culture and our nature at the same time. To Greeks *physis* meant the 'way of growth'; 'The nature of a thing . . . is how it grows, and everything in the universe, physical and social alike, has a *physis* of its own, a distinctive way of growing, a life-cycle'.[15] Everything has its own *physis*, being neither the arbitrary decision of gods nor the object of unregulated human action. 'Would you be willing to define the work of a horse or of anything else to be that which one can do only with it or best with it? . . . Is there anything else with which you can see except the eyes? . . . Could you hear with anything but ears? . . . Is not that the work of a thing which only it can perform, or it can perform better than anything else?' Socrates kept asking Thrasymachus, as Plato tells us.[16] Greek thought turned obsessively on the notion of the ordered universe, in which the determined merges with the achievable, and the free-dom of *techne* fulfils itself through submitting to the necessity of nature. They attacked the idea from numerous angles. Beside the already mentioned *physis*, the Socratic *psyche* and the famed Aristotelian *telos* (form) can be, the subtleties of their semantic uniqueness notwithstanding, shown to be varia-tions on a single theme. Παιδεία, so penetratingly dissected by Werner Jaeger,[17] belongs to the same semantic family. It obstinately defies any attempt to map it unambiguously in the semantic field of modern languages. It com-prises much more than any single term we use to express our way of splitting the continuum of being. As Edward Myers aptly remarked, it is 'a conception which includes more than is suggested by either "culture" or "education": it includes the humanistic ideal of an ethical-political culture'.[18] Alas, the most perspicacious formula stops short of conveying the richness of the original meaning. We try in vain to assemble the indivisible monolithic concept by patching together incoherent bits and pieces of our modern experience.

The cultural-natural ideal of the ancient Greeks was not subdivided into the realms we are used today to distinguishing so meticulously; the morally good was at the same time aesthetically beautiful and closest to the truth of nature. The pre-ordained unity of achievement-and standard-dimensions was most fully expressed in the much-discussed concept of Καλοκάγαθια, broadly dealt with by all thinkers of the classical period from Herodotus to Aristotle. The second part of the concept, γαθόζ, is an adjective derived from the verb αγαμαι, roughly corresponding to the English 'admire' and 'praise'. The first part, Καλόζ, is more complicated; it meant, simultaneously, the physically beautiful, handsome and attractive; the functionally beautiful, as of an object which is made to measure for its goal or its calling; the morally beautiful, the noble and virtuous; and the socially (politically) beautiful, as of a person ready to perform eagerly his civic duties, dedicated to his community and deserving to be rewarded for his public activity. The concept was used as indivisible; those who employed it seemed to be fully satisfied that the many virtues we usually treat as separate in fact go together and condition each other. Together they constitute the natural vocation of the human being; still 'only those who act achieve Καλοκάγαθιαυ in their lives'.[19] Wherever there is virtue, there is a choice; a person can choose inaction, he can fail to achieve his calling even if acting, when behaving irrationally or allowing himself to be diverted from the path of righteousness. The natural character of the ideal does not make its actualization any easier or smoother. It still demands ἀγών, strife and competition, the idea taken over by the philosophers of spiritual perfection from pre-Socratic times; it was Heraclitus who put forward the idea that the strife 'has shown some to be Gods and some mortals, has made some slaves and others free'.[20] It seems that the post-Socratics preferred to assign the same 'unveiling' function to strife in both the fields that Heraclitus was still inclined to distinguish. They would hardly have been prepared to comprehend Sir Henry Maine's sharp distinction between the achievement and the ascriptive principles.

The innate equivocality of the hierarchical notion of culture in general, Καλοκάγαθία in particular, brings to mind Gellner's charming, Swift-like dissection of the not-too-imaginary phenomenon of 'bobility'.[21] With unerring aim Gellner lays bare the social sense of the apparently absurd, ambiguous and inherently contradictory concept: 'Bobility is a conceptual device by which the privileged class of the society in question acquires some of the prestige of certain virtues respected in that society, without the inconvenience of needing to practise them.' That is what 'bobility' indeed means sociologically. It is true again that it is always possible to exert 'social control through the employment of absurd, ambiguous, inconsistent and unintelligible doctrines'. But is it entirely convincing that juxtaposing two notions that we usually distinguish makes the resulting concept necessarily absurd? What are the other criteria a sociologist may employ to judge the 'absurdity' or 'rationality' of a social phenomenon apart from its social structural context? Would not rather the semantic coherence of a socially functional concept be measured against the structure it denotes and operates? And, secondly, though many privileged classes use 'bobility'-like concepts to foster and defend their rule, the inverse is not necessarily true. One can imagine – and indeed point out – instances in which a socially accepted and approved hierarchical concept of culture may be anchored in the social structure through other functions than the protective device of a well-entrenched hereditary elite.

As to the first reservation, it was Georg Simmel[22] who provided us with the right clue to assess the aristocracy and its ideals against the intrinsic logic of a social structure of which it is a constitutive part. Simmel sees the phenomenon of aristocracy as a derivative of a particular type of society which can exist only if it turns out perpetually an aristocratic-type stratum and aristocratic-type cultural principles. As we know, in a caste society each new group, whatever its discriminating feature, tends to assume attributes of a caste and to accommodate itself in the web of castes; in a society organized on the basis of a functional co-existence of mutually impenetrable, hermetically closed groups, the ruler-owner class inevitably assumes the same character. Like other classes or *Stände*, it is closed above and below; like other groups, it is entitled or forced to avail itself of particular cultural symbols, and exploit particular goods because it holds a particular segment of the total social structure (and not the other way round, as is the case in a mobile and open society). It is the structural locus of the group as a whole which gives every single member of the group his social identity. If we now consider cultural symbols against their natural semantic context – the social structure they simultaneously signify and bring into being – it will seem only logical and rational that their distribution is based on the assumption that 'each member of an aristocracy participates in and avails himself of whatever is most valuable in all members of the group. It is as though a substance of lasting value runs through the blood of the various members of an aristocracy, generation after generation'.[23] There is a clear correspondence between the organizing principle of the social structure and the first axioms of the accepted 'ideology' of culture. Since both the signs and their assumed referents belong obviously to the same semantic context and vouchsafe, respectively, their meaningfulness and operative relevance, the recrimination of 'deceit', 'absurd exploitation' etc. can be substantiated only by referring to an outside, alien sociological logic. Intrinsically, the merger between individual virtues and the structural allocation of the group to which the individual belongs seems to be well founded on the 'objective logic' of the social structure.

Everett E. Hagen attacks the same topic from the vantage point of the structurally determined personality type. A traditional society – one conducive to an aristocratic elite – is a society in which authoritarian personalities abound (not to be mistaken for Adorno's famous concept). The point is that according to Hagen the occurrence of this peculiar personality-type is not limited to any particular social class of such a society; it permeates all class boundaries and tends to be as widespread in the aristocracy as in the peasantry. 'It seems likely to me that a key causal force shaping both the pattern of social relations and the personality of the peasant is his awareness of the limited extent of his power.' The aristocratic elite, on the contrary, seems to be all-powerful:[24]

> Their power, however, depends on their inherited position, not on individual achievement. It is worthwhile to note how greatly their view of the sources and limitations of their power resembles that of the peasantry. The absolute amount of the economic and political power of an individual member of the elite classes is not fixed. He may be able to gain power at the expense of someone else. However, to each member of the elite this possibility is a threat as well as a promise; and apart from this possibility of shifts of power within the group, life seems greatly dominated by forces beyond their control, just as life does to the peasantry.

Though starting from original concepts very different from Simmel's, we arrive at the very similar conclusion of a close correspondence between the 'bobility'-like concept of cultural ideal and the inherent logic of the structurally (and, according to Hagen, technologically) determined logic of 'lived' processes.

However, even if the censure of the 'bobility'-like cultural ideas as an absurdity turned into a class weapon could be anchored in the reality of the society under discussion; even if, in other words, the reservations raised so far could be fully rejected, the question would still remain whether it explains away all instances of the hierarchical concept of culture. The instance we have chosen as representative of the concept, the Greek notion of culture, does not fit very well into the 'bobility' framework; it could perhaps have been brought under the heading of 'bobility' in its pre-classical, ἀρετή stage, in which the chivalrous ideal of aristocratic warriors approximated to the hereditary privilege to rule; this, however, is much less true in the classical period of a Rousseauesque political, social and economic democracy – unless, of course, we are prepared to treat, not entirely unjustly, all the free citizens of Athens as the aristocrats of a slave society. The assessment of the role played by the hierarchical concept in a conflict-ridden society depends obviously on the structural frame of reference we choose. So far we have not come across a single case in which a frame, turning the hierarchical concept into another version of 'bobility', cannot be found. We begin to ask whether the hierarchical concept can be cleared of the charge of being class-bound at all. We have tried to opt for the social-structural logic which clears away the seeming absurdity and logical inconsistency of hierarchical concepts of culture. But, even if rational in this way and logically consistent, is this concept 'classless'? Can it become 'classless' at all?

Ideally, the answer is yes. In 1924 Edward Sapir tried to resurrect the Greek approach to culture by supplying the commonsensical evaluating concept with a scholarly footing. His simile of 'genuine culture' (versus 'spurious') borrowed heavily from the Greek heritage of 'individual refinements' and 'ideal form'.[25]

> A genuine culture is perfectly conceivable in any type or stage of civilization, in the mould of any national genius. . . . It is merely inherently harmonious, balanced, self-satisfactory. . . . It is a culture in which nothing is spiritually meaningless, in which no important part of the general functioning brings with it a sense of frustration, of misdirected or unsympathetic effort.

One can easily notice the relativistic slant present in Sapir though entirely absent in Aristotle; one can notice also the humble acceptance of alternative cultural solutions, which would have been hardly comprehensible to the self-assured contemporaries of Plato. Still one point remains beyond discussion: in a given society one and only one ideal form can be deduced which is simultaneously the right and the true (genuine, in short) *physis* of the human being. The yardstick Sapir provides to measure this superior culture bears a close resemblance, to be sure, to the Aristotelian ideal of *sophrosyne*; but it clearly belongs with the powerful stream of the romantic opposition to the individual *hubris* preached in the gospel of industrial society. It can pass for a classless phenomenon only if we are prepared to write off the powerful case made by numerous authors for the class anchorage of modern romanticism. This time however, unlike the case of 'bobility', the class-commitment means dissent. Far from being instrumental in preserving the current system of rule and privilege, the hierarchical ideal of culture conveys in one of many possible shapes the discontent of one of many deprived and unprivileged groups. It is a fighting ideal, aimed at change and reform, whether it is conscious of its future-directedness or,[26] much to its adherents' subsequent surprise, apparently aimed backwards. It looks as if the hierarchical concept of culture, while remaining class-committed in each case, is not necessarily establishment-oriented. Some very influential modern thinkers would say that no genuine cultural ideal can be establishment-oriented. Were Herbert Marcuse using the term 'genuine culture', he would have certainly applied it to the postulates of dissenting classes only; it is his contention that[27]

> the historical validity of ideas like Freedom, Equality, Justice, Individual, was precisely in their yet unfulfilled content – in that they could not be referred to the established reality, which did not and could not validate them because they were denied by the functioning of the very institutions that were supposed to realize these ideas.

It is the fate of cultural ideals, says Marcuse, that they always portray the restiveness and hankering of destitute and/or ascending classes. The moment they are adopted as descriptive devices of the social reality and cease to provide an independent fulcrum for alternative societal forms, they forfeit their creative force either irretrievably or temporarily until they are adopted again by a new class, once again as critical devices.

It seems that, in the rotation of conflicts, revolutions and institutionalization of new systems, hierarchical concepts of culture, always present, play an important though changing role. They emerge as war-cries of the oppressed and dissenting; usually they end up as 'bobility'-like legitimations of a new establishment. Sometimes (as in the case of the ideal of freedom, continuously re-appearing in Western history, each time with an enlarged semantical referent) they resume their long-forgotten militantly critical role, but then are re-formulated as a partial component of a broader principle.[28]

Our epoch is apparently distinguished by the lack of a hierarchical concept of culture comparable to the ancient Καλοκάγαθία or to the more recent nobility (or, to the same effect, the Berber *baraka* discussed by Gellner). Though our times are indeed saturated with partly universal, partly competitive hierarchical cultural ideals to an extent perhaps unknown to our ancestors, we reject emphatically the objective (to wit, pre-human) existence of cultural standards. Since at least the times of Sir Henry Maine we are able and indeed used to grounding our sociology-of-knowledge explanation of this novel stance on the contractual-achievement principle of the modern social organization; any reference to a pre-established hierarchy of any kind would have been at odds with the *Weltanschauung* of a class which has chosen accomplishment as the paramount legitimation of its rule. We do not, however, attach enough importance to the influence exerted on the modern stance by the rising social status of the intellectuals who increasingly are in a position to determine in their own way the standards and the content of the dominating socialization trends. The intellect, the real or alleged driving force of the intellectuals' advance (and at any rate the hub of their own class legitimation), shares with money, as Simmel prophetically proclaimed, the unique quality of being simultaneously multi-final and multi-genetical; it leads to many different socially definable goals and it may be used as an implement by incumbents of many different social locations, armed with different types of original assets. That is why intellect along with money was, and still is, used willingly as the vehicle of upward social mobility by exactly the individuals to whom the more traditionally regulated (and thus more specific) privileged routes are inaccessible.

The relative impartiality and availability of the materialized sediment of intellect – knowledge – was instrumental in the rapid elevation of the new influential, prestigious and well-to-do class of intellectuals. The elevation of this class, however, meant inevitably the parallel elevation of symbols which supposedly discriminate the elevated class. Indeed they have been hallowed and sacralized as *the* modern standard of hierarchical culture. Being at odds with the 'bobility'-principle (knowledge is by its very definition something to be acquired, achieved, accumulated by one's effort – *learned*) they cannot be, and indeed are not, depicted in the manner practised in the case of ἀρετή or nobility of spirit. Nobody, except a few solitary geniuses, can be possibly earmarked as a possessor of knowledge by any other sign than the knowledge itself. As a result, the way we speak and think about the modern version of the hierarchical cultural ideal conceals the way this ideal functions in the social reality. We not only substitute the 'right type of school' for the 'right type of family', forgetful of the role the 'right family' plays as the 'right school's' gatekeeper (or, perhaps, of this gatekeeper's role in turning the given school into a 'right' one); we believe that people become members of the institutionalized 'knowledgeable' communities because they are learned scholars in their own right – while in practice we assume that X is a learned scholar when told that he is a member of the above-mentioned community. Moreover, we meticulously observe a complicated procedure of apprenticeship, whose real function consists in decisions by the institutionalized communities themselves on who does and who does not deserve to become one of their number. It does not seem to be an historical accident that the guild prerogatives accompanied by intricate rites of passing and initiation – a device made originally to measure the aristocratic, corporate society – were preserved intact and indestructible precisely in the sphere which supplies the focus of the modern hierarchical cultural ideal, while withering away in virtually all other social fields. We have come a long way indeed since Francis Bacon's solitary battle for the legitimation of scientific values. Alongside the brilliant career of scholarship as a cultural ideal, scholars (who perform the same function toward the new ideal as holders of the quality of Καλόζ performed in the times of Aristotle) become more and more definable as employees of scholarly organizations.

In the light of our argument, Gellner's phenomenon of 'bobility', far from being a case of an absurd, illogical concept employed for class purposes, does not seem to be limited in its application to aristocratic society alone. It does not apply to many cultural ideals, and to none of them in their militant, dissident stage; it is very likely however that 'bobilization' is the inescapable ultimate fate of all historically known and eventually triumphant hierarchical ideals of culture.

**Culture as differential concept**

In its second meaning the term 'culture' is employed to account for the apparent differences between communities of people (temporally, ecologically, or socially discriminated). This usage locates the differential concept of culture among numerous 'residue concepts', contrived frequently in the social sciences to explain away the sediment of deviant idiosyncrasies unaccountable for by the otherwise universal and omnipotent regularities (where it shares the ascribed function with ideas, tradition, life experience etc.).

The above remarks refer most fully (perhaps only) to the modern applications of the differential concept, though the concept itself was not totally unknown to the ancients. The Greeks did encounter 'other peoples' and were poignantly conscious of their distinctiveness. Indeed, they developed a unique penchant for conscientiously putting on the record the puzzling divergences between other peoples' habits and their own. Still they saw these distinctions precisely as curious deviations from the normal pattern: competent descriptions of Caucasians, Egyptians, Scythians, Babylonians and many other 'aliens' by Herodotus are built up of sentences beginning in most cases with the phrases 'They do not' and 'contrary to us'.[29] The world of the Greeks was neatly divided into Hellenic nucleus and uniformly barbarian sheath. Philosophically, the reconciliation between the assumption of pre-formed standards of truth, beauty and moral righteousness and the recorded variability of accepted folkways must have produced insurmountable obstacles. It seems however that Greeks never came to grips with the issue in theoretical terms. Classifying explicit dissimilarities indiscriminately as alien curiosities can be seen as a way of circumventing the problem rather than solving it.

What probably prevented Greek thinkers from using whatever stood for our 'culture' in the plural was their unquestionable assumption of the basically innate nature of life standards and of the merely 'grinding' role of educational processes. The educator was a midwife facilitating the delivery of a product not of his own creation. Whatever his virtues, non-compliance and nonconformity did not count among them. One can probably interpret this otherwise remarkable assumption of non-controversial unity between the active process of individual growth and self-perfection and allegedly immutable and non-manipulable standards as a philosophical reflexion of a culturally uniform and socially closely knit community; however, even if one detests this sort of a crude sociology-of-knowledge explication, there seems to be a strong case for the epistemologically restrictive role of a highly developed social integration. Coming across cultural differences does not necessarily mean noticing them; and noticing them does not automatically imply conferring an equal existential status on contradicting ways of life.[30] Relativity of cultural standards was conceived historically only when the burgeoning modern social structure had undermined the former unity of the individual and his community.

The bequest of the Greek hierarchical and absolutistic vision of culture enthralled European minds long after Locke, in 1690, came out with the full list of the intellectual ingredients which the differential concept required. In 1750 Turgot, much in tune with the prevailing intellectual *ambience*, tried to escape from the philosophical impasse by furnishing the hierarchical concept of culture with universal (this time explicitly on the mankind-scale) value: 'The primitive dispositions are equally active among barbarians and civilized peoples. . . . The chances of education and circumstances develop them or let them be buried in obscurity.'[31] But then the Lockean revolution was already in the making. The devastating question, 'Where is that practical truth that is universally received without doubt or question, as it must be if innate?'[32] had already been asked, and the magic key of the 'empty cabinet' had unlocked hitherto unbreakable intellectual fetters.

It is true that Locke drew his crucial arguments against innate standards mainly from the ethnographic data (scarce and misleading as they were at the time). But it would be naive to believe that Locke's conclusions were intrinsically present in the very diversity of human kind, waiting for a suitably inquisitive mind to lay them bare for everybody to see and accept. The differential concepts of culture, like all other concepts, are intellectual frames imposed on the accumulated body of recorded human experience. They are aspects of human social practice; its cohesiveness *in toto*, as in the case of any other systemic whole, is not necessarily divisible into cohesiveness when any fragment is taken apart. The concepts are indeed immured in the totality of human practice, but they are not always linked most intimately with those elements of experience to which they are semantically ascribed. Their association with their semantic referents usually records and enshrines some amount of active human arbitrariness; while genetically they are usually rooted deeply, and much less arbitrarily, in the historically determined organization of the human condition itself, the most deeply felt and lived part of human existence. The relationships are, of course, much more complicated than we have succeeded in epitomizing; there are plenty of feedback- and backlash-type effects of any element on the totality of practice. We shall certainly come back to this issue in due course; we have turned to it already at this stage only to explain why we are inclined to trace Locke's discovery to structural changes in the English society of the seventeenth century rather than to explorations of new continents by maverick merchants, saints and pirates. Alternative ways of life had to win their legitimate status inside a community unified by a single source of legitimacy to make possible the abrogation of an absolute and unrivalled social system and its sacralized image, the absolute standards of morality, beauty, decency.

The moment the differential concept of culture emerged from the ashes of its absolute and hierarchical predecessor, it was buttressed by several tacit (sometimes explicit) premises which were to remain its undetachable attributes throughout its history.

(1) By far the most important, indeed the seminal assumption is the Lockean belief, which, if re-stated in a milder form, boils down to a contention that human beings are not entirely determined by their genotype; the innate equipment of a human being, rich as it can be, still leaves men basically unprepared for the human way of life; plenty of loose ends may be tied up in many different ways, and natural determinants do not favour any of the ways eventually chosen. The only thing these determinants do stipulate is that some choice should be made to endow a *homo sapiens in potentia* with the characteristics of the *homo sapiens in actu*; indeed, if restricted to his somatic, biological aspects, a potential human being is incomplete, truncated, monstrously infantile. Quite recently Clifford Geertz, one of the ablest and most penetrating minds among living anthropologists, invited us to look at cultures[33]

> less and less in terms of the way in which they constrain human nature, and more and more in the way in which, for better or for worse, they actualize it. . . . Man is the only living animal who needs [cultural] designs for he is the only living animal whose evolutionary history has been such that his physical being has been significantly shaped by their existence and is, therefore, irrevocably predicated upon them.

In the well-informed ratiocination which preceded the above conclusion Geertz called upon the modern view of human biological pre-history to build a reinforced foundation under the famous profession of faith that 'the biological bases of cultural behaviour in mankind are for the most part irrelevant', while 'historical factors are dynamic',[34] which was virtually

unchallengeable after it was transformed into the identity tag of cultural differentialists.

(2) From the assumption of the basic incompleteness of the human being
in his purely biological capacity immediately follows the second premise of
the differential concept of culture: that various, even mutually exclusive,
socio-cultural forms may correspond to a single set of non-social (biological,
natural-environmental, ecological) conditions. Ruth Benedict, again, says in
her celebrated allegory:[35]

> The cultural pattern of any civilization makes use of a certain segment of the great
> arc of potential human purposes and motivations, just as we have seen in an earlier
> chapter that any culture makes use of certain selected material techniques or cul-
> tural traits. The great arc along which all the possible human behaviours are
> distributed is far too immense and too full of contradiction for any one culture to
> utilize even any considerable portion of it. Selection is the first requirement.
> Without selection no culture could even achieve intelligibility, and the intentions it
> selects and makes its own are a much more important matter than the particular
> detail of technology or the marriage formality that it also selects in similar fashion.

The ancient Aristotelian duality of the active, moulding form (spirit, *telos*)
and the passive, moulded substance (matter, body) has been reiterated in an
updated disguise. 'Active cultural factors operate on the relatively static materials of race and physical environment,' is the blunt statement of C. Daryll
Forde.[36] Culture is the human energetic activity set against immobile nature.
The same motif is repeated assiduously whenever the culture-as-differential
tune is played, though the actual melody varies over a wide range. The rather
extreme and embarrassing voluntarism of Benedict, assigning well-nigh
unlimited freedom to purely cultural choices, has been recently replaced by a
more cautious attitude. Leslie A. White, though aiming at ordering known
cultures into a single evolutionary sequence (a procedure traditionally associated with a rather unequivocal rejection of relativism), is still emphatic that
culture is an 'extrasomatic, temporal continuum of things and events *dependent upon symbolling*'.[37] But his is not the tone which dominates nowadays.
Another neo-evolutionist, Julian H. Steward, is probably closer to the recent
mood when concluding that[38]

> if the more important institutions of culture can be isolated from their unique set-
> ting so as to be typed, classified, and related to recurring antecedents or functional
> correlates, it follows that it is possible to consider the institutions in question as
> basic or constant ones, whereas the features that lend uniqueness are the secondary
> or variable ones.

What is more important, recent writers shun considering the obstinate diversity of cultures as one of the unproblematic 'brute facts', which ought to be
ascertained but can hardly be referred to any 'deeper' layer of empirical reality. On the contrary, they treat the fact that 'cultures' resist amalgamation and
tend to retain their distinctive features as a problem to be explained.
Increasingly conscious of the basic unity of the human species, they tacitly
assume that if peoples do not succumb to a set of unified standards, there
must be some factors operating which prevent them from doing this, and

that these factors should be pinpointed and duly analysed.[39] Marshall D. Sahlins, an anthropologist of remarkable synthesizing capacity, singles out, among 'devices that insulate peoples against cultural alternatives', the 'negatively-charged ideas about conditions and customs in neighbouring societies'. This ethnocentric ideology is largely responsible for 'adapted and specialized, mature cultures' being 'conservative, their reactions to the world defensive'.[40] Once a choice has been made, the resulting culture acts as the main hindrance to the acceptance of other peoples' choices; the empirical diversity of cultures does not necessarily imply an immanent relativity of cultural standards or the impossibility of conceiving a universal scale of these standards' relative superiority, a belief, which helps its holders round the most awkward corners of extreme, and no longer respectable, cultural relativism.

(3) Obviously, the differential concept of culture is logically incompatible with the notion of cultural universals (which does not mean that efforts to locate these universals cannot be made without drawing logical conclusions and rejecting the differential paradigm; in fact they have been made repeatedly, as we shall see later). Using the term 'culture' with the indefinite article makes sense only if supported by an implicit assumption that nothing universal can be a cultural phenomenon; there are, to be sure, numerous universal features of social and cultural systems, but they do not, by definition, belong to the field denoted by the word 'culture'. Unfortunately, this type of logical self-awareness is seldom made manifest. Many an anthropologist takes great pains to 'prove' that the alleged cultural similarities are not cultural at all, and would have been better referred to some psycho-biological, proto-cultural phenomena. The lucidity of thinking displayed by David Kaplan (who *defines* culture as something that 'does not appear to be explainable by an appeal to either genetic or panhuman psychic traits')[41] remains a rarity in anthropological literature. What was from the very outset a partisan option for one of several current meanings of the term has been insistently presented as an empirical, descriptive assertion, though the definitional *a priori* decision determined the way empirical data were selected and (if collected by others) interpreted. Thus, to Lowie's mention of 'universals of the human mind' (1920) Sapir retorted angrily though self-assuredly that any widespread social trait can be shown 'to be not [the] immediate and universal psychological response that we would have it, but an originally unique, local phenomenon that has gradually spread by cultural borrowing over a continuous area'.[42] Diffusionism was an inescapable complement of a consistent differentialism. If we define culture – following, for example, Clyde Kluckhohn – as '*a way* of thinking, feeling, believing', as the '*group's* knowledge stored up . . . for future use',[43] then to assume that several cultures are capable of arriving independently at an identical solution will be as implausible as the probability that in several separate intra-breeding populations the same mutations will appear spontaneously and evolve into parallel genetic trends; and thus the hypothesis of diffusionism turns automatically into the most plausible explanation of cultural similarity.

David Aberle made a cogent case for early linguistical structuralism (in the shape it assumed in the heyday of Ferdinand de Saussure's posthumous triumph) having played the role of the main inspiration of cultural differentialism. The easy analogy between language and culture (both phenomena serve as constitutive factors of respective *communities*) seemed to have strengthened enormously the position of those social scientists who pushed to the fore the discriminating function of cultures. Among numerous contiguous points specified by Aberle, two are particularly important in the present context: like language, culture 'is selective', each being 'a unique configuration. There are no general categories for analysis.'[44] Once again, what was in the first place a methodological postulate (of an enormous heuristical value, to be sure) was reincarnated in the cultural analogue in the garb of a pseudo-descriptive statement.

(4) Obviously the other side of the same coin is the emphatic rejection of cultural universality. The only idea of universality compatible with the differential concept of culture is the universal presence of some sort of a culture in the human species (exactly as in the case of Saussurean language); but what is meant in the above statement is rather a universal feature of human beings, not of culture itself.

There is an apparent contradiction between our generalization and the notorious attempts of differential culturologists to draw inventories of, precisely, 'cultural universals'. Marvin Harris traces this search for 'universals' back to the eighteenth century, when the term 'universals' was not used, and when ethnographers made no bones about the nature of their descriptive categories, aimed, purely and simply, at bringing some order into the chaotic field data and some discipline into their collection. Joseph Lafitau (1724) organized his findings under the headings of religion, political government, marriage and education, occupations of men, occupations of women, warfare, commerce, games, death and burial, sickness and medicine, and language; J. N. Demeunier (1776) modified and extended the list, making room for such refined items as standards of beauty or body disfigurement.[45] But not until Clark Wissler did the unassuming authors of such inventories pretend to discover universals instead of simply describing the items they were looking for. The unpretentious headings waited until 1923 to be promoted, by Wissler, to the impressive rank of 'universal culture patterns',[46] while their number shrank to eight (speech, material habits, art, science and religion, family and social systems, property, government, and war). With George P. Murdock the list grew up again into an enormous series of alphabetically arranged items, including, among many others, courtship, eschatology, gestures, hair styles, joking, mealtimes, pregnancy usages and soul concepts.[47] The authors remained curiously blind to the fact that the alleged generalizations reported nothing but the questions asked by field workers and shaped a *priori* by their own trained habit of splitting the universe into discrete phenomena.

The genuine procedure, through which the universals of the discussed kind were arrived at, was seldom made explicit. One of these rare cases provides the programmatic statement by E. E. Evans-Pritchard (1962), from which we learn, that the task of the anthropologist consists in understanding the significant overt features of a culture, disclosing the latest underlying form of it, and then in comparing 'the social structures his analysis has revealed in a wide range of societies'.[48] Thus comparison is the focal point of the whole method. In fact, the so-called universals are only similarities laid bare by the process of comparing separate cultural entities.

Alas, no amount of comparing is likely to bring us any closer to the discovery of what really can be called 'universals' without violating the accepted rules of the logic of science; and that is not only because of the notorious inborn deficiencies of inductive thinking. The real trouble with the procedure proposed by Evans-Pritchard lies in the impossibility of specifying universally valid and uncontroversial criteria for choosing the 'one and only' frame for comparison and subsequent classification of cultures. The choice is in fact ineluctably weighted by the first stage of the whole procedure, by the allegedly inherent, though usually imported, logic of the anthropologist's own local ethnographic scene. If a student of culture wishes to transcend the embarrassing parochialism of local contingencies, he will choose to compare, following Radcliffe-Brown's advice,[49] cultures viewed through the prism of commonsensical categories, like economy, politics, kinship etc. If he succeeds, he will be rewarded with another set of classificatory types. Their arbitrariness will be disguised only by the sham glare of empirical exactitude. Still no amount of empirical precision will save his creation from being dismissed, again without conclusive argument, by another – neither better nor worse – commonsensical classification.

The inexorable inconclusiveness, and thus meagre informative load, of classificatory ventures provides the main target for Edmund Leach's devastating critique. Not that Leach doubts the cognitive value and possible applications of comparative classifications; what he demurs at is substituting classifications for universal generalizations, and the illusion that, once classifications are produced, the problem of cultural universals is done with. Leach's contention[50] is that

> comparison and generalization are both forms of scientific activity, but different. Comparison is a matter of butterfly collecting – of classification, of the arrangement of things according to their types and subtypes. . . . Radcliffe-Brown was concerned, as it were, to distinguish wrist watches from grandfather clocks, whereas Malinowski was interested in the general attributes of clockwork. But *both* masters took as their starting point the notion that a culture or a society is an empirical whole made up of a limited number of readily identifiable parts, and that when we compare two societies we are concerned to see whether or not the same kinds of parts are present in both cases. This approach is appropriate for a zoologist or for a botanist or for a mechanic.

Leach believes that anthropology should be close to neither of these fields, and to find its proper method should turn to mathematics. An engineer by training, Leach is too intimate with mathematics to boil it down – in line with many dumbfounded proselytes – to quantifying and arithmetic. His polemic does not revolve around an imaginary dividing line between the exactness and precision of quantifiable formulas and the unreliability and haziness of humanities. He readily concedes that classificatory hair-splitting is as precise and even as empirically trustworthy as one can desire. What Leach is after is something far more ambitious, something of which mathematics is the genuine embodiment for those properly conversant with its very essence: he wishes, following the Cartesian recipe, to penetrate the realm of the necessary, invariant, certain. He is not interested in the patchwork-like correction of individual fallacies in what is basically the right analytical strategy; he aims at transplanting the whole issue of cultural universals from the theatre of contingency, accidentality, temporality, into the soil of invariant principles to which it really belongs. But this is already another problem, to which we shall return in due course.

(5) Having deprived themselves of the universal, generic analytical frame of reference, the users of the differential concept must strain themselves to the utmost to construct a vicarious frame on which to pin their findings. The initial modesty of Franz Boas, who urged his followers to concentrate on individual cultural traits considered separately, soon proved to be self-defeating when confronted with the logarithmic pace of data-collecting. To make sense of the facts amassed at enormous speed, and to screen the future flow of the recorded bits of reality carved out as 'facts', it was necessary to construct a systematic model in which the 'facts' could be safely and suitably accommodated and so made intelligible. The vital importance of this task was eventually, though not early enough, admitted by Boas himself. His disciples were quicker to respond. The address to which they turned for help in the first instance was, quite naturally, the 'natives', the members of investigated cultural communities themselves.

At first this quest did not go far beyond the standard Weberian stipulation of 'understanding'. Loyal to his German philosophical upbringing, saturated with *Weltanschauung* and *Volksgeist*, Bronislaw Malinowski was among the first to formulate the task of ethnographer as 'grasping the native's point of view, his relation to life', and realizing '*his* vision of *his* world'.[51] Malinowski did not intend simply to turn his colleagues' attention to one of the many routine chapters of any standard ethnographic report. Native ideas were not only one of many curiosities to investigate and describe, but the focal clue to the real meaning of everything the ethnographer saw and noticed in the field. The sense attached by Malinowski to his programmatic statement can be best decoded in the light of the neo-Kantian 'absolute presuppositions' of the Baden philosophical school, much in vogue and very influential in the formative years of Malinowski's epistemological stance. The basic ideas of the school were succinctly epitomized in Wilhelm Dilthey's methodological prescriptions:[52]

> The fundamental relationship on which the process of elementary understanding rests, is that of the expression to what it expresses. . . . Understanding tends towards articulate mental content which becomes its goal. . . . The expression of life which the individual grasps is, as a rule, not simply an isolated expression but filled with a knowledge of what is held in common and of a relation to the mental content.

The disparate field data can be properly assessed and understood – it follows, if one wishes to extrapolate to the ethnographer's predicament – if referred to their 'mental content', to the ideas their authors wished to express in the artefacts under study. 'A culture' is in the first place a spiritual community, community of shared meanings.

Franz Boas' conversion, the similar philosophical background notwith-standing, was clad in a much less metaphysical garb, perhaps because it happened at such a late date, after the prolonged exposure of Boas' mind to the rather secular and mundane intellectual climate of America. Boas saw, as Malinowski did, in the 'relation of the individual to his culture' 'the sources of a true interpretation of human behaviour'. But instead of elusive 'values' and 'world vision' (never, to be sure, consistently pursued by Malinowski either, in defiance of his own postulates), he resorted to the behaviouristically pedestrian 'social psychology' of the 1920s: 'It seems a vain effort to search for sociological laws disregarding what should be called social psychology, namely, the reaction of the individual to culture.'[53] Whatever the relations between the practical field performances of their proponents, Boas' and Malinowski's analytical strategies are located at the opposite poles of the philosophical spectrum. Malinowski sees the intrinsic cohesion of 'a culture' in the meaningful project the 'natives' impose on and express by their cultur-ally standardized behaviour; the human beings he studies are to be seen chiefly as subjects. Boas locates the issue in the realm of behavioural patterns. His 'natives' are, to begin with, the trained reactive objects of culture. The fol-lowers of Boas in the culture-and-personality school were initially closer to Malinowski's *Volksgeist* than to Boas' dalliance with behaviourism. In his seminal essay on the concept of culture, Clyde Kluckhohn defined 'a culture' by relating it to the shared, and historically created, 'definitions of the situa-tion' rather than to the distinctive 'ways of life' which are their manifestations.[54] A. L. Kroeber seemed to ascribe paramount theoretical sig-nificance to the notion of 'cultural ethos', the total quality of a culture, defined as 'the system of ideals and values that dominate the culture and so tend to control the type of behaviour of its members'.[55] The closest recent approximation to the Kroeberian version of *Volksgesicht* can be found prob-ably in the concept of style offered by Meyer Schapiro to denote the manifestation of the culture as a whole, the visible sign of its unity. The style reflects or projects the 'inner form' of collective thinking and feeling.[56] Historical antecedents of the discussed attitude can be found in great number, long before articulated philosophically by Dilthey or Windelband, deeply ingrained in pre-scientific popular common sense. They were copiously quoted by Margaret T. Hogden in her enchanting study of sixteenth- and sev-enteenth-century anthropological ideas.[57] In fact, the habit of defining distinct 'nations' through their 'vices, deficiencies, virtues, and honest properties' through their *ethos* or *style* – goes back well into the Middle Ages.

At the more mellowed stage of its history the culture-and-personality school accommodated the Freudian two-way link between civilization and human psychology to brush away the awkward dilemmas and ensuing incon-sistencies of the earlier theory. Having incorporated the psychoanalytical

paradigm of early experience as simultaneously culture-determined and cul-
ture-determining, the school ceased to be haunted by the embarrassing choice
between German metaphysics and American behaviourism. The culture-and-
personality theorists have finally found their missing link; the fact that it was
located in the sphere of the unconscious seemed to provide the desired proof
of the verisimilitude of the culture-and-personality hypothesis. The intimate
bond between culture and personality seemed now to have been firmly established. The new spirit of the school was adequately expressed by Ralph
Linton in his foreword to Kardiner and his associates' codifying treatise:[58]

> The basic personality type for any society is that personality configuration which is
> shared by the bulk of the society's members as a result of the early experiences
> which they have in common. It does not correspond to the total personality of the
> individual but rather to the projective systems or, in different phraseology, the
> value attitude systems which are basic to the individual's personality configuration.
> Thus the same basic personality type may be reflected in many different forms of
> behaviour and may enter into many different total personality configurations.

Theoretically and empirically (as, for example, in Ruth Benedict's demoniza-
tion of Japanese toilet training or Gorer and Rickman's morbid
preoccupation with Russian swaddling habits) 'personality configuration' or
'type' became ultimately the alternative term for 'cultural pattern' or 'ethos'.
The school has been fairly consistent throughout its history; the final semantics were in fact pre-figured by early conceptual choices, which set the school
from the outset in quest of a suitable, Freudian-type psychological theory and
made their marriage imperative. The future evolution of the school was in fact
already contained *in potentia* in Ruth Benedict's statement of 1932: 'Cultures
are individual psychology thrown large upon the screen, given gigantic proportions and a long time span.'[59]

Theory-constructing begins always in cutting out, from the sensed reality,
of a 'black box' of the student's choice. The selection of the black box determines obliquely what variables become for the researcher the 'inputs' and the
'outputs' of the investigated phenomenon. Only they remain exposed to
empirical assessment and only they require recording. The theory-maker ends
up eventually with two series of recorded data on his desk; the task consists
in constructing a model which accounts for discovered relations between
'inputs' and 'outputs' – which depicts, in other words, the 'outputs' as the
function of 'inputs' (in the mathematical, not biological or sociological sense
of the word 'function'). The intimate affiliation, in fact identity, of culture and
personality was not 'discovered' by the school under discussion; it was pre-
determined by the school's initial decision to select the psychologists' black
box as the starting frame for its own theory-making: the experimentally inaccessible space between external stimuli and outward, manifested responses to
these stimuli. Exactly as psychologists do, the culture-and-personality school
tries to fill the unknown content of this space by hypothetical 'intervening
variables', which, in turn, delineate further research strategies and focal theoretical concepts. To make the long story short, what was misleadingly
presented as empirical conclusions, was in reality an *a priori* decision woven

into the selection of disparate behavioural patterns as the subject-matter of culturological research; a direct and inevitable outcome, to be sure, of opting for the differential concept of culture.

Of course, the void between inputs and outputs can be filled with many diverse theoretical models, as indeed has happened in the last decades. A whole range of models can be found, from id-formative agonies of the embryo to conscious, cognition-framing knowledge ('ethnoscience', recently called 'ethnomethodology') of adult members of the community. Still all these models, their diversity notwithstanding, can and should be safely classified in the same category, as all of them are alternative solutions to the same issue framed originally by the shared decision as to the location of the 'black box' of culture. This decision constitutes the common paradigm of all approaches founded on the differential concept of culture, whatever their latent or manifest controversies and animosities. Though Ward Goodenough would not probably consider himself a representative of the same kind of anthropology of which Robert Redfield has been for many years the acknowledged spokesman, their recommendations to fellow-anthropologists, the two offshoots of one paradigmatical root, bear a striking resemblance and offer an eloquent testimony to the decisive role of conceptual options. Thus Redfield[60] reminds his readers that

> in attempting to describe a little community in terms of world view the outsider withholds his suggestions for systematizing the whole until he has heard from the natives. The outsider waits. He listens to hear if one or many natives have themselves conceived an order in the whole. It is *their* order, *their* categories, *their* emphasis upon this part rather than that which the student listens for. Every world view is made of the stuff of philosophy, the nature of all things and their interrelations, and it is the native philosopher's ordering of the stuff to which we, the outside investigators, listen.

And in unison with Redfield, though employing different terminology, Goodenough reiterates the same ideas:[61]

> A society's culture consists of whatever one has to know or believe in order to operate in a manner acceptable to its members. . . . It is the form of things that people have in mind, their models for perceiving, relating, and otherwise interpreting them. . . . Ethnographic description, then, requires methods of processing observed phenomena such that we can inductively construct a theory of how our informants have organized the same phenomena.

It seems that the differential concept of culture goes inescapably together with an assumption of the intrinsic cohesion of each separate culture-unit's being anchored 'over there', either in the subconscious furnishing of human personalities or in typical ways of cognitive mapping inculcated in the members' minds. The most explicit attempt to transform the tacit assumption into an elaborate methodological principle has been so far expressed in terms of the alternative of 'emic' and 'etic' approaches – the modernized edition of the time-honoured German dilemma of *Natur- und Kultur- Wissenschaften, Erklärung und Verstehung*, etc.

The terms, recently broadly used, sometimes abused, by the followers of

Harold Garfinkel (who call themselves alternately 'ethnomethodologists', 'phenomenological sociologists', 'sociologists of everyday life'), were introduced by Kenneth L. Pike, a maverick linguist blazing his trail to the study of society with tools borrowed from his training in structural phonology.[62] The difference between phonetics (the 'etic' approach) and phonology, or the study of phonemes (the 'emic' approach) in linguistics can be expressed in crude terms as the distinction between the study of actually produced sounds and their elementary units (which can be done without knowledge of the actual meaning of words in the language under study and expressed in purely physical terms) and the study of those aspects of sounds only which are indeed operative in creating and conveying words, e.g. meaningful sequences of sounds (which can be accomplished only if the language under investigation is conceived – 'understood' – as an ordered arrangement of meanings and their sound forms). According to Pike, taking the stock of behavioural patterns of a culture, as seen from outside, by an observer unaware of the 'semantic' side of the behaviour he describes, will be the sociological analogue of phonetics. To avail ourselves however of the achievements of structural linguistics we must be able to construe a sociological correlate of phonology. Hence the need of an 'emic' approach as a vital methodological postulate.

It is the focal assumption of Pike's strategy that 'when people react to human behaviour in their own culture they react to it as if it were a sequence of separate particles of activity'.[63] These particles, which alone convey the meaning intended by the actor and elicit the culturally prescribed response from the native perceiver, can be looked upon as 'emes' of the culture in question. To apply the 'emic' approach to the study of cultures, means, consequently, to siphon out the elements or aspects of visible behaviour which are meaningful in the above sense to the natives. The second stage will consist in reconstructing from the 'emes' and their contextual usages (which are necessary for elucidating their paradigmatical and syntagmatical relations) the latent configuration which constitutes the backbone, or the grammar, of the culture's specificity and distinctiveness. In other words, though the anthropologist will ultimately arrive at a theory of his own creation, this theory must be a model of the meanings the natives actually employ and of the ways they employ these meanings. We are once again in the familiar realm of *Verstehende Soziologie* and *Einfühlung*, but this time the old issues are expressed in the language inspired by the intoxicating accomplishments of structural linguistics (as we shall see, Pike's and his followers' is not the only way in which structuralist achievements may be exploited by students of society).

Pike's programme raises two important issues. The first is of a purely technical nature: to what extent *behaviouremes*, discrete, sememe-like units of observable human behaviour, are at all identifiable. This question requires a long series of empirical studies, which surely must overcome numerous obstacles to be successful (for example, the fact that any human behaviour employs many languages – gestures, dress, loci, and even several tiers of verbal expressions). Still the second question is more essential. Is the extraction of discrete and repeatable behavioural units the only condition which will make the behaviour-language parallel legitimate? Is not non-verbal human behaviour a phenomenon parallel rather to the use of language in social context (sociology of verbal communication) than to the detached relationship between two isomorphic systems of 'signifyings' and 'signifieds'? And, consequently, is the realm of subjective, lived and intended meanings the proper correlate of the semantic field of language as analysed in the frame of linguistics? The whole, composite and multi-sided, issue is far from being obvious; what is more important, the solution seems to depend on a more or less arbitrary theoretical option rather than on theoretically neutral research. If so, then the attempt to harness the authority of structural linguistics to bear out a modernized version of neo-Kantian cultural idealism seems, to say the least, rather one-sided.

We do not usually feel any need to apologize for using the term 'language' in the plural. We consider it an objective, easily ascertainable, self-imposing fact that there are not only many languages, but that each language constitutes 'in reality' a separate, relatively well-defined entity. We do not expect insurmountable obstacles in establishing the boundaries of either 'linguistic communities' or 'linguistic systems'. We look at languages as separate entities because they are, by themselves and independently of any research interest, separate entities.

Not so however with cultures. True, the differential concept of culture has been riveted onto the current paradigm to the extent that few anthropologists feel 'the fact' of plurality and separatedness of cultures as something which requires arguing or verifying proofs. Still, contrary to the case of language, the differential concept of culture is not (or, in any case, not as much as the term 'languages') implied by the immediately given reality independently of researchers' activities. It is implied rather by the empirical strategy chosen by students of culture. It seems 'natural' and beyond argument only in the framework of specific field conditions. The excuse for the lengthy quotation from Manners and Kaplan which follows is that it contains what is probably the best analysis of the influence exerted by research method on the general theoretical attitude.[64]

Along with the positive contributions of the emphasis on field work seem to have come certain negative consequences for the development of anthropological theory. There has been a strong tendency for the individual anthropologist to immerse himself so completely in the intricacies and unique features of the people he studied that it became difficult for him to discuss the culture except in terms of its uniqueness or special flavour. Indeed . . . many anthropologists have seen this portrayal of the unique as the main mission and contribution of the discipline.

Many others who were willing to work toward more general formulations found themselves so intimidated by the sheer weight of ethnographic detail that they retreated in dismay from an essential task of theory formation, namely, abstraction. Thus, ironically, anthropology's empirical riches have tended often to act as a deterrent rather than a stimulus to theory formation.

On the one hand, the extreme particularists, pluralists, humanists, or radical relativists have insisted on the uniqueness of each culture – either by referring to its genius, flavour, configuration, style, pattern, and so forth, or by emphasizing the self-evident, that 'no two cultures are exactly alike'. Because they were right, in the sense that no two anything are exactly alike, their opposition to generalizations, speculations about cross-cultural regularities, or cause-and-effect statements applied comparatively carried enough weight to discourage free theory formation in anthropology. It always turned out that 'my people don't do it that way'.

However self-defeating and shaky the differentialists' pretensions may seem when laid bare by Manners and Kaplan, they do not appear to loosen their grip on anthropologists' minds. The sway under which the logic of empirical situations holds all theoretical activity is apparently overwhelming. People involved deeply in field practice find it difficult to be detached enough to neglect details which – so they were indoctrinated – constitute the pith and marrow of any contribution they can possibly make to human knowledge. Quite naturally, they do not see the relationship between their field methods and the concept of culture they cherish in the way Manners and Kaplan do. They are indeed convinced that the 'uniqueness' of what they see and describe is an attribute of the phenomenon described and not of the very low level of particularity they have deliberately chosen or unknowingly inherited. Thus, to give one example, Robert Redfield, while embarking on an audacious venture of generalized typology, thought it possible and desirable to absolve and exculpate those who would have recoiled from following his lead:[65]

> In reading Radcliffe-Brown on the Andamanese one finds no important account of anything outside of the little communities he describes. And, indeed, it was true that these primitive communities could in fact be regarded without reference to anything much outside of them; they could be understood, more or less, by one man working alone. Nor need that man be a historian, for among those non-literates there was no history to learn. . . . The anthropologist may see in such a system evidence of elements of culture communicated to that band or tribe from others, but he understands that the system as it now is keeps going by itself; and in describing its parts and their workings he need not go outside the little group itself.

In other words, it is not that 'a culture' is seen as an isolated and unique entity because, for these or other reasons, the differential concept of culture has been applied. It is rather that the culture is in fact a self-contained system of traits which distinguishes one community from another; and so instead of co-shaping the vision of an anthropologist, the differential concept reflects the objective truth he discovered.

The peculiar vision of cultural field associated with the differential concept of culture begets a wide range of specific issues on which research interests tend to be focused. The paramount issue is, of course, the phenomenon of 'cultural contact'. If any culture constitutes by definition a unique, cohesive and self-contained entity, then any situation of ambiguity, equivocality, lack of visible unilateral commitments, even of apparent lack of cohesion, tends to be viewed as 'encounter' or 'clash' between otherwise separate and cohesive cultural wholes. This impact of the differential concept of culture is already so deeply ingrained in popular thinking, that we employ and perceive the notion of 'cultural clash' as self-evident, commonsensical truth. A look backward into the intellectual past of the Western world however casts serious doubts on the timelessness and spontaneous origin of the belief. Margaret T. Hogden discovered that the enormous travel-literature left by numerous pilgrims to the Holy Land in the late Middle Ages contained no single proof that intelligent Europeans of those times experienced anything comparable to the nowadays fashionable and 'commonsensical' cultural shock: 'They expressed little or no curiosity about their fellows, little interest in alien ways, little reaction to cultural diversities.' Similarly, there is no evidence that the Indians brought to Europe by Columbus – in an advanced stage of the Renaissance – stirred any noticeable commotion among the enlightened public.[66] The notion of cultural clash apparently became an integral part of popular thinking following recent experiences of modern society; but it also played an active role in articulating these experiences and moulding their mental image.

Viewing the world through the spectacles of the differential concept, students of culture are forced to trace the roots of any change to some kind of a contact between the culture under study and another culture. Trying to arrange all the data related to the studied community around an internal axis of cohesion, they destroy by the same token potential analytical tools necessary to locate the 'inside' causes of change. Homogeneous, cohesive is the culture of a 'slowly changing' society; since the cohesion of any culture is achieved through successful re-creating, in the process of early training, of the same basic personality type, cohesion and homogeneity become synonymous terms for a sluggish pace of change (the change must not be vigorous to the point of creating significant discontinuities between the conditions in which two successive generations are trained). Inconsistent, heterogeneous cultural conditions (one hesitates to use the term 'culture', which implies a systemic nature of the whole) become, on the other hand, inextricably bound up with the continuous presence of 'full secondary culture contacts' (mingling of individuals brought up in conditions already affected by contacts) or at least 'primary cultural contacts' (encounters between individuals brought up in homogeneous but disparate cultures).[67]

Advocates of the differential concept of culture are often too much concerned with vindicating the self-identity and uniqueness of 'a culture' they study to withstand the temptation of viewing any contact and any mixing of 'cultures' as something intrinsically abnormal, if not undesirable and evil. Sometimes this attitude finds an ethical expression, as in Ruth Benedict's famous metaphor of the broken cup. In most cases the same attitude is embodied in allegedly descriptive, empirical terms; it is, for example, broadly accepted that the conditions of 'cultural contact' are conducive of a relatively high rate of mental disorders and psycho-somatic diseases. Nobody seems to care that the crucial act of referring respective statistical data to the clash between the expectation fed into immigrants by their native cultures and the new cultural reality is an arbitrary theoretical decision, not an empirical result. What is allegedly borne out has been in fact assumed from the outset. Were an alternative theory employed, the same phenomena could have been explained by, say, peculiar factors operating in self-selection of prospective immigrants, or by the exceptional severity of economic, social etc. obstacles

piled up in the way of an immigrant in comparison with the settled inhabi-
tants.

The differential concept of culture is not an accidental concomitant of the
intellectual climate of modernity. It affirms several of the focal assumptions
of modern thinking by lending them the spurious air of empiricism. But it
also helps to bridge some disconcerting discrepancies between these assumptions and a number of stubborn facts of observable reality. Both functions
make it indispensable.

To begin with, the axiom of biological equality of the human races and
genetical uniformity of the whole genus of homo sapiens is continuously and
jarringly at variance with the obstinate differentiation of historical achievement and performance. This contradiction can be conveniently explained
away by the contingencies of cultural values and traditions. In its extreme, the
method takes the shape of the Weberian formula: beliefs→behaviour→social
structure and process, a formula far more persistent and fertile than even the
extensive argument over the role of protestantism at the cradle of modernity
would suggest.[68] Hagen would point to the watershed between cultures which
turn out authoritarian personalities and those which rear innovators;[69] F. S.
C. Northrop[70] would try to demonstrate the aesthetic orientation of oriental
cultures as opposite to the rationality of the West. And hosts of theoreticians
and field workers would try to enumerate innumerable culture-determined
barriers to modern ways of life.[71] In each case culture, in the differential sense
of the term, is saddled with the principal responsibility for the disparate destinies of peoples equally endowed genetically and confronted with, allegedly,
an identical array of economic opportunities.

Secondly, the differential concept of culture sometimes fills the intellectual
gap left by the supernatural and providence; the explanatory powers of these,
once omnipotent, intellectual tools shrank considerably with the dawn of the
modern age, but the function they used to perform by no means disappeared.
The modern epoch proclaimed human freedom from supernatural fetters.
By the same token it produced a new demand for man-made necessities to
account for involuntary, not immediately manageable ingredients of the
human condition. Hence the unique intellectual appeal of the differential
concept of culture, according to which 'culture systems may, on the one hand,
be considered as products of action, on the other as conditioning influences
upon further action'. Culture, when understood as 'historically created
selected processes that channel man's reaction both to internal and to external stimuli',[72] fits perfectly both requirements to which the desired
explanatory device must conform. It is simultaneously a man-made and a
man-making entity; submitted to human freedom and constraining this freedom; related to the human being in his quality of subject as well as object.
When armed with the differential concept of culture, one can easily eschew
the twin horrors of methodological voluntarism and over-determinism; one
may intelligibly account for the evident confines of human liberty without
detracting the tiniest bit from the principle of man's freedom of choice.

Thirdly, picking culture as the principal differential of the human condition fits well the master-command role assigned by modern thinking to knowledge and education (for reasons already discussed above). The belief in the well-nigh uninhibited potential of intellectual discourse and socializing exertions penetrates deeply practically every diagnosis of our time as well as our attempts to deal with what we consider social, economic, or political 'problems'. The differential concept of culture is in this respect analogous and complementary to the similarly differential concept of education. Their plights are intimately related, both concepts having been riveted deeply into the very foundations of modern reality-handling.

And finally, as Peter Berger aptly remarked, 'one cannot throw a sop to the dragon of relativity and then go about one's intellectual business as usual'. For better or worse, ours is the age of relativity. 'History posits the problem of relativity as *a fact*, the sociology of knowledge as *a necessity of our condition*.'[73] For 'sociology of knowledge', on which Berger's polemical wrath is focused, we can as well read 'modern informed mind'. It would be odd indeed if the differential concept were not pushing its hierarchical predecessor beyond the confines of what passes for the legitimate scholarly endeavour. Nearly all spokesmen for the Modern Mind (though some joyfully, and others with sorrow) have proclaimed that the only absolute element in our condition is the end of the Absolute. Whatever are the reasons, we find it increasingly difficult to believe in absolute and universal standards of good or beauty. We tend to treat moral norms as well as aesthetic raptures as matters of mere conventionality. No wonder that 'comparative cultures' look to us like collections of curios, sharing first and foremost the feature of being equally unfounded in anything but human, past or current, options.

To put it briefly, the differential concept of culture seems to be an indispensable constituent of the modern world-image, closely related to its most sensitive articulations. In this intimate affinity lies the genuine source of this concept's intellectual forcefulness and perseverance.

## Generic concept of culture

The generic concept of culture feeds on the overlooked and the unsaid parts of the differential one. In this sense it is an inescapable corollary to its major adversary. The more successful the differential concept is in splitting the human scene into a multitude of unrelated, self-sufficient enclaves, the more strongly the need is felt to tackle the problem of the essential unity of mankind. It is not a biological, pre-cultural unity which is sought – unity of this sort is, in fact, ubiquitous in all discussion of culture – it is a theoretical foundation of the relative autonomy and distinctiveness of the cultural sphere in general, the differential concept in particular. Cultural differentiation is not, conceptually, at odds with the assumption of essential pre-cultural unity. On the contrary, the idea of cultural differentiation was called for to account for empirical variations unexplained by the modern, egalitarian, humane view of basic identity in the biological endowment of human races. Not so in the case of unity of the culture itself, a unity situated entirely in the realm of the cultural; although this idea does not necessarily entail refusal to appraise cultural variations and their significance, it does mean a fateful shift of emphasis, of the focus of theoretical and research interest, and, above all, in the type of issues with which one wishes and is able to grapple. If the hierarchical notion of culture puts in the limelight the opposition between 'refined' and 'coarse' ways of life as well as the educational bridge between them; if the differential notion of culture is an offspring of, and a bolstering to, concern with the countless and endlessly multipliable oppositions between the ways of life of various human groups, the generic notion is construed around the dichotomy of the human and the natural world, or, rather, around the time-honoured, ancient issue of European social philosophy – the distinction between '*actus hominis*' (what happens to man) and '*actus humani*' (what man does). The generic concept is about the attributes which unite mankind in the way of distinguishing them from everything else. In other words, the generic concept of culture is about the boundaries of man and the human.

For reasons easy to understand in the light of the discretional function of culture (see chapter 2), the drawing of this frontier-line seems to bear enormous emotional significance to human beings. It expressed itself, in primitive solutions recorded by anthropologists, in an ingenuous though utterly efficient expedience of stretching the man-nature borderline between one's own cultural community and the rest of the world – which comprised, in the event, tigers as well as other tribes with incomprehensible and inscrutable ways of life. This solution however remained efficient as long as the group which employed it stayed self-sufficient, to wit, free not to enter normatively patterned and reciprocally accepted relations with the aliens. Then the issue of demarcation moved to a new field, that lying between the whole lot of humans on one side and non-human living creatures on the other. With the web of regular and institutionalized bonds spreading all over the continuously expanding *oikoumene* (the known part of the habitable world), establishing an absolute border in a constantly shifting and mobile universe acquired a paramount importance. The inductive way of enumerating accepted members of the human club would have been impractical – it simply would not stave off future ambiguities; an absolutistic, universally applicable answer was required. Quite naturally, in the era of substituting the territorial criteria for kinship and affinity in defining human groups, there was a pronounced tendency to situate the frontier in geographical space. Hence the famous 'ubi leones' of Roman cartography, and Scylla and Charybdis in Greek mythology. Hence, above all, the ambiguous, half-human, terrifying and repulsive monsters, employed by ancient and mediaeval geographers to delineate the confines of (and thus to define) human kind. The fringes of the explored world were invariably inhabited by such monsters in the writings of the highest authorities of the time: Pliny the Elder, Pomponius Mela, Caius Julius Solinus Polyhistor, Bishop Isidore of Seville, Albertus Magnus, Vincent de Beauvais. The frontiers of the *oikoumene* in Isidore's etymologies were filled with fearsome ogres; there were headless creatures with mouths and eyes in their chests, noseless creatures, creatures with protruding lower lips under which they hid when asleep, gargoyles with one outsize foot on which to rest for hours at a stretch, or with mouths so tiny that only liquid food could be sucked through a straw.[74] Even more repellent and awe-inspiring were the customs of these devilish oddities: Peter the Martyr's detailed account of the Anthropophagi tells that

> such children as they take they geld to make them fat as we do cock chickens and young hogs, and eat them when they are well fed: of such as they eat, they first eat the entrails and extreme parts, as hands, feet, arms, neck, and head. The other most fleshy parts they pounder for store, as we do of pork and gammons of bacon. . . . Such young women as they take, they keep for increase, as we do hens to lay eggs.[75]

Two parallel developments led to shifting the frontier-layout efforts from space to the time dimension: the first was the consistent elimination of the remaining blank spots on the earth map and the resulting scarcity of lands which could accommodate fabulous beings, the second was an emerging awareness of history and its single-directional nature. In modern times Pithecanthropus, Sinanthropus and Australopithecus took the place of the Anthropophagi. The high intensity of the emotions they stirred, beyond any comparison with other scientific issues, can be reasonably explained only by their latent delimiting function. Phenomenologically the generic notion of culture belongs in the same category with Anthropophagi and Australopithecus. The fixed attention paid to it, far in excess of its purely scientific significance, bears again eloquent witness to its more general, semiotic aspects. It is the modern, mankind-scale version of the perennial concern with group self-identity.

In its simplest form, the generic concept of culture consists in attributing to culture itself the quality of a universal feature of all men and of men only. Clifford Geertz's is a typical statement to this effect.

> Man is the toolmaking, the talking, the symbolizing animal. [In this form the articulation of the peculiarity of human nature follows the pattern set by Leslie A. White in his discussion of symbol and tool,[76] and, through him, the ideas of Friedrich Engels.] Only he laughs; only he knows that we will die; only he disdains to mate with his mother and sister; only he contrives those visions of other worlds to live in which Santayana called religions, or bakes those mudpies of the mind which Cyril Connolly called art. He has . . . not just mentality but consciousness, not just needs but values, not just fears but conscience, not just a past but a history. Only he [the argument concludes in grand summation] has culture.[77]

Geertz's phrasing of this already widespread idea seems to be among the most comprehensive in the category. It combines arguments drawn from the modern philosophical analysis of the human existential plight with psychological findings and seminal methodological principles of the humanities in general. The culture, as described in the quoted paragraph, is much more (or much less) than the differentialists' cluster of norms and patterned customs; it is, indeed, a specific approach, human through and through, to the drama of life, entrenched in the last analysis in the specifically human ability of the mind to be intentional, active and creative. Other proponents of the generic concept of culture are often much closer to the already mentioned traditional and dull 'common denominator' approach, though situated in the context of the historical passage from the animal to human world.[78]

Even Geertz's formula however remains at the level of phenomenal description. It simply states the most conspicuous peculiarities of the human race; it refrains from all attempt to organize the disparate tenets into a cohesive structure; it abstains even from designating one of the many planes of reality as a privileged locus of *explanans*, and others, respectively, as the site of *explanandum*. These elements are being provided continually by other students of culture. The issue remains one of the most contentious in the whole science of culture, and numerous alternative, not always compatible, solutions are being offered. The following is an attempt to classify the most influential among them.

(1) One alternative is to define culture from the outset as one, total and indivisible set of symbolized meanings and tools, ascribable solely to mankind in its entirety. Thus, according to Leslie A. White, 'the culture of mankind in actuality is a one, a single system; all the so-called cultures are merely distinguishable portions of a single fabric'.[79] Robert H. Lowie holds a similar view: 'A specific culture is an abstraction, an arbitrarily selected fragment. . . . There is only one cultural reality that is not artificial, to wit: the culture of all humanity at all periods and in all places.'[80] Obviously this is better said than done. The trouble with a 'totalistic' notion of culture of the above sort becomes transparent the moment one tries to recast it into the tool of specific analysis. What does, exactly, 'the culture of all humanity' mean? Is this a system *sensu stricto*, e.g. a set of interrelated and communicating units? If so, what are the units, if not 'specific (national, tribal, group-based in general) cultures', which are dismissed as 'arbitrarily selected fragments' or 'merely distinguishable portions'? In what sense does the culture of mankind as a whole constitute a totality in reality, and not only analytically, as a product of empirical comparisons and theoretical syntheses? One reason why we are likely to find these questions cumbersome and embarrassing is the notorious lack of corresponding, analytically distinguished units among the theoretical constructs of sociology (defined as a social-structure approach to the study of human life). Sociology, as it came of age in the bosom of Western civilization and as we know it today, is endemically national-biased. It does not recognize a totality broader than a politically organized nation; the term 'society', as used by well-nigh all sociologists regardless of their school loyalties, is, for all practical purposes, a name for an entity identical in size and composition with the nation-state. Terms like 'humanity', 'mankind', etc., if they do appear in professional sociological literature, are either used in a non-specific, metaphorical, or shorthand sense, or are understood as analytically hollow labels for an aggregate of societies proper; aggregate, to be sure, but not a system; a set of units, but not of interrelationships between them. Sometimes, we must admit, some sociologists (more often social psychologists) discuss regularities, if not laws, related to 'man' as such, whatever his national, geographical or historical specification. This is, however, a 'man' as a random

sample of the species, not a substitute for 'totality of mankind'; this concept is a product of an analytical process of abstraction, not of synthesis, and it can hardly serve as a brick of which one can build up a model of a single society, to say nothing of mankind as a totality. The concept of culture as a mankind-scale total system is therefore left very much in the void, lacking all 'substantive' foundation to rest on. No wonder that White or Lowie did not go very far, in fact not a single step beyond their programmatic statements; it seems that until sociology develops analytical concepts of a comparable scale statements of this kind are doomed to remain declarations of faith without direct relevance to the actual cognitive procedure. If employed prematurely for analytical guidance, they will rather lead the student along the well-trodden path of the 'common denominator' hunters.

(2) Another alternative draws inspiration from the structural-functionalist model of the social system. The generic character of the culture concept it promotes is buttressed on the assumption of universality of prerequisites, which must be met to ensure the survival of any imaginable social system. Whatever system we choose as a take-off point, we can always spell out an inventory of essential needs which must be satisfied in this or another way. Some needs cannot be satisfied but through artificial, human-made institutions; hence a universal frame which must be filled up by any specific culture, whatever its idiosyncratic features.

Though there is an obvious affinity between the strategy applied here and the one originated and cultivated by Talcott Parsons, some of its applications are notably illuminating and inventive. Thus, for example, Edward M. Bruner,[81] apart from more traditional and routine 'prerequisites' like control of aggression and allocation of women and property, specifies, as universal elements of human culture, imposing the necessary delay between wish and gratification; repressing of inadmissible desires into subconsciousness and sublimating them in socially beneficial motives; providing makeshift gratifications for repressed drives in fantasy, literature, drama, folk tales, play, religious ritual; specifying persons and groups whom it is proper to hate; defining persons approved as sexual objects; developing rules regulating the acquisition of goods. Clyde Kluckhohn, writing a decade earlier, was somewhat less imaginative and more anxious not to travel too far from the safe ground of 'common denominators'; but he did spell what amounted to the principles of a 'functional prerequisites' approach to culture as generic phenomenon:[82]

The facts of human biology and of human gregariousness supply . . . certain invariant points of reference from which cross-cultural comparisons can start without begging questions that are themselves at issue. As Wissler pointed out, the broad outlines of the ground plan of all cultures are and have to be about the same because men always and everywhere are faced with certain unavoidable problems which arise out of the situation 'given' by nature. Since most of the patterns of all cultures crystallize around the same foci, there are significant respects in which each culture is not wholly isolated, self-contained, disparate but rather related to and comparable with all other cultures.

The last quotation, to the extent to which it may be legitimately classified in the category presently under discussion, renders conspicuous the genuine nature of the whole 'functional prerequisites' approach to culture in its generic sense. The approach in question seems to be very close indeed to the preoccupations of 'butterfly collectors'. Most authors are concerned, in the first place, with finding a convenient frame of reference for comparing basically distinct and self-enclosed cultures. This frame of reference should take the form of a list of items or chapter headings. What can be called 'the human culture' has only the ontological status (if any) of a derivative of many real entities, i.e. individual cultures. This approach seems to be more variable and less jarringly off the mark precisely because it is much better adjusted, in contradistinction to the one previously discussed, to the currently available analytical outfit of sociology. It is, in fact, cut to the measure of the nationally-biased sociology of today.

The important point is that this type of generality in culture is a by-product, if not an artefact, of mankind *not* being united into a whole; of it being, on the contrary, split into separate units which must in the first place adjust to the neighbourhood of other human groups and defend themselves against merging with them and losing their own group identity. In other words, the most generic element in culture is precisely its dividing, differentiating function. In this sense again the concept under discussion is the true offshoot of a sociology dominated by the national-state paradigm in general, and its sophisticated, structural-functional version in particular.

(3) The same bias, injected into the blood of the modern study of culture in its infancy, in the form of the Durkheimian vaccine, by its midwives, Malinowski and Boas, colours the 'ethical universals' brand of the generic concept of culture. This has been introduced again by Kluckhohn in search (in Kroeber's classic 'butterfly collection' style, which blends, as usual, statements about reality and postulates about methodology) of 'categories, which remove cultures from the states of completely isolated monads and make some valid comparisons possible'. There are, as we see, cultures in the plural in states in the plural. For some reason, however, we want them to be incomplete monads rather than complete. This is where 'general categories' come in; they enable us to make *some* comparisons between them. How cultures are expected to surrender a part of their monadic nature by having been compared, is doomed, of course, to remain the secret of Kroeber's epistemology.

Be that as it may, Kluckhohn pins his hopes for comparative categories on ethical universals. These can be of two kinds: '(1) Rules approving or forbidding specific kinds of acts (e.g. truth-telling and incest); (2) General principles or standards of evaluation which make for the stability and continuity of groups and for maximizing the satisfactions experienced by individuals.'[83] The second phrase, which utters in one breath 'stability of groups' and 'satisfaction of individuals' and makes them dependent on the same 'general principles', reaches, in its happy-go-lucky unproblematic frivolity, well beyond Durkheim, into the naiveties of utilitarianism. But the most surprising statement follows: 'Ethical universals are the product of universal human nature, which is based, in turn, upon a common biology, psychology, and generalized situation.' As to the last item, we recognize the common mistake of ascribing an ontological status to what is, in the last instance, a frame of analytical reference applied universally by scientists, and rooted in the familiar national-state bias. The new and bizarre element is the first two items, whose presence in the quoted explanatory statement amounts in its final effect to announcing a non-cultural, or, rather, pre-cultural nature of the universal component of culture. What is 'generic' in culture is allegedly an alien body, a foreign component, imposed on cultural phenomena proper by sets of factors not submitted to a truly cultural regulation. Nothing has been said by Kluckhohn to help us solve the riddle of, say, the rule of truth-telling being determined by human biology. And, in particular, how the prohibition of incest, the first really human act, the first clamping of an artificial, human-made order on otherwise randomly distributed biological occurrences – how this very embodiment of cultural act can be explained away by omnipresence of pre-cultural qualities.

But for the last oddity, most of the 'ethical universals' concepts are notoriously lumbered with the structural-functional view of the human world. This is clearly visible, for example, in David Bidney's pronouncement:[84]

> For all cultures the perpetuation of the society takes precedence over the life of the individual and hence no society tolerates treason, murder, rape, or incest. All societies recognize mutual rights and duties in marriage and condemn acts which threaten family solidarity. Similarly all societies give recognition to personal property and provide some techniques for the distribution of economic surplus to the needy.

The association is inevitable, since the structural-functional approach to ethics is very nearly the only one admitted in current sociological theory. Modern sociology does handle the whole issue of ethics as a corollary of the 'central value cluster', the updated substitution for the Durkheimian *conscience collective*, responsible, presumably, for holding together the precarious web of social bonds between biologically egoistic individuals. The association is in fact so close that we do not risk forsaking too much of its content if we simply treat 'ethical universals' as another name given to the previously discussed undisguisedly structural-functional version of the generic concept of culture.

(4) Priority of the social over the individual makes sense – though upholders of this methodological principle in analysing culture are reluctant to admit it – only if a society without culture is possible or, for that matter, imaginable. Indeed, if cultural norms are brought to life by a society struggling for its survival, it follows that society must have been born in some way other than cultural, in fact with no cultural means whatsoever in use. The supposition is hardly palatable. Society without culture seems to be a monstrosity comparable to the proverbial headless calf. And so the idea that a culturally patterned individual behaviour is as much a precondition of society as a society-based culture is a precondition of a social individual dawns every now and again in sociologists' minds. If men created society – had both a need and the ability to do it – they must have been endowed with qualities

instrumental in structuring both society and the way they think of it and choose their attitude toward it. Logically, culture is to the same extent pre-social as it is societally generated. Historically, they emerged and grew, it seems, simultaneously and in close collaboration, feeding and helping each other, each one exteriorating, in the reality of the other, the condition for its own development.

Once social scientists set to explore the common root of culture and society, the surest and safest choice is, obviously, human psychological endowment. The decision to focus attention on the general qualities of human perception is the first step on a long way leading as far as the sophisticated heights of the modern semiological structuralism of Vygotsky, Piaget or Lévi-Strauss. The beginnings are, however, modest and commonsensical, as in a lecture given in 1957 by Robert Redfield:[85]

> There is that phenomenon of the mind we call 'self-consciousness'; all men are aware of self, distinguish an I and a Me; and, farther, they relate themselves to others who are also known as selves to themselves. All men look out upon a not-self, a universe, in which people are distinguished, one from another, as persons, and in categories, some of the categories, such as kinship, being universal. All are disposed to feel and think more intimately and kindly toward the members of their own immediate groups than they think and feel about people in more remote groups in situations where a choice of loyalties is required.

The basic idea belongs obviously to the Lockean-Kantian tradition. The field in which the idea is anchored is the one tilled diligently by the phenomenological psychology of Alfred Schutz or Erwin W. Strauss. But the theoretical context is still well within the traditional confines set by American cultural anthropology. It may well be that the quoted statement by Redfield represents the highest point traditional anthropology could reach in its search for generic components of culture prior to the assimilation of the achievements of phenomenology and structuralism.

(5) Among all the qualities of human psychology, as distinct from the animal, one feature in particular was discussed by numerous authors, separately and at length, as the one most conspicuously exclusive to human beings and thus the most likely candidate for the role of the foundation of culture in its generic sense. This one, preferentially treated, feature was the human ability to think symbolically; in particular, to produce arbitrary symbols and to assign collectively accepted meanings to them. 'The man differs from the dog – and all other creatures – in that he can and does play an active role in determining what value the vocal stimulus is to have, and the dog cannot,' says Leslie A. White.[86]

The idea of language as a distinctive feature of human creatures is established in our intellectual tradition from times immemorial. In the intellectual history of the West it goes back at least to St Thomas Aquinas and through him to Aristotle. Still it was only recently that the hitherto unexplored languages of peoples defined as 'primitive' were put on the record and their vocabulary and grammatical structure investigated. The impact was immediate and far reaching. By a happy concatenation of events, taking the stock of 'primitive' languages took place much later than the first inventories of other cultural fields, like forms of marriage and family or labour implements; so much later that the evolutionary ideas which had dominated the minds of the first explorers of exotic families and stone axes were already on the wane, if not actually becoming objects of derision. Students of languages, therefore, unlike their predecessors, did not miss the obvious; from the outset they realized that whatever can be said of the relative level of development of this or another society, their languages cannot be arranged on an evolutionary scale; there are not 'more perfect' or 'more primitive' languages, if measured by the only criterion which can be reasonably applied, the sureness and efficiency of conveying information in the native context. Perhaps this aspect of the historical fate of ethno-linguistics explains in part why language, or symbol-making in general, was so quickly and with no noticeable resistance acclaimed the universal and essential core of human culture as well as its foundation.

The initial discovery of the unique role of symbol-reading and symbol-producing in the particularly human way of life inspired increasingly ingenious research into animal use of symbols. The original hypothesis was put to a strict test, and very little of the supposedly obvious truth withstood it. Quite a number of allegedly human features of symbol-exchange were gradually discovered in animals, and not necessarily among those noted for their extensively sophisticated intra-species communication, like bees, apes and dolphins. The hypothetically sharp and unequivocal dividing line between human and animal handling of symbols became even more blurred when scientists began to experiment instead of record their observations, when they shifted their attention from the actual use of symbols by animals in their intra-species communication to their mental and physiological capacity for using them when confronted with a learning situation, with a human being playing the role of the situation-partner.

The first victim to fall to the tightened scrutiny was the belief quoted above in White's formulation: that only humans use symbols. If we define symbols as 'mediators' in the chain of communication, as entities constructed of stuff different from what is being communicated, entities into which the content of information is translated by the sender and from which it is re-translated by the recipient of the message, then most animals have symbols in widespread use indeed. Still at least three important differences between animal use of symbols and the human use were possible:

(a) in the relation between symbol and what is symbolized; this relation may be 'natural' or 'arbitrary', and the distinction may be valid in a double sense. First, in the sense of presence or absence of some kind of physical resemblance between a symbol and its referent. Second, and more important, is the difference between a situation in which a given symbol, even when it does not bear the slightest resemblance to its referent, is produced 'automatically' in a causal association with its referent, and a situation, in which the symbol-using creature may or may not produce the symbol when its referent occurs, and when, moreover, it can produce this symbol without any temporal, or spatial, physiologically mediated contiguity with the referent;

(*b*) in the type of referent to which symbols are attached. Symbols can contain information about the 'subjective' state of the symbol-producing organism at the moment of actually producing the symbol; or they can convey information concerning things and events 'objectifiable', e.g. detachable, both spatially and chronologically, from the symbol-producing organism at the moment of producing it. Another way of putting it is to distinguish between a 'cool', 'unemotional' symbol-use (when it is possible to discuss 'fire' without actually experiencing either fear of flame or escape drive) and a symbol-use as an integral, undetachable component of a complex, unified pattern of emotionally-organized behaviour (when the cry 'fire' appears only simultaneously with actual flight). In this wording the distinction now under discussion seems to be very close indeed to the first one;

(*c*) in the way the use of symbols is internally structured. This concerns not so much an isolated symbol as a system of symbols – symbol as an element of code, definable as a patterned web of relations between symbols. There are codes, like the three-part colour code of traffic lights, in which symbols cannot combine to produce a new meaning, and where combinations of symbols which are meant to be used separately, can produce only confusion (= overlapping of incompatible meanings). And there are codes of different kinds, in which a relatively small amount of units may produce, through the applications of the rules of combination, a practically endless multitude of meanings. This second quality, typical of human language, was named by André Martinet 'double articulation'.[87]

> Ce qui paraît distinguer le langage humain de formes d'activité qu'on constate chez d'autres êtres animés et qu'on pourrait être tenté d'appeler aussi 'langage', n'est-ce pas le fait que l'homme communique au moyen d'enoncés articulés en mots successifs, alors que les productions vocales émises par les animaux nous semblant, sur le plan du sens, aussi bien que celui de la forme, être des touts inanalysables? Il apparaît donc que le langage humain est, non seulement articulé, mais doublement articulé, articulé sur deux plans.

To the double articulation human language owes its unique richness and flexibility, its capacity of producing, with practically no technical limitations ever new meanings, and so introducing ever new subtle distinctions into the universe referred to in the acts of communication.

The three distinctive features combined make for the summary peculiarity of human language against all animal symbol-use: symbols used by animals bear their meaning, we may say, openly and immediately; they are in a sense identical with their meanings, even in the case of a symbol 'arbitrary' from the point of view of its likeness to the referent. The immediate transparency and availability of the meaning comes from the fact that any symbol is unilaterally mapped into one and only one type of situational context; the meaning of the symbol is derivable from the one-to-one relationship between an individual symbol and an individual referent. Not so in the case of human-made symbols, which are arbitrary (in the sense of being undetermined), possessive of objectified referents, and integrated into a code-system. 'The full meaning of a word,' as Colin Cherry put it in his classic treatise on human communication,[88] 'does not appear until it is placed in its context.' But this context is not provided by the non-linguistic events, like a particular state of the symbol-producing organism or emotion-generating facets of its immediate environment. The context, from which the meaning can be deduced, is made of other words; those actually present in the immediate neighbourhood of the same utterance-string, or those present only *in potentia* – as meaningful alternatives to the words actually used. Thanks to this new plane of structured relationships, the linguistic plane *sensu stricto*, human communication can handle not only individual things or events, but relationships between them; these relationships are the true referents of human language. As the Russells expressed it recently, true (human) language 'involves the free combination of symbols limited only by logical rules of grammar and syntax, which themselves express *relations between* symbols and hence symbolize *relations between* things and individuals and events'.[89]

As we shall see later, this unique capacity for re-producing and producing new structures rather than the simple skill of introducing symbolic go-betweens into the space which divides awareness of the event from the event itself, endows human language with its culture-generating potential and transforms it into the true foundation of culture as a generic phenomenon. That is why the question of the generic component of human culture – of the essence of *the* culture – brings us inevitably, at a relatively early stage of our enquiry, to the issue of structure and structuring. Being structured and being capable of structuring seem to be the twin-kernels of the human way of life, known as culture.

The point seems to be of crucial importance for any attempt to assess culture in its generic sense. Human language is a unique blend of thinking (intelligence, according to Piaget's terminology) and symbol-producing. The two activities are by no means identical, nor are they inextricably connected. Elements of sound-language, or speech, developed in fact along lines different from those of embryos of thought, as was well argued by L. S. Vygotsky.[90] In his estimation the sounds produced by the higher apes, though bestowed with symbolic meaning, are singularly unfit for developing into 'true language' precisely because they are invariably immured in an intensively affective context; and intense emotions are at odds with the intelligent regulation of behaviour. 'The close correspondence between thought and speech characteristic of man is absent in anthropoids.' The capacity to produce sounds subordinated unilaterally to some non-symbolic events is a widespread quality in animals. Incipient elements of analysis and synthesis – the two mutually complementary processes of thinking – are traceable as well in the behaviour of many animals. But only in humans, in cultural beings, do they meet and blend. Pure symbol-use, before it transcends the threshold of structuring capacity, seems to be a blind alley; no amount of new symbols added to the number already in employment is likely to combine them into a true language. There seems to be indeed a qualitative abyss between ordinary symbols and human language. Structure, therefore, rather than symbol-use is, probably, the genuine gravity centre of culture as a universal attribute of humans.

The final conclusion to this effect was drawn by Jean Piaget: 'Whereas other animals cannot alter themselves except by changing their species, man can transform himself by transforming the world and can structure himself by constructing structures; and these structures are his own, for they are not eternally predestined either from within or from without.'[91] Thus the peculiarity of man consists in his being a structure-generating and structure-oriented creature. The term 'culture' in its generic sense stands precisely for this exceptional ability. This is however an elliptical statement unless the meaning in which the terms 'structure' and 'structuring' have been used is made specific.

The amount of books and papers conceived above all as discussions of the precise meaning of 'structure' is constantly growing, and one would be hard put to it even to enumerate and classify the definitions or rules of usage they propose or claim to have discovered. It is not, however, certain that the result of such a time-consuming effort will be sufficiently valuable to counterweight the expenditure of time. The term 'structure' made a very rapid career in the 1950s and 1960s and there are always many contenders eager to join the *cortège* of ascending celebrity; the fashionable concept tends then to be overloaded with meanings, since too many tinsel-blinded zealots try to stretch or distend its scope, each from his own side, to accommodate his own concerns and research topics. The limits of the term's application, at present diffuse and contentious, will probably continue to fluctuate for some time yet, before a semblance of *consensus omnium* will emerge. What follows is, therefore, nothing more than another attempt at phenomenological analysis of the term, as it is understood in modern thinking; an attempt to extract the kernel of the constitutive, necessary intention from the husk of the incidental and the changeable.

In 1968 Raymond Boudon, keeping a wary eye on the spate of self-appointed structuralists, published an acute analysis of disparate uses and abuses of the term under the symptomatic title 'A quoi sert la notion de structure?',[92] meaning, one can guess, that the notion does not always serve the right cause. It is Boudon's contention that the word is, in its present usage, simultaneously a member of a family of synonyms, and as such redundant, and a cumulative heading for a family of homonyms, and as such too general to specify any precise content. His visible resentment against the over-exploited word, particularly manifest in the introductory declaration of the author's intention, does not stop Boudon from coming nevertheless to terms with the concept and, for that matter, treating the reader to an exemplary, orderly and systematic review of an assortment of selected scientifically modelled structures. Still it is his belief, and, in fact, the outspoken principle of the whole book, that the word, when put into the two different, above-mentioned, contextual settings, means two things having little in common but their names. As a synonym of many other better established words, 'structure' means simply 'being systemic' (in opposition to 'being an aggregate'), or 'being organized' (as distinct from 'being disorderly'). It is used 'pour souligner le caractère systématique d'un objet'. As a family name for a set of homonyms, 'structure' as such has hardly any describable meaning; by this name various scientists call their theories of the object they investigate;

deductive-hypothetical models of a given part of reality, consisting above all of axiomatic assumptions and rules of transformations. In this case, 'structure' is almost as broad a notion as 'theory'. The more specific meaning of a particular structure, not structure as such (i.e. structure of kinship or structure of grammar), 'ne fait que résultér indirectement de l'analyse d'un material particulier'. Now, Boudon chose to discuss 'structure' in its first context in terms of 'définition intentionelle', and in the second in terms of 'définition effective'.[93] Why he did so, is not entirely clear. He perhaps set out initially to define structure, but thought better of it and did some splendid study of what structured entities indeed are; but the original conceptual framework remained, rather obfuscating the most significant message of the book. What Boudon discriminates as two kinds of definitions are, in fact, two successive stages in structure-modelling; we usually discover first the systemic, i.e. structured, character of the object under study and then try to model actual regularities which warrant our original impression. In both stages the 'definition', or, more precisely, our understanding of the conditions on which we are allowed to apply the term 'structure', remains largely the same. We shall try below to enumerate these conditions. Without, however, going into details at this stage, we assume for the moment, that we all agree on what we mean when using the term 'structure', as, broadly, an antonym to 'disorder'. In this wide sense we can say, that culture as a generic quality, as a universal attribute of mankind as distinct from all other animal species, is the capacity to impose new structures on the world.

Whatever we say on the diiference between a structured and a disorderly state, the set of ordered states is always less numerous than the set of all possible unordered states. Structure, therefore, is a less probable state than disorder. The other way of saying this is that structure means always limitation of possibilities. Limitation is achievable by splitting a broad category of undifferentiated elements into a series of sub-categories differing from each other in probabilities of their occurrence. Biologically, all women falling into a fairly broad range of ages are indiscriminately fit as potential sexual partners. Through dividing them into mothers, sisters, maternal uncle's daughters etc., discriminated in their eligibility for sexual intercourse, the set of possible sexual couplings is drastically reduced. Physically, the temperature of the human environment oscillates within a very wide range of probable values. By introducing mediating artefacts between the human body and the natural environment (built-up enclosures, clothes etc.) the actual variation in the immediate vicinity of the body is again drastically reduced. Physiologically, probabilities of possible outcomes of a duel between two animals (one of them homo) are determined by factors beyond the combatants' control (dexterity of brawn, fangs, claws); when one of the adversaries modifies the capacity of his own, or his enemy's, natural equipment by inserting mediating artefacts into the process of the struggle, the relative probabilities of various results are drastically changed.

These three examples represent three alternative ways of 'structuring': through (a) differentiating meanings ascribed to various parts of the environment; (*b*) introducing regularity into an otherwise more erratic and less predictable environment; (*c*) manipulating the distribution of probabilities by 'biasing' the situation in favour of one of the sides involved. All three constitute the principal and universal processes, in fact the essence, of human culture. It is easy to see that all three, though in varying proportion, imply participation of two types of patterns (meaning, in this context, simply regularities): (*a*) patterns relating specific states of the environment to specific 'after-states' of the human organism (states of environment being inputs, 'after-states' of the organism being the output of the human being as a cybernetic 'black box'), and (*b*) patterns relating specific states of the human organism to the specific 'after-states' of the environment (inputs and outputs changing their places, with environments in the role of the 'black box'). The cultural process of structuring the universe of abstract possibilities is, therefore, subdivided into two interrelated structurings: (*a*) of the human behaviour, (*b*) of the human environment.

In this sense we can conceive of the cultural process as an extension, or subcategory, of a much more general relation of adaptation, entered by all living organisms and – at the other end of biological-cultural evolution – by manmade self-regulating mechanisms, in short, by all 'open systems', i.e. systems which cannot survive without some input of energy and/or information from the part of the universe beyond their confines. According to Piaget, this process of adaptation, compellingly initiated by the life-cycle of the open system, consisted of a two-faceted relation of assimilation and accommodation.[94] The first is the outward aspect of adaptation; various elements of the environment are assimilated by the subject, either energetically, or informatively, or both. The second is the inward aspect of the same relation: the intrinsic structure of the system itself undergoes constant modifications required if the exchange with the environment is to be perpetuated. Adaptation is achieved if, and only if, assimilation and accommodation are reciprocally equilibrated; or, rather, adaptation *is* an equilibration of assimilation and adaptation.

Now, we have described adaptation in terms sufficiently broad to account equally for both factors, usually sharply discriminated – body and mind. Adaptation, as well as its two facets, if described in the above terms, and so far as their definitions are held within the universe of meaning warranted by these terms, is neither 'bodily' nor 'mental'. What is being described in other contexts as the bodily or the mental we can depict as two correlated forms or applications of adaptation, retaining however an identical structure; as, definitionally, two reflections of one structure, imprinted on two different kinds of medium. It is hard to conceive how mental processes like thinking or intelligence could be defined in any other way than by indicating structures and their transformations. Applying 'mind' as an explanation of a system's behaviour seems to be a logical error, since, as Anatol Rapoport put it, 'mind' is only a name invented to distinguish the class of things which 'behave' or 'perform actions' as distinct from those which only 'participate in events'. Rapoport indicates 'plasticity of response, the ability to modify the response to a given stimulus' as recognizable symptoms of 'intelligence';[95] in other words, the one thing we can say reasonably about the concept of 'intelligence' is that we apply it whenever the above symptoms are actually present. Similarly, according to the classic study by A. M. Turing, unless we define mental processes in a way which compels us to agree with a statement that the only way by which one can be sure that a machine thinks is to be the machine and to feel oneself thinking, the only alternative way of solving the question of 'machine thinking' is to test a machine's performance in a situation usually describable as requiring intelligent behaviour.[96]

The generic notion of culture is coined, therefore, in order to overcome the persistent philosophical opposition between the spiritual and the real, thought and matter, body and mind. The only necessary and irreplaceable component of the concept is the process of structuring, together with its objectified results – man-made structures.

The continuous and unending structuring activity constitutes the core of human praxis, the human mode of being-in-the-world. To carry on this active existence man is supplied with two essential instruments – *manus et lingua*, as Aquinas put it; tools and language, according to the Marxian tradition. With these two implements man handles – through structuring – the world he lives in and himself. This 'handling' consists in drawing energy and generating information. The two components of the human mode of existence tend to be perceived in different ways. Energy is what man needs; in gratifying this need he is dependent on the forces which are not entirely under his rule. This state of dependence man perceives as being-an-object, as being exposed to a manipulation he cannot avert precisely because he cannot survive unless complying with the conditions his dependence sets for him. Information he experiences as something he wishes; in generating it he subjects hitherto elemental and unbridled forces to his will. This state of creation man perceives as being-the-subject, as exposing the world to his own manipulation. Hence the continuous persistence in human thinking of the world of the multi-named dichotomy of spirit and matter, mind and body; and the invariable tendency to associate the first with freedom, the second with thraldom.

Culture is a perpetual effort to overcome, to remove this dichotomy. Creativity and dependence are two indispensable aspects of human existence, not only conditioning, but reinforcing each other; they cannot be transcended conclusively – they overcome their own antinomy only by re-creating it and re-building the setting from which it is generated. The agony of culture is therefore doomed to eternal continuation; by the same token, man, since endowed with the capacity of culture, is doomed to explore, to be dissatisfied with his world, to destroy and to create.

### Notes

1 W. J. M. Mackenzie, *Politics and Social Science*, Harmondsworth, Penguin, 1967, pp.190–1.

2 Cf. E. E. Evans-Pritchard, *Social Anthropology*, Oxford University Press, 1951, p. 40 (italics added).

3 Cf. *Culture: A Critical Review of Concepts and Definitions*, Papers of the Peabody Museum, Cambridge, Mass., 1952.

4 Cf. 'A formal analysis of definitions of "culture"', in *Essays in the Science of Culture*, ed. Gertrude E. Dole and Robert L. Carneiro, New York, Crowell, 1960.

5 *Culture, Language, and Personality*, University of California Press, 1949, pp. 79–80.

6 For the philosophical expositions of this theory, cf. for example, L. Wittgenstein, *Philosophical Investigations*, Oxford, Blackwell, 1953; Gilbert Ryle, 'Ordinary language', *Philosophical Review*, 1953, pp. 167 ff, or G. E. Moore, 'Wittgenstein's lectures in 1930–33', in *Philosophical Papers*, London, Allen & Unwin, 1959.

7 Gilbert Ryle and J. N. Findlay, Symposium, *Proceedings of the Aristotelian Society*, Suppl. vol. 35,1961, p. 235.

8 For the difference between language and speech from this point of view, cf. ibid., pp. 223 ff.

9 A. J. Greimas, *Sémantique structurale*, Paris, Larousse, 1966, p. 44.

10 Luis J. Prieto, *Messages et signaux*, Paris, Presses Universitaires de France, 1966, pp. 18, 20.

11 J. Burnet, 'Philosophy', in *The Legacy of Greece*, ed. Sir Richard Livingstone, Oxford University Press, 1969, p. 76.

12 Cf. Harry Levin, 'Semantics of culture', in *Science and Culture*, ed. Gerald Holton, Boston, Houghton Mifflin, 1965, p. 2.

13 De *Anima*, ii i. 1.

14 Cf. *Phaedo*, 245 c – 246 a.

15 Robert A. Nisbet, *Social Change and History*, Oxford University Press, 1969, pp. 9, 22.

16 Cf. *Republic*, 352 d – 354 a.

17 Cf. *Paidea, Die Formung des griechischen Menschen*, Berlin, Walter de Gruyter, 1959.

18 *Education in the Perspective of History*, New York, Harper, 1960, p. 80.

19 Aristotle, *Nicomachean Ethics*, 1. 9.

20 E. H. Diels, *Die Fragmente der Vorsokratiker*, Berlin, 1903, vol. 53.

21 Cf. 'Concepts and society', reprinted in *Sociological Theory and Philosophical Analysis*, ed. Dorothy Emmet and Alistair MacIntyre London, Macmillan, 1970, pp. 139–41.

22 *Soziologie*, Leipzig, Duncker und Humblot, 1908, pp. 732–46.

23 According to the pertinent summary of Simmel's concept by Donald N. Levine, 'Some key problems in Simmel's work', in *George Simmel*, ed. Lewis A. Coser, Englewood Cliffs, N.J., Prentice-Hall, 1965, pp.108–9.

24 *On the Theory of Social Change*, University of Chicago Press, 1962, pp. 65,75.

25 Reprinted in Edward Sapir, *Culture, Language and Personality*, University of California Press, 1949, p. 90.

26 According to the rule articulated by the prominent Polish social philosopher Kazimierz Kelles-Krauz as the law of 'the upheaval retrospection'; cf. *Pisma Wybrane*, vol. 1, Warsaw, Książka i Wiedza, 1962, pp. 241–77.

27 'Remarks on a redefinition of culture', *Science and Culture*, ed. G. Holton, Boston, Houghton Mifflin, 1965, p. 225.

28 Cf. the law-like formulation of the rule by Karl Marx in K. Marx and F. Engels, *The German Ideology*, London, Lawrence & Wishart, 1968, chapter 1.

29 Cf. Herodotus, Oxford text, ed. C. Hude, i. 193–4, 202–4; ii. 35; iv. 75.

30 In the mediaeval view of cultural differences deviation belonged conceptually and functionally to an entirely distinct category of intellectual phenomena.

31 *Plan de deux discours sur l'histoire universelle*, Paris, Guillaumin, 1844, p. 645. Quoted by Marvin Harris, *The Rise of Anthropological Theory*, London, Routledge & Kegan Paul, 1968, p. 15.

32 *An Essay Concerning Human Understanding*, Oxford, Clarendon Press, 1894, p. 66.

33 'The transition to humanity', in *Horizons of Anthropology*, ed. Sol Tax, London, Allen & Unwin, 1965, p. 47.

34 Ruth Benedict, *Patterns of Culture*, London, Routledge & Kegan Paul, 1961 (originally 1935), p. 170.

35 Ibid., p. 171.

36 *Habitat, Economy, and Society*, London, Methuen, 1963 (originally 1934), p. 7.

37 *The Evolution of Culture*, New York, McGraw Hill, 1959, p. 3 (italics added).

38 *Theory of Culture Change*, Urbana University Press, 1955, p. 184.

39 That is, quite obviously, only one of the possible explanations. Another one, always plausible, is an omnipotent tendency to project the hierarchical concept of culture onto a 'we-group' image, incorporating, this time, the totality of mankind. Our standards are convincingly superior (more efficient, more convenient, more human etc.); why, therefore, should anybody reject them?

40 'Culture and Environment: the study of cultural ecology' in *Horizons of Anthropology*, ed. Sol Tax, pp. 140, 141.

41 'The superorganic: science or metaphysics' in *Theory in Anthropology*, ed. Robert A. Manners and David Kaplan, London, Routledge & Kegan Paul, 1969, p. 22.

42 Quoted by David F. Aberle, 'The influence of linguistics on early culture and personality theory', in *Theory in Anthropology*, p. 311.

43 *Mirror for Man*, New York, McGraw Hill, 1949, p. 23 (italics added).

44 Aberle, op. cit., pp. 305, 306.

45 Marvin Harris, *The Rise of Anthropological Theory*, London, Routledge & Kegan Paul, 1968, pp. 17–18.

46 Cf. *Man and Culture*, New York, Crowell, 1923, pp. 50 ff.

47 'The common denominator of cultures', in *The Scene of Man in the World Crisis*, ed. Ralph Dinton, Columbia University Press, 1945, pp. 145 ff.

48 'Social anthropology, past and present', in Robert A. Manners and David Kaplan, op. cit., pp. 51–2.

49 Quoted by Sol Tax, *An Appraisal of Anthropology Today*, University of Chicago Press, 1953, p. 109.

50 *Rethinking Anthropology*, London, Athlone Press, 1966, pp. 2, 6.

51 *Argonauts of the Western Pacific*, London, Routledge & Sons 1922, p. 25.

52 *Gesammelte Werke*, vol. VII, Stuttgart, Teubner, 1926, pp. 207–9. English edition by H. P. Rickman in *Wilhelm Dilthey, Pattern and Meaning in History*, New York, Harper & Row, 1962, pp. 119–21.

53 *Race, Language, and Culture*, London, Macmillan, 1948 (originally 1932), pp. 258–9.

54 Cf. Clyde Kluckhohn, *Culture and Behaviour*, New York, Free Press, 1962, p. 52.

55 Cf. *Anthropology*, New York, Harcourt, Brace, 1948, pp. 293–4.

56 'Style', in *Anthropology Today*, ed. Sol Tax, University of Chicago Press, 1962, p. 278.

57 *Early Anthropology in the Sixteenth and Seventeenth Centuries*, Philadelphia, University of Pennsylvania Press, 1946, pp. 179 ff.

58 *The Psychological Frontiers of Society*, New York, Columbia University Press, 1945, p. viii.

59 'Configurations of culture in North America', *American Anthropologist*, vol. 34, 1932, p. 24.

60 *The Little Community, Viewpoints for the Study of a Human Whole*, University of Chicago Press, 1955, p. 88.

61 1957. Quoted by William C. Sturtevant, 'Studies in Ethnoscience, *American Anthropologist*, vol. 66, 1964, p. 101.

62 Cf. *Language in Relation to a Unified Theory of the Structure of Human Relations*, part I 1954, part II 1955, part III 1960, Summer Institute of Linguistics, Glendale, California.

63 Kenneth L. Pike, 'Towards a Theory of the Structure of Human Behaviour', in *Language in Culture and Society*, ed. Dell Hymes, New York, Harper & Row, 1964, p. 55.

64 'Notes on theory and non-theory in anthropology', in *Theory in Anthropology*, London, Routledge & Kegan Paul, 1969, p. 4.

65 *Peasant Society and Culture*, University of Chicago Press, 1956, pp. 6,

66 Cf. M. T. Hogden, *Early Anthropology in the Sixteenth and Seventeenth Centuries*, Philadelphia, University of Pennsylvania Press, 1946, pp. 86, 114.

67 Cf. Margaret Mead, 'Character formation and diachronic theory', in *Social Structure, Studies Presented to A. R. Radcliffe-Brown*, Oxford University Press, 1949, pp. 21–6.

68 Small sample of studies collected by Robert W. Green in *Protestantism and Capitalism*, Boston, Heath, 1959, offers a fair over-view of the multi-faceted argument.

69 Cf. *On the Theory of Social Change*, Dorsey Press, Homewood, Ill., 1962; particularly pp. 86 ff.

70 Cf. *Meeting of East and West*, New York, Collier-Macmillan, 1960.

71 Cf., for example, the following tiny fraction of the immense literature: *Tradition, Values, and Socio-Economic Development*, ed. Ralph Braibanti and Joseph J. Spengler, Cambridge University Press 1961; W. Ian Hogbin, *Social Change*, London, 1958; Leonard W. Doob, *Becoming More Civilized*, University of Chicago Press, 1960.

72 Clyde Kluckhohn, op. cit., pp. 73, 31.

73 Peter Berger, *A Rumour of Angels*, Harmondsworth, Penguin. 1971.

74 Cf. Ernest Brehaut, *An Encyclopaedist of the Dark Ages, Isidore of Seville*, New York, 1912, pp. 207–21.

75 Cf. M. T. Hogden, op. cit., p. 30.

76 Cf. *The Science of Culture, A Study of Man and Civilization*, New York, Grove Press, 1949.

77 'The transition to humanity', in *Horizons of Anthropology*, ed. Sol Tax, p. 37.

78 Cf., for example, F. Clark Howell, 'The humanization process', in *Horizons of Anthropology*, ed. Sol Tax, p. 58.

79 *The Evolution of Culture*, New York, McGraw Hill, 1959, p. 17.

80 'Cultural anthropology: a science', *American Journal of Sociology*, vol. 41, 1936, p.305.

81 'The psychological approach in anthropology', in Sol Tax, op. cit., pp. 73 ff

82 'Universal categories of culture', in *Anthropology Today*, ed. Sol Tax, University of Chicago Press, 1962, p. 318.

83 Clyde Kluckhohn, op. cit., pp. 275, 285.

84 'The philosophical presuppositions of cultural relativism and cultural absolutism', in *Ethics and the Social Sciences*, ed. Leo R. Ward, University of Notre Dame Press, 1959, pp. 62–3.

85 'The universally human and the culturally variable', in *Human Nature and the Study of Society*, University of Chicago Press, 1962, p. 451.

86 *The Science of Culture, A Study of Man and Civilization*, New York, Grove Press, 1949, p. 29.

87 *La Linguistique synchronique*, Paris, Presses Universitaires de France, 1965, p. 2.

88 *On Human Communication*, MIT Press, 1966 (originally 1957), p. 10.

89 Claire Russell and W. M. S. Russell, 'Language and animal signals', in *Linguistics at Large*, ed. Noel Minnis, London, Gollancz, 1971, p. 167.

90 Cf. 'The genetic roots of thought and speech', in *Thought and Language*, English trans. by Eugenia Hanfmann and Gertrude Vakar, MIT Press, 1970, pp. 33–51.

91 *Structuralism*, English trans. by Chaninah Maschler, London, Routledge & Kegan Paul, 1971, pp. 118–19.

92 Lost, unfortunately, in the English trans. by Michalina Vaughan, published under the title of *The Uses of Structuralism*, London, Heinemann Educational, 1971.

93 It is difficult to understand why 'la définition effective' has been substituted, in the English translation, by 'operational definition'. This last term has a precise meaning in the methodology of social sciences – a meaning hardly intended by Boudon. What Boudon did have in mind was, rather, a 'positive' definition in opposition to a merely 'intentional'.

94 Cf. *La Naissance de l'intelligence chez l'enfant*, Neuchâtel, Delachoux et Niestlé, 1959, Introduction. Also published as *The Origin of Intelligence in the Child*, trans. M. Cook, London, Routledge & Kegan Paul, 1953.

95 'An essay on mind', in *Theories of the Mind*, ed. Jordan M. Scher, New York, Free Press, 1962, pp. 285–7.

96 'Computing machinery and intelligence', *Mind*, vol. LIX, 1940. Reprinted in *Minds and Machines*, ed. Alan Ross Anderson, Englewood Cliffs, N.J., Prentice-Hall, 1964.

# 2

# CULTURE AS STRUCTURE

The second law of thermodynamics states the universal tendency of all isolated systems to pass from more to less organized states; this passage is called 'increase of entropy'. Increase of entropy is, if considered within the confines of the given isolated system, an irreversible process; the system cannot 'on its own' return to a more organized state. There is an interpretation of entropy[1] as energy, which must be applied to bring the system back to its initial condition. This amount grows unremittingly as a function of time flow. No isolated system can draw the required energy from its internal resources; it must be, if at all, brought in from the environment of the system.

The only remedy against the otherwise inescapable maximization of entropy (described by thermodynamics impressively as 'thermic death') seems to be to break the boundaries of the system open to exchange with what was previously its outside, and unrelated, environment. This transformation of an isolated system into an open one amounts, in fact, to the inclusion of the environment in the orbit of the system; or, rather, to the system and its environment entering a network of constant and regular mutual relations, e.g. a larger, more spacious 'meta-system'. The initial, lesser system will now constitute that part of the meta-system in which the process of entropy rise has been arrested or even reversed – at the expense of the other, 'environmental' part of the meta-system (let us be clear-minded concerning the purely relative meaning of the term 'environment' in this context; environment is definable solely as the 'other part' of the meta-system). That is what is indeed happening in the case of all living organisms. According to the famous adage of Schrödinger, living creatures 'suck negentropy' (= negative entropy) from their environments. They are, as Anatol Rapoport put it in another celebrated dictum, tiny 'islands of order' on a sea of increasing disorder. The same may be said of 'organisms' of a different kind – the human socio-cultural systems.

A digression does not seem out of place. The analogy between a living organism and human society is ill-famed to the point of being held in constant and malevolent suspicion. Many a scientist does not, in fact, consider it as eligible for serious scholarly argument. This almost universal distrust was, perhaps, well justified historically by vagaries of some nineteenth-century minds intoxicated with the then modish biological syndrome (particularly by the fanciful ideas of Novikov in Russia, Schäffle in Germany, Worms in France; to some extent, Spencer in England). It is hardly as justified now, when nobody is likely to go far enough with, say, P. Lilienfeld,[2] to agree that the same biological laws explain and explain away the processes of a single cell and the behaviour of a human individual. We are nowadays sophisticated enough (or, perhaps, mindful of how painful singed fingers can be) to reject disdainfully the baits of simplistic analogy. Still, the modern, cybernetically-inspired equation between biological and social *systems* bears only a very superficial resemblance to nineteenth-century biological expansionism. What is at stake today is not a light-hearted reasoning from one structure to another, of a very different kind, warranted by a merely phenomenal likeness, but a painstaking effort to penetrate the deep-seated, essential homo- and iso-morphisms. As A. Rapoport put it,[3]

> Arguments based on ordinary analogies are seldom conclusive. For example, just because it is true that natural selection benefits the survival of the species, it does not follow that economic competition is indispensable for the vigor of a nation. Nor is the justification of capital punishment convincing on the basis of its analogy with surgery applied to a diseased part of the body. A mathematical analogy, however, is a quite different matter. Such analogy is evidence of similar *structure* in two or more classes of events, and a great deal can be deduced from such similarity.

If there is, therefore, a universal component in every case of a struggle against the rise of entropy, it is certainly situated in the general qualities of structure and structure-formation. Similarly, if we are interested in culture in its capacity as an anti-entropy device, we have to begin by investigating its structure.

## The concept of structure

As was indicated already in the first chapter, structure is, in the first place, an antonym of 'disorderly state'. Both notions are intimately related to the concept of probability. A disorderly state is, in the final account, a set of events in which probabilities of actual occurrences are distributed entirely at random; everything is equally possible, everything can happen with the same degree of probability; in other words, nothing is exactly predictable. In a state completely devoid of order (structure), no amount of data will suffice to predict the further sequence of events (future states of the field in question). Structure, on the contrary, implies some differentiation of actual probabilities among the states which are theoretically conceivable. Some future states of the field are more probable than others. The future states of a structured whole are indeed predictable, and the more structured (orderly) a given whole is, the less information is required to make a reasonably reliable forecast.

This unique and indeed rare quality of structured wholes (systems) is ascribable to the presence of repeatable patterns. The exact nature of these patterns is often misunderstood. There is a tendency in the social sciences to generalize the universal attributes of systems from a much less universal class of attributes of a sub-set of structured wholes, represented mainly by individual living (in the biological sense) organisms. The peculiar feature of these systems consists in their 'defensive' character; they usually possess narrow limits of tolerance towards flexibility of their own variables, and their 'sys-temness' manifests itself mainly in the action of specialized 'equilibrating' units which (*a*) avert excessive oscillations of variables which can jeopardize the survival of the whole, and (*b*) bring the whole of the system back within the limits set by rigid and unfaltering boundary parameters. This quality of the systems in question indicates their frailty, the limitation of their systemic nature, their vulnerability to the adverse conditions which tend to upset their anti-entropy resistance; it boils down, in the last analysis, to the circumstance that whatever constant relationships there are between sub-units of the system (which are at the bottom of their defying the entropy law), they hold only within the definite limits which the boundary parameters outline. This unwar-ranted 'organic analogy' is persistent to the point of being well-nigh endemic in sociological concepts of the social system. Originated in modern times by Durkheim and Pareto, there is a fixed tendency in social system theory to identify the issue of the system's survival with the defence of one, rigid and unyielding, network of relationships. This tendency has found its fullest and most sophisticated elaboration in Parsons' view of the social system. Its intrinsic faultiness has been pinpointed recently by Walter Buckley in the following remark:[4]

> Whereas mature organisms, by the very nature of their organization, cannot change their given structure beyond very narrow limits and still remain viable, this capac-ity is precisely what distinguishes sociocultural systems. It is a major adaptive advantage, in the evolutionary scheme, of this latter level of organization.

Now the trouble with the approach under discussion is not the assumption that there are limits to the viability of the system – boundaries within which sub-units of the system remain related to each other in a definable way; there are, in fact, limits in this sense to any system and every imaginable structure. Nor can the intuitive concept of 'narrowness' of the limits, which will proba-bly defy all attempts at empirical specification, serve us as a reliable guide in our effort to disentangle universal qualities of structures from their specific organistic manifestations. Indeed, it does not seem that the intuition which prejudices us against extrapolating the biological model into the field of socio-cultural systems can be meaningfully and profitably articulated in terms of qualitative and 'substantive' discrepancies. At the heart of the matter there is rather a quantitative difference, sufficiently conspicuous however to inspire – and, in fact, require differentiation of the questions asked about bio-logical organisms on the one hand and socio-cultural systems on the other.

When modelling structured images of biological organisms, our attention is usually deliberately focused on the way in which the system attempts suc-cessfully to keep itself within the limits. There is nothing illegitimate in this stance as such. We have indeed every possible right to select the same cogni-tive focus, when dealing with socio-cultural systems, as most sociologists, trying to grapple with the notorious Hobbesian query, actually do. This is, however, a vantage point which opens to our scrutiny frontiers of 'systemness' rather than the nature of the 'systemness' phenomenon. If 'being structured' is related above all to resistance to the entropic tendencies toward an increasingly disorderly state, the crucial issue is the ability of some chosen sectors of the world to structurize, to 'negentropize', rather than simply to keep intact and frozen an already 'structured' structure. Hence our objections to the half-way nature of Buckley's indictment. When Buckley mentions the 'given structure' of mature organisms, he obviously means an established network of relationships between the parts. But the inapplicability of the biological approach to socio-cultural systems, which Buckley rightly preaches, is not the result of concentrating the biologists' attention on a 'given structure' only in the above sense; the underlying assumption behind Buckley's critique is an essentially static, immobile nature of structure as such. Logically, he coins a separate term, 'morphogenesis', to denote a system built in the way which does not give preference to any particular 'given structure'. What, however, will be 'systemic' about this kind of a system? The attribute of possessing a 'given structure' is precisely the only quality which distinguishes an ordered, systemic-like part of reality, from its chaotic and unorganized outside. The structure, therefore, by its very definition is something relatively stable and constant, resistant to entropic erosion. The crux of the problem is, however, that this endemic constancy of the structure does not necessarily manifest itself, on the empirical level, in monotonous repetitiousness of its phenomenal outcomes. On the contrary, broad and practically limitless empirical variety can still correspond to a constant, even inflexible, underlying structure. There is, let us repeat, nothing intrinsically wrong with focusing one's attention, whether a biologist's or a sociologist's, on discovering a 'given structure' (assumption of many – how many? – structures in a system, instead of one, would amount, in fact, to the denial of systemness). What is wrong indeed is confusing the empirical and the structural plane. If one locates the structure on the empirical level, and takes for the structure proper the constancy of statistical correlations between phenomena, then, and only then, reasoning from biological organisms to socio-cultural systems becomes dangerously misleading. What seems to be the seminal fault of Parsons' image of the social system is not his assumption of the constancy of the structure, but location of this structure on the plane of actual social relations and, consequently, the assumption, that defence of the system's structure is tantamount to the defence of the current network of its empirical actualizations.

We can return now to the discussion of the nature of patterns which constitute the distinctive feature of structured wholes. We remember that structured wholes are those in which 'not everything can happen'; or, rather, the probability of some states, defined by the logic of the given structure as incoherent, is minimized. Therefore, the units of the whole must be interrelated. The other way of saying this is that there is *communication* between units. In fact, communication is the defining feature of the status of 'being a member of the system'. According to Oscar Lange, system is to be defined as a collection of 'communicating elements': 'Every unit of the system either communicates with at least one other unit of the system, or is communicated with by at least one unit of the system. In the system there are, therefore, no isolated units, e.g. such units which neither communicate, nor are communicated with by other units of the system.' A unit $x$ communicates with another unit $y$ (again according to Lange), if some components of $x$'s output become components of $y$'s input (we assume, of course, that the output of any unit taken apart is in some constant way related to its input).[5] This intimate association between systemness and communication (in its modern, extended and generalized sense) is the guiding idea of cybernetics. It has been elaborated, in particular, by W. Ross Ashby.[6] He emphasizes insistently the limitation as the major component – the content, in fact – of any act of communication. If, given a state $S^x_1$ of the unit $x$, another unit $y$ can assume all imaginable states $S^y_n$ contained in the space of possibilities – then, says Ashby, there is no communication at all between $x$ and $y$. The meaning of communication is, in short, coextensive with the concept of limitation. The radical generality of the modern concept of communication, as well as its paramount role in defining any kind of structure, has been explicitly stated by Abraham Moles. He defines communication as 'establishment of an unequivocal correspondence between a spatial-temporal universe A $(x,y,z,t)$, the sender, and a spatial-temporal universe B $(x^1, y^1, z^1, t+t')$, the receiver'. This definition is, quite obviously, spacious enough to accommodate a great many notions normally introduced independently of each other. What the term 'communication' refers to is not only its commonsensical referent – exchange of messages between two separate agents – but also: anamorphosis (transformation) of one and the same medium, if it takes place between moment $t$ and $t+t'$, and remains in an 'unequivocal correspondence' with the state of the medium at the initial moment $t$; translation – or the 'transfer from one symbolic space to another'; explanation – or the 'transfer from one space of symbolic attributes to another'; and understanding – or the 'transfer from the phenomenal field to the field of symbols combined ("reliés") in a structure'.[7] All these types of relations of communication, as well as others, unnamed (if only isomorphic), may constitute a structure.

An alternative way, therefore, of saying that structure is a limitation imposed on a universe of possible events is to say that structure is a network of communication within a set of elements. The alternative way of saying that communication consists in an unequivocal correspondence between two sets of components is to say that the set second in the sequence (not necessarily temporal) may be, theoretically, depicted as a function of the first – B = F(A). The structure may be defined, therefore, as a set of rules of transformation of, and between, a group of interrelated elements. Since event-generating transformations defined on a given space of possible events are subjected to rules (patterns), the pool of actual occurrences is a limited sub-set of the total universe of possibilities.

The actual occurrences are situated on the level of perception (phenomenal, or empirical level). Not so the structure; this is not directly accessible to sensory experience. Neither is it derivable directly from processing the experiential data, e.g. through computing statistical distribution of certain variables in the pool of recorded events. The structure's relation to empirical phenomena is a reflection of the relation of abstract models to sensory impressions (and the other way round; it would be useless to thrash out on this occasion the time-honoured argument about priority, as both reflections are attainable to our knowledge – exist for us – either together or not at all). The important point is that there is no one-to-one relationship between a given structure and a corresponding set of empirical events. One structure can generate highly diverse sets of occurrences; vice versa, any set of empirical events can be generated as an output of various underlying structures. Which, of course, makes the demand to prevent the confusion between the levels particularly momentous.

Let us note as well the intimate connection between the notion of structure, as we have defined it here, and the modern concept of information as elaborated, above all, by C. E. S. Shannon and W. Weaver.[8] Both structure and information are related directly to the limitation imposed on the universe of possibilities. The measurement of information proposed by Shannon and Weaver is, as we know, homologous to the measure of entropy; the higher the degree of entropy in a given aggregate of elements, the more information is conveyed when exact description of the state of the aggregate is achieved. In other words, the more structured a given aggregate is (the more limited the pool of its possible states), the less information is needed to eliminate completely all uncertainty as to its actual state. If we wish to compute the amount of information contained in a specific message, we should deduct the residue of uncertainty which was left after the message from the degree of uncertainty which had existed before the message was sent. Again, if we wish to express how 'structured' a given aggregate actually is, we can deduct the amount of information actually needed to describe fully its state from the amount which would have been necessary were the aggregate entirely random.

One possible conclusion deserves our particular attention. as seminal to the generic concept of culture. We have seen that, with the growth of entropy in an aggregate, the scope of information actually available (e.g. the possibility of eliminating uncertainty as to its state) falls. On the other hand, the more successful we are in reducing the entropy of the aggregate, the more information becomes immediately available. Now, reduction of entropy is achievable, as we remember, only at the expense of an intake of energy from outside the aggregate (recall 'sucking of negentropy'). What follows is exchangeability of energy and information, the possibility of increasing the scope of attainable information through application of energy. Several scholars have shown indeed a remarkable homology of equations which express transformations of energy and of those which describe the processing of information (principle of duality of energy and information).[9] Let us take good note of this phenomenon, which seems to bear paramount importance for the proper understanding of culture as structuring.

Yet another comment seems timely. Basic theorems of the theory of information, if not recorded in mathematical terms, are frequently wrapped in a language suggestive of psychological phenomena (cognition, knowledge) or, for that matter, of a conscious mind, as constitutive factors in the very act of bringing information into being. In keeping with the commonsensical seman-tic referents of the word – superfluous from the vantage point of Shannon's theory and in no way adopted by this theory – the term 'information' is time and again used in conjunction with an 'observer', who is (or was) uncertain, to whom information has been passed, who has employed the information he received to disperse his (subjective) uncertainty etc. Indeed it is difficult, thanks to the vernacular origin of the term, to dispense entirely with the 'observer' without risking clumsiness and artificiality in the non-mathemati-cal descriptions of the phenomena related to information. Unavoidable as it probably is, the unfortunate usage may contribute to the already profuse ten-dency to interpret information in subjective terms and to put it to the task of reinforcing and warranting the mentalistically focused theory of culture. Still the presence of the ubiquitous 'observer' in verbal versions of information theory is, as a matter of fact, entirely redundant theoretically, and motivated solely by the convenience of expression (or, possibly, by the wish to bring an unfamiliar notion closer to the reader's experience). The notion of informa-tion does not require the concept of the observer's mind as a constitutive component any more than the notion of entropy does. 'Uncertainty', the cornerstone of information theory, is by no means a subjective phenome-non; it means the objectively real random distribution of probabilities that certain members of a set of events will indeed take place. Even the 'conveying' of information does not refer to an actual exchange of knowledge between two conscious minds; the above expression stands for a change which occurred, again in an objectively real sense, in the distribution of probabilities. Passage of information is above all a transformation of the medium described in informational terms; it is a real, objectively tangible operation performed on a sector of objective reality. Increase and decrease in the volume of avail-able information is an objective process which goes on and achieves its complete form whether there is, or there is not, an 'observer's mind' around to watch it and to avail itself of its benefits. True, practical, human relevance of the oscillations of information volume consists, in the last analysis, in the opportunity, given to whatever mind is placed in the position of observer, to ascertain the situation, make the right prediction and select the proper behav-iour. In the framework of this self-orientation process, however, human beings do not enter the informative processes as operative factors which co-deter-mine the actual volume of available information. They do enter these processes, if at all, in another role, that of bearers of practice, producers and manipulators of environment. Those who assume the first and the second role are not necessarily the same persons.

## Ontological and epistemological status of structure

The ascending role played by the notion of structure in the logic of modern science revives a number of essential arguments related to the nature of cog-nition and knowledge. All of them have a very long history and occupy a prominent place in the Western intellectual tradition born of the seminal clash between two major currents of ancient Greek philosophy. Two of them, however, are particularly worth mentioning in the present context, since they are, manifestly or latently, at the bottom of the present discord inspired by the advent of structuralism as the major adversary of the positivistic establishment in the social sciences. The first is the controversy between knowledge of the 'certain' and of the 'contingent'; the second – between the ontology of the 'transcendent' and of the 'immanent' object of cognition.

Plato was the first to articulate the former paradigm, though, as was at that stage customary, in ontological terms. Parallel to the distinction between soul and body, the 'thought' and the 'sensed', came two layers of the universe, intimately interwoven, to be sure, but still separate and enjoying, each of them, its own, distinct and unique, existential mode. Changeability and immutability respectively were among their most significant distinctive features. Plato summarized the pre-Socratic history of Greek philosophy as a process dominated by the clash between two major tendencies, represented by 'Ionians' (from Thales on) and 'Italians' (Parmenides and his school); the main issue of philosophy had, in his view, sedimented from this continuing argument, as the battle between 'Giants' and 'Gods': 'On the side of the Gods are all who at any time believe that unseen things are the true realities; on the side of the Giants all who at any time believe that the real is nothing but body which they touch and handle.'[10] In the words of one of the personages of the *Sophist*,[11]

> One party is trying to drag everything down to earth out of heaven and the unseen, literally grasping rocks and trees in their hands; for they lay upon every stock and stone and strenuously affirm that real existence belongs only to that which can be handled and offers resistance to the touch. . . . And accordingly their adversaries are very wary in defending their position somewhere in the heights of the unseen, maintaining with all their force that true reality consists in certain intelligible and bodiless Forms.

Behind this difference of opinion lies, of course, the argument about the nature of reality, arising, in the last analysis, from a deeply rooted distrust of the reality of movement and change. 'The many things that bear the same names as the Forms are perpetually changing in all respects; and these are the things we see and touch, whereas the Forms are unseen.' It is thus laid down that there are two orders of things: the unseen, exempt from all change, and the seen, which change perpetually. Finally it is argued as probable that soul, which is unseen, most resembles the divine, immortal, intelligible, simple, and indissoluble; while the body most resembles the human, mortal, unintelligible, complex, and dissoluble. 'The Friends of Forms take unchangeableness as the mark of real Being, variability as the mark of Becoming. . . . The Forms admit no sort of change, whereas the many sensible things never remain the same.' In the *Phaedo* and *Republic* the ideal world is constantly spoken of as excluding any change, and this was always treated as the necessary condition for the existence of knowledge.[12] The downright identity of the 'real', the 'true' and the 'unchangeable' was the cornerstone of the Platonic tradition in the theory of knowledge. What demonstrates its existence simply through being accessible to the senses cannot claim true reality: it has no firm basis to buttress its claim to reality, since it is accidental, haphazard, fleetingly elusive. What is real, must be such for ever, instead of submitting its reality to the hazardous test of continuous sensory presence.

At this point the first issue merges with the second. Plato solves the intricate problem of the way in which the 'real', since independent of the authority of sensory evidence, can be grasped at all by assuming the immortality of the soul. The immortal soul is introduced as a logical conclusion from the fact that the real is accessible to us 'from within': 'If the truth of things is always in our soul, the soul must be immortal; hence you may confidently set about seeking for and recovering the memory of what you do not know, that is to say, do not remember'; 'seeking and learning are nothing but recollection'; since the immortal soul 'has seen all things, both in this world and in the other, there is nothing it has not learned'.[13] The form is given once and for all; the status of immutable εἴδη must be superior to the modality of things which 'change forms', challenge the boundaries of essential entities – which can be genuinely real only in so far as they remain identical with themselves.

This line of thought gave birth to the science of logic, as it emerged in Aristotle's teaching and bloomed in mediaeval scholastics, in the form of the science of 'necessary', to wit, immutable relationships, unrestrained by sensory evidence. It achieved new heights in the teaching of Descartes. By this time the conceptual separation of 'certainty' and existential proof was complete. The new logic, that of empirical investigation, was in full swing, but the opinion prevailed, and indeed was codified by Descartes, that no amount of empirical evidence of actual 'existence' of events can lead eventually to genuinely 'certain' knowledge. And vice versa, without the Platonic supporting assumption of the immortal soul amassing the true knowledge of forms, certainty ceased to be a proof of actual existence. Descartes distinguishes 'that faculty of our understanding by which it has intuitive awareness of things and knows them from that by which it judges, making use of affirmation and denial'. The last sort of judgments are doomed to remain inconclusive, as they account for 'complex natures', which are contingent, which may appear, but may not as well, and so cannot be ascertained for sure. 'Deduction is thus left to us as the only means of putting things together so as to be sure of their truth. . . . Mankind has no road towards certain knowledge open to it, save those of self-evident intuition and necessary deduction'; we can acquire certainty only in those cases in which we do not take 'great trouble to ascertain whether they [the natures we analyse] are actually existent or not'.[14] The whole issue was thus stripped of its ontological veneer and translated into a wholly epistemological language. It ceased to be a matter of immutable forms; it became, instead, the question of certainty, which is pivoted, in the last instance, on intuitive self-evidence, and which can be extended, with the help of logic, to judgments arrived at through deduction.

Two major pillars of the Platonic concept of knowledge remained, however, intact: the distinction between 'necessary' and 'contingent', and identification

of the true, better, superior, unfailingly reliable knowledge with the first category. It was left to modern empiricism, proclaiming that *nihil est in intellectu,
quod non prius fuerit in sensu*, to challenge these two essential principles of the
rationalistic theory of knowledge. The assault reached the peak of intensity
when the empiricist premises were given positivistic treatment. Intuition was
ridiculed, self-evidence dismissed as a residue of metaphysics, and human
knowledge reduced to what can be derived, by proper handling, from the primary data of immediate sensory experience. The issue of eternal, indubitable,
necessary truths was dismissed rather than contested. The rule of phenome-
nalism, one of the few outspoken principles of positivism, stated flatly that
human knowledge is and must remain unidimensional, fully accommodated
on the plane of empirical data. The supporting rule of nominalism assigns to
general concepts and statements the ancillary role of shorthand, convenient
recordings of the essentially individual fact-events. There is no room left for
'self-imposing', self-evident truths, much less for perennial and unchangeable
'essences' rooted somewhere in the infrastructure of the contingent, empirically accessible chain of occurrences.

The two rules we have mentioned do not preclude accommodation of the
notion of structure into the body of the positivistically defined knowledge.
Still, of course, the notion must undergo a fairly substantial change; indeed,
quite a large portion of the attributes we have ascribed to the concept of
structure are not admissible by the rules of experiential austerity. Above all,
structure is denied any sovereign, or even superior or prior, status with respect
to the data of experience. The very discussion of the status of structure, as distinct from the status of fact-records, is ominously reminiscent of metaphysics.
Structure, in the framework of positivist knowledge, would be accorded the
meaning of a mere arrangement of primary data; the kind known well from
the statistical tables depicting the distribution of observed facts from a chosen aspect, or, rather, informing how the observed events divide into classes
devised, for the sake of parsimony and convenience, by the researcher.
Structure is a result of measurement and a way of recording the quantified
findings, which is, of course, a different way of defining structure from that,
say, of Lévi-Strauss, who is indeed emphatic on the lack of necessary connection between measure and structure.[15]

The fatuous disdain with which positivism continuously treated all not
strictly observable data repeatedly inspired resentment in scientists worried by
the manifest feebleness and precariousness of the ground on which faith in
the validity of human knowledge would rest were the positivist premises
unreservedly accepted. The notorious loopholes and inconclusiveness of
inductive reasoning, and the obvious contingency of what, from the positivist
perspective, passed for 'facts', pushed scholarly activity far away from the persistent scientific ideal of 'certainty'.

The most celebrated in this century was the phenomenological broadside
on the fortress of positivism. The object of true knowledge was again transferred from the realm of the 'transcendental' into the one of the 'immanent'.
In Husserl's famous slogan *Zu den Sachen selbst!* 'things' were re-defined as

the purified essence of the direct object of *Bewusstsein*; this, in its turn, as the sort of existence an object of knowledge assumes when it is known, e.g. given to the consciousness. Thus the traditional dichotomy between *cogito* and *cogitatum* seems to have been finally transcended; both partners in the cognitive act fuse into one, accessible directly to analytical scrutiny. By this expedient Husserl hopes to lay firm foundations under human knowledge; to reach, once again, for the necessary, essential knowledge – 'contingent existence cannot change what reason has recognized as the very essence of its object'; knowledge, which will comprise the objective essences of things, 'independent of any arbitrary meaning which a subject *wants* to give them'.[16] The fact of 'existence' is assigned again a role of hypothesis, yet to be verified; it is however irrelevant to the pursuit of essences – existence does not belong among their necessary attributes. 'For me the world is nothing other than I am aware of and what appears valid in such *cogitationes*. The whole meaning and reality of the world rests exclusively on such *cogitationes*.'[17] This assumption makes possible the categorical statement, that 'analysis of essence is *eo ipso* general analysis; cognition of essence in terms of essence, in terms of essential nature, in terms of cognition which is directed to universal objects'.[18] Not only have the basic ideas of Descartes been vindicated, but in his virulent inroads against the positivistic dissipation of knowledge Husserl in fact ventured onto a slushy ground where Descartes would not have dared to hazard himself. One can say that Husserl applied to Descartes the same type of radical treatment that Fichte exercised on Kant's legacy. The haunting dichotomy of the necessary and the existing has been pushed away instead of being solved. The ἐποχή – suspension of the existential issue committed at the very outset of phenomenological *cogitationes*, has never, in fact, been rescinded. The validity of human knowledge has been rescued at the expense of empirically accessible information, for which phenomenology has no employment precisely as positivism has none for the essential truths. No wonder that the herculean project of the master boiled down, in the practice of his heretical disciples, to a hardly Husserlian, but obviously spiritualistic methodological rule (manifested, for example, in Maurice Natanson's definition: phenomenology is a generic term 'to include all positions that stress the primacy of consciousness and subjective meaning in the interpretation of social action';[19] in this caricature of the Husserlian stance the world 'over there', surreptitiously re-admitted to the realm of definite judgments, is again categorized in the old terms of subjective 'primacy' which Husserl claimed, with no success, to have chased away).

The quest after certainty, the desire for knowledge of the necessary, were however at the very fount of the Husserlian brand of anti-positivistic rebellion. It would seem that in the framework of this overwhelming intention the only modality available for the 'structure' was that of '*Sache*' in the Husserlian sense, i.e. one of the essences definable and describable entirely in terms of intentions; it was, in fact, a mode akin to Boudon's 'definition intentionelle'. The particular intentions constitutive of structure would be those of order, consistency, logical cohesion. The question of existence would be, precisely as in the case of all other '*Sachen*', overruled by the principle of ἐποχή. The only discipline to which structure, as '*Sache*', is submitted is that of meanings imposed by its constitutive intentions. The prerequisite of necessity being the paramount intention, structure cannot but be the very epitome of the 'certainty' and 'necessity' of things.

The suspension of the phenomenal world is however hardly assimilable in the universe generated by the assumptions of science. As has been amply shown by the offshoots of phenomenology intended to produce a practical methodology of the social sciences (Merleau-Ponty, Schutz, Natanson), necessity and certainty in the Husserlian sense are the first victims of any effort to stretch phenomenological principles enough to cover the field constitutive of sociology. Exactly these two ideals seem to be out of place, resisting any attempt to square them with the task of handling the phenomenally accessible reality of Man. Any notion of structure which is calculated to stand a chance of being adopted and utilized in the practice of science must be defined in the way in which the total set of issues arising from the admission of the authority of phenomenal evidence plays a major role. But then the pure, Cartesian-Husserlian notion of certainty, offered by knowledge of the necessary alone, becomes, perhaps, untenable. What is then left of the old Platonic εἴδη is the idea of constancy, invariance, stability hidden behind the stream of variable, diversified and apparently chaotic phenomena. The 'essence' is still the supreme goal sought by science in defiance of the positivistic *sophrosyne*, but now it is tainted with the impure blood-relation to the phenomenal plane, irretrievably vested with supreme legitimizing authority under the protracted positivist rule.

The present position, somewhat astride the barricade separating excessively radical adversaries, has been expressed succinctly by Jacques Monod:[20]

> La stratégie fondamental de la science dans l'analyse des phénomènes est la découverte des invariants. Toute la physique, comme d'ailleurs tout développement mathématique, specifie une relation d'invaliance. . . . Quoi qu'il en soit, il y a et il demeurera dans la science un élément platonicien qu'on ne saurait en distraire sans la ruiner. Dans la diversité infinie des phénomènes singuliers, la science ne peut chercher que les invariants.

What Monod had left unsaid is the utterly un-Platonic way in which the old Platonic goal is now being pursued by scientists: through reason turned on the phenomenal universe rather than upon itself. Indeed, nothing esoteric has been left in the notion of the 'constant' and 'invariant', endowed by Plato with the quality of an Absolute, accessible only through the memory of an immortal soul; or – even if we peel off, generously, the metaphysical husk of the idiosyncratic terminology – still available by an alternative route, essentially distinct from the one leading to the fixing of empirical data. To Monod, 'les invariants' pursued by his science, biology, can be discovered in laboratory analysis of the live substance, and only there. These are structures and functions of the living organisms, riveted 'over there', 'transcendental' as Husserl would anxiously note, and accessible solely through the only reality which simultaneously opens them to, and conceals them from, the inquisitive human mind: through empirically approachable phenomena. 'C'est la repro-duction, *ne varietur*, à chaque génération cellulaire du texte écrit sous forme de séquence de nucléotides dans l'ADN, qui assure l'invariance de l'espèce.'[21]

The structure defined above all by its invariance, but hardly 'necessary' in the sense of being the only imaginable, the only logically possible, seems to provide as well the cognitive task Lévi-Strauss is after. His famous formula, coined in *The Structural Study of Myth*,[22]

$$F_x(a) : F_y(b) \equiv F_x(b) : F_{a-1}(y)$$

is precisely of this kind. The commentary,

> here, with two terms, *a* and *b*, being given as well as two functions, *x* and *y*, of these terms, it is assumed that a relation of equivalence exists between two situations defined respectively by an inversion of *terms* and *relations*, under two conditions: (1) that one term be replaced by its opposite (in the above formula, *a* and a–l); (2) that an inversion be made between the *function value* and the *term value* of two elements (above, *y* and *a*),

refers to the logic of mythological thinking, discoverable, if at all, through analysis of myths; no amount of phenomenological analysis of intentional meanings will reveal that the two above described relations are equivalent, or what specific conditions an inversion must meet for this equivalence to be admitted by the logic of myths. Logical rules of this kind may be invariant, but obviously they are not necessary, i.e. the only imaginable rules which can generate a language serving effectively the task of ordering the universe. Similarly, another logical rule, formulated temporarily on a less abstract (and so less universal) plane, like 'jaguar est à fille indisposée comme la chauve-souris est a jaguar'[23] (or, if recorded via its application, 'généralement tenue pour responsable d'une ouverture corporelle et d'une émission de sang, la chauve-souris se transforme . . . en responsable d'une fermeture corporelle et d'une résorption d'excréments'), may be, perhaps, proved an invariant principle of the logic of myths, but can be hardly considered as representing a transformation which is 'obviously' or 'intuitively' true.

Again, Noam Chomsky is utterly explicit as to the finality of the divorce between 'certainty' and 'necessity', and the second marriage which 'certainty' entered, this time with 'invariance', sometimes named universality. After describing several of the many structural rules of language, Chomsky emphatically draws a hardly Platonic conclusion:[24]

> There is no *a priori* necessity for this to be true. These characteristics of language, if true, are empirical facts. It is reasonable to suppose that they are *a priori* for the organism, in that they define, for him, what counts as a human language, and determine the general character of his acquired knowledge of language. But it is easy to imagine systems of language that would depart from these principles. . . . Such principles, we may speculate, are *a priori* for the species . . . but are not necessary or even natural properties of all imaginable systems that might serve the functions of human language.

To put this in different words, the invariant rules of language may appear necessary from the vantage point of the individual subjectivity of any member of the species Homo Sapiens as it historically emerged on the earth; for every human being they are given once and for all as indispensable constituents of his intelligible universe and can be, perhaps, laid bare by 'reason turned upon itself'; but in this sense the term 'necessity' does not add much to the notion of universality, which is an empirical fact. That is this 'here and now', experimentally identifiable necessity which is itself an artefact of the long historical process of development, owing its *a priori* position toward a specific, individual or group, experience, to the fact of its being *a posteriori* to a history-long collective experience of the species. The history of the species led to crystallization of some of the structures as the constitutive elements of the intelligible and meaningful universe of every single member of this species.

We can say that the life-process of the human being as a person (the individual entity defined by his values and the ends he pursues, teleologically organized, future-oriented) is possible, and indeed takes place, only in the framework of his existence as an epistemic subject; this existence, in turn, is immersed into a historically structured and organized human world, in which isomorphism of human thought and practices has been accomplished. In the most general terms, the relationship between the activity of the individual and the structural framework provided by the universe he lives in may be compared to the relationship between worker and machine, as described by Marx in his *Grundrisse*:[25]

> The worker's activity, limited to a mere abstraction, is determined and regulated on all sides by the movement of the machinery, not the other way round. The knowledge that obliges the inanimate parts of the machine, through their construction, to work appropriately as an automaton, does not exist in the consciousness of the worker, but acts through the machine upon him as an alien force, as the power of the machine itself.

This dialectical relation between the thought which makes the universe of humans real and that which makes it intelligible and amenable to meaningful interaction is put in more general terms in the *German Ideology*:[26]

> The social structure and the state continually evolve out of the life-process of definite individuals, but individuals not as they may appear in their own or other people's imagination but rather as they really are, that is, as they work, produce materially, and act under definite material limitations, presuppositions, and conditions independent of their will.

In other words, individuals not as persons, but as epistemic, or rather epistemic-productive beings. As persons, they can experience the clash between their value-organized project and the law-organized, transcendental medium to which the project is to be applied; they may even try to overcome the opposition in the way typical of a person, i.e. through reducing both sides of the opposition to the same philosophical principle, the one which guides the value-organized, meaningful, projecting side. As epistemic entities, however, they participate in the universe submitted in its entirety to one set of structuring-structured rules of transformation; were they not participants, they would hardly exist at all, neither as thoughtful persons, nor as living organisms. Maurice Godelier seems to hit the bull's eye when indicating,[27] that if the future science of man concentrates on the laws which govern the emergence and evolution of structures as created by and creative of the human universe, the now hallowed and unencroachable oppositions between psychology and sociology, sociology and history, history and anthropology (in Lévi-Strauss's sense) will become sterile. Then, let us add, the original programme of Marx will be vindicated; and among the oppositions now haunting the science of man, which will be overcome, the alleged contradiction between individual and society will figure prominently.

To recapitulate: the structure sought by the structuralist understanding of culture is the set of generative rules, historically selected by the human species, governing simultaneously the mental and practical activity of the human individual viewed as an epistemic being, and the range of possibilities in which this activity can operate. Since this set of rules precipitates into social structures, it appears to the individual as transcendental law-like necessity; owing to its inexhaustible organizing capacity it is experienced by the same individual as his creative freedom. That is, however, the basic assumption of the programme under discussion, that both elements of the basic human experience – his existence and his essence, his objective and his subjective modality – grow ultimately from the same stem; and to it they should, and may, be traced back.

## A synopsis of the structuralist programme

It should be clear by now that it is the author's contention that the structural approach as described in the preceding paragraphs opens new vistas before sociological analysis. In particular, it promises to solve several peculiarly obnoxious problems, which so far have mounted allegedly insuperable obstacles on the road of the science of society and culture. It should be emphasized, however, as strongly as the above statement, that the author does not intend to offer the structuralist approach as a substitute for everything sociology so far has invented and tried. One can easily point to innumerable analytical problems of supreme significance which can be dealt with, efficiently and fruitfully, with the tools already in sociologists' employment. It seems that the prospect of one, all-embracing theoretical model, fit to account for all and any cognitive issues which can be legitimately raised by a social scientist, belongs to the category of attractive but unattainable utopias. The multi-faceted and multi-levelled human praxis – the ultimate source of all interests re-phrasable as cognitive issues – effectively escapes every attempt at reducing its variability to a single principle. The principle of the structured-structuring nature of the praxis itself, submitted to the rule of a sort of a 'generative meta-grammar', is no exception. That is why, instead of promulgating another revolutionary manifesto (which has become fairly frequent in recent sociology), it seems to be much more reasonable to enumerate these moot and matted problems of social science, which – according to a widespread, if not the universal, opinion – have not so far been handled in an intellectually satisfying manner, but are more likely to become solvable if approached in the fashion devised by the structuralist view of culture.

(1) First, and probably most attractive, comes the chance to grapple, for the first time in a serious manner, with the problem of cultural and social universals (not to be confused, let us emphasize again, with the Murdock-like *a posteriori* generalizations derivable from the statistical treatment of phenomenal data). The problem is far more important in that it is plain and realizable at the first glance. Not only the patent lack of success in pursuing the universals of human existence, but also the total lack of analytical tools relevant to the task, constitute an apparently endemic malaise of the social sciences. With hardly any exception, all the concepts and analytical tools currently employed by social scientists are geared to a view of the human world in which the most voluminous totality is a 'society', a notion equivalent for all practical purposes, to the concept of the 'nation-state'. Above the level of the nation-state we can engage merely in 'comparisons', leading eventually to the discovery of statistical distributions of features which are meaningful only on the nation-state level; or we can apply the approaches of the game theory, whose objects must meet one condition only to become analysable in the terms the theory provides: they must be 'unified' in their compliance with the rules of the game. The notorious ineptitude of the social sciences to transcend their own limitations in the field of universals sanctified in practice, for many decades, the confusing and harmful distinction between sociology, as a scientific endeavour, and philosophical anthropology, as a branch of the arts. There seems to be little justification for this division, which renders only those human affairs which are located below the nation-state level suitable for scientific treatment. One can hardly legitimize the remarkable surviving power of the distinction without referring to the original sin, committed at an early stage of the institutionalization of modern sociology as an academically established science. Otherwise, the significant watershed between the arts-type and the scientific treatment of the dual human existential status would hardly overlap with the frontiers of the nation-state organization.

Recently Gideon Sjöberg and Ted R. Vaughan have aptly traced the flagrant inhibition of sociology in dealing with supra-societal issues back to the formative years of modern social science.[28] They have picked on Durkheim and Weber as the major culprits, to be blamed for the so far incurable affliction of sociology. Durkheim's decision to rivet his vision of human existence into the framework of the society, equated with a politically organized nation, squared well with the inherent logic of his theory of man; one, we should notice, which went back far into the past of French social philosophy, to Jean-Jacques Rousseau and further back to Blaise Pascal: to their vision of the human being as split into two essentially incompatible halves, the beastly and egoistic, and the heavenly and altruistic; and, in particular, to Rousseau's theoretical stratagem of reconciliation between the two, the idea of morality as achievable only through the common will, constitutive of the politically organized community. Thus, long before Durkheim, the French philosophical tradition vested the ultimate moral authority in the nation-state and announced the ultimately moral origin of everything social in the human individual. It was left to Durkheim merely to codify the already common-sensical knowledge in what was to be taken in future for the language of the science of the social. It was only logical, therefore, that supra-national entities had to be denied a rightful place in the system of sociology. They could be admitted into the system, if at all, only if capable of warranting their status as sources of moral authority; but, as we have seen, such a source had been already identified, by definition, with a politically organized community. There is, therefore, an air of circular argument in Durkheim's statement, which Sjöberg and Vaughan quote without noticing the intrinsic tautology: 'In contrast with the nation, mankind as source of morality suffers this defi-ciency: there is no constituted society.'[29] As long as moral integration remains the main preoccupation and organizing topic of sociology, the nation-state must be the empirical incarnation of 'society' in its highest form, while any concept referring to supra-national entities will remain 'scientifically' hollow, if not illicit. Sjöberg and Vaughan associate this restrictive bias, characteris-tic of Weber and Parsons in the same measure as of Durkheim, with the sociologists' proclivity to nationalistically confined ideologies. In whatever direction, however, the causal chain points, sociology in the currently domi-nant form has no use for human universals; neither has it a language relevant to the task of their description. It was admirably shown by Robert A. Nisbet[30] that modern sociology began when 'the idea of the abstract, impersonal, and purely legal state is challenged by theories resting on the assumed priority of community, tradition, and status'. There is, perhaps, an intimate connection between the priority of the community (or nation-state) over the individual as the corner-stone of sociology and the sociologists' endemic inability to for-mulate the problem of universals instead of mere 'comparative classifications'. The genuine universals may be established, if at all, on the level of factors operative in shaping both 'epistemic beings' and 'praxis actors', i.e. both human individuals and networks of their relationships.

Another inherent limitation thwarting many an attempt of current sociol-ogy to deal meaningfully with human universals is the tacit and compliant acceptance of the institutionalized 'branch division' of society. The intra-breeding populations of sociologists duplicate the established 'specialization of power'; we are, mostly, sociologists of industry or of education, or of reli-gion, or of politics etc. It is only natural, in these circumstances, that the structures or generative rules common to all spheres of human activity tend to be overlooked. Acceptance of the institutionalized frontiers of a domain involves, though only inadvertently, adoption of the functional values oper-ative in their institutionalization: it involves, consequently, appropriation of the relevant, sight-narrowing frame of analytical reference. To spot the real universalities, one has to transcend the boundaries which – being placed on the superficial, phenomenal level – blind the observer to the infrastructure shared by all institutionalized fields. The same generative rules govern human praxis in politics, industry, agriculture, religion and whatever else; they are, in fact, prior to functional divisions and may be traced only if the vision of the analyst is enlarged to embrace, in one scanning effort, the totality of human praxis. Even if focused, to be empirically viable, on one chosen sector of the praxis, it must be organized by the strategy of stripping off precisely those phenomenal aspects which owe their origin and presence to functional differentiation. Once again, the structural approach to culture offers what seems to be the right and long sought-after vantage point.

(2) Another chance offered by the structural approach is a fresh look at the concept of function, worn out to the point of frustrating disenchantment. The traditional usages, with almost no exception, have been ominously reminiscent of the Aristotelian *telos*; indeed, from Malinowski to Parsons the idea, if not the concept, of 'systemic prerequisites' has been the indispensable companion to the notion of function. Logically, if not genetically, the concept of societal system holds priority over the idiom of function: in fact, to this concept the present meaning of function owes its intelligibility. Whatever case can be built up against the indictment of teleologism, the truth is that, to make any sense at all, the concept of function may be introduced only as a successive link in a chain of reasoning beginning with an existential statement about an accomplished, 'completed' society which 'tends' to survive, and which, to 'achieve this goal', 'demands' specific patterns, 'promulgates' specific values etc. However useful may be the notion of function as a heuristic device, the endemic feebleness of its theoretical foundations remains an inexhaustible source of embarrassment for its upholders. The logical sequence which the notion of function in its current interpretation inevitably presumes is, additionally, conducive to an unbridgeable gap between the synchronic and diachronic dimensions of sociological analysis: indeed, if the existence of a mature societal system capable of generating effectively its 'prerequisites' is the prior condition for the notion of function to be meaningfully applied, then the sociological analysis organized around the concept of function is unable to account for how the society could emerge in the first place; neither is it able, short of unseemly antics, to render intelligible the continuous dynamics of the communal form of human coexistence.

Whatever factor sociological theory will eventually select as its central analytical concept, it will be well advised to beware of choices innate in the irritatingly barren argument over societal-individual priorities. It must be a factor operative on both levels. It must account for both, inextricably interwoven, facets of human existence: subjective and objective, determining and determined, creative and created, socializing and socialized. Then and only then can it be utilized in building models at once syn- and dia-chronical, and bridging the so far isolated levels of individual situation and social structure in a way which does not beg the phony question of the 'priority' of one of the two modalities of human existence.

The idea of sign-function seems to be the obvious candidate, equipped with all the required merits. Indeed, the sign, as 'an act of simultaneously cutting out two amorphous masses,' as an act of creating and conveying the meaning, which is 'an order with chaos on either side',[31] is coextensive in its modalities with the human praxis itself; as an analytical concept, it looks as if it was the praxis' mirror reflection, faithful in the ideal, though rare, sense of co-dimensionality. Analysing cultural patterns in terms of their sign-function (i.e. in semiotic terms) we thus relate them directly to the human praxis, without prejudicing the question of analytical level. It is a dynamic concept of function, capable not only of preserving, but of generating forms; something ascertainable not in the relation to an accomplished, inflexible and, by assumption, stabilized entity, but in relation to a process, to the endless and open-ended chain of human activity. In this sense the function of cultural patterns consists in creating order and orientation; or, rather, in the two-pronged process of ordering societal environment and human-behaviour-in-this-environment. Neither of the two reciprocally constitutive sides of human praxis claims priority over the opposite side.

Now, the sign-function of the cultural patterns is brought into effect through the operations, of 'discrimination' or 'delimitation',[32] directed towards the environmental medium of action and the action-orienting programme at the same time. These two basic operations order, through differentiating, the otherwise amorphic planes, 'reality' and 'cognitive-motoring map'. Hence, 'a single term-object has no meaning at all; any meaning presupposes the existence of a relation; it is on the level of structure that we should seek the elementary meaningful units, not on the level of elements'.[33] It is the relation between various signs applicable in a situation which really counts as meaningful; and precisely that relation – the presence of one sign being simultaneously the absence of another – which is amenable to the functional treatment. The meaning-value of any cultural sign-pattern 'depends entirely on their opposition to other elements, on their being different from other elements. They are, therefore, characterized not by any positive quality of their own, but by their oppositional quality and differential value'. The signs owe their functionality precisely to their active, ordering capacity – their faculty of re-shaping both the cognitive mind and its object. In Luis J. Prieto's words,[34] sign

> puts itself in relation not only to the possibility which comes into effect, or to the possibilities with which the one it signifies belongs, but to all possibilities involved. It cannot be otherwise, since if the sign indicates the possibility which comes into effect, or the possibilities with which it belongs – it does it only due to the fact that it eliminates other possibilities.

To take the simplest possible example, a 'No entry' door-plate is meaningful only in so far as there are other doors which bear no such inscription, since the function of the sign 'No entry' does not consist in designating a peculiar one-to-one relationship between the idea conveyed by the inscription and specific doors bearing the tablet; it does consist, instead, in active differentiating of the people who approach the door from the side with the plate and those who approach it from the other side, as well as in informing all potential readers of the difference between the people residing behind the 'No entry' plate and those people who are deprived of a similar defence.

(3) As partly follows from the above remarks, the structural approach to

human praxis promises a new chance of a satisfying solution to the contro-versial culture-social structure paradigm. Whatever the well-known differences between the many available definitions of, respectively, culture and social structure (and however intensive the feelings aroused by the con-stant argument, which tend to magnify distinctions of relatively minor importance), the two concepts, whenever they appear as antonyms, are essen-tially rationalizations of the constantly and commonly experienced dual nature of the human condition; on the one hand, human beings experience their own existence as a set of unflinching, recalcitrant confinements, with-standing defiantly every attempt to cast them into the mould of human will; on the other, they learn continuously of their own intellectual projects and emotionally coloured will, which appear as directly manageable, flexible, mal-leable – as the realm of freedom manifested in creativity. This basic experiential distinction, the avowed root of most of Western philosophy, is, of course, an epistemological byproduct of the clash between *Sein* and *Sollen*, between what is and what ought to be; in a perfectly integrated society, free of ambiguous meanings and of the necessity of choice (as, for example, in the artificial world created by Kurt Goldstein for his psychiatric patients who suf-fered loss of the capacity to think 'abstractly') this distinction would hardly have occurred to human beings at all. It has all the same, been constantly pre-sent, since the times of the lyrical poets of ancient Greece, in the intellectual formula of human expelience characteristic of Western civilization. The same basic experience, depending on the focus of interest or level of analysis, is sub-sumed in other seminal pairs of oppositions, like subject and object, spirit and matter, mind and body, norm and reality, value and fact.

All three categories of the concept of culture which were distinguished in the first chapter, belong to the same half of the semantic universe of philo-sophical discourse which in other contexts is organized by terms like mind, norm, spirit, value etc. It accounts for the universe of norms or normative patterns, traceable in principle to human creation, perhaps ultimately to the generating capacity of the human mind, while the social structure, even if reduced to a set of institutionalized behavioural norms, is treated as a poten-tial adversary of the norm *in actu*, as an entity essentially tougher, more resistant, in some sense 'more real' (or even 'substantial').

Now, throughout the history of Western civilization there is an obstinate and pronounced tendency to reduce the above duality of our world-image to a single element, through representing one adversary as a corollary of the sec-ond. Our brief review of the historical destinies of the Platonic dichotomy offered us a cursory insight into the specific forms in which the above ten-dency may manifest its presence. Within the analytical frame now under discussion the proposed stratagems assume, understandably, the form of ontological assertions. The alternatives range from the concept of downright generation of the cultural superstructure by the societal infrastructure (in some positivistically coloured brands of Marxism) to its direct opposite, a view of the social structure as 'typified' and so a monotonous sediment of normative cultural patterns (both in Parsons and in Berger and Luckmann, however different they may be in other respects). Even the outright adversaries agree however, as we can see, that the relation between the social structure and the culture is that of determination or generation, sometimes supplemented by a functional one. The history of the argument is reminiscent of the fitful swings of a pendulum rather than of a chain of conclusive solutions, and only the notorious amnesia of social science to its own past can explain the amazing fact that an impressive number of theoreticians still hope to arrive at something enlightening through exploring blind alleys walked endlessly to and fro by their predecessors.

Once again the structural, semiotic approach to human praxis offers a chance of a new and cogent solution of the old problem. The clue is provided by the dialectics of *signifiant* and *signifié*, convincingly analysed by Ferdinand de Saussure.[35] The two welded aspects are distinguishable in all signs, not necessarily linguistic. It is likely that in a cultural act, considered from the semiotic perspective, the two intimately linked though analytically distinguishable aspects can be organized respectively into two isomorphic structures: the one, called usually culture, and the second, dealt normally with under the heading of 'social structure'. If we now view the second as a network of dependencies and constrictions built into the flow of energy (learning of the essential constructive principles of all self-regulating and self-programming wholes, including human society, from cybernetics), then the first may be interpreted as the code through which information on the second is expressed, conveyed, deciphered and processed. The two participate jointly in the basic human endeavour to reduce the incertitude of the human condition, ordering it, making it more predictable and so more manageable.[36] So far as this interpretation holds, the relation between culture and social structure is one of signification (which is, let us repeat emphatically, an active process throughout); and the exact methods, elaborated for analysing isomorphic sets, can be employed for its study.

(4) Common misinterpretations notwithstanding, a chance to bridge the conceptual chasm between synchrony and diachrony is also built into the analytical equipment of modern structuralism. The numerous statements to the contrary, frequent as they have been (Lévi-Strauss himself belonged at a time with the major culprits, responsible for the current association of structuralism with disbelief in the contribution of historical knowledge to system description), have been elicited by the understandable, though not necessarily convincing, passion of the devout preachers of an undoubtedly revolutionary idea. Defence against the truculent orthodoxy seems to require emphatic tabooing of all ambiguity. Since the heresy long ago turned into respectable routine, it has become manifest that the most sophisticated synchronic analysis does not require abandonment of the diachronic perspective; on the contrary, 'some connection between diachronic process and synchronic regularities must exist since no change can produce a synchronically unlawful state and all synchronic states are the outcome of diachronic processes'.[37] Moreover, genetic and structural aspects are understandable only in their reciprocal processual and analytical interdependence,[38] and socio-cultural

changes, as well as the structure of social and cultural systems, are analysable with the same conceptual set.[39] The conceptual tool which most readily comes to mind in this connection is that of 'unmarked' and 'marked' signs (the 'primitive' opposition of Trubetzkoy between 'merkmaltragend' and 'merkmallos' members).[40] The 'unmarked' sign, usually the simpler and more sketchy of the two, denotes initially the whole class of phenomena indiscriminately; then an attribute possessed by a sub-class only, becomes for some reason important, and then part of the unmarked sign's applications receive a 'mark' to distinguish just this sub-class. The hitherto monopolistic unmarked sign stands now in opposition to the new marked one; so far neutral toward the marked feature, it now conveys the information on its absence. V. V. Martynov[41] has developed recently a fairly convincing theory employing the concept of 'markers' showing how diachronic processes of change are constantly generated by synchronic structure in virtue of its endemic rules. There is no doubt that no serious consideration impedes substituting cultural items for linguistic terms in Martynov's models. I shall return to this point later.

There is much more to the great structuralist promise than we have succeeded in showing by enumerating only some of its main points. No wonder that in spite of the outspoken criticism voiced by the more traditional representatives of anthropology and sociology the ranks of scholars who try to apply the achievements of linguistics to socio-cultural analysis are getting wider every year. In anthropology the application of structuralist ideas brought remarkable accomplishments to which works by Edmund Leach and Mary Douglas in Britain testify convincingly.

Still the case is being reinforced again and again against the linguistic analogy, and not all of it can be dismissed as a tribute paid to the conservatism of institutionalized science. Those who tried it, and those who did not, warn us against attaching exaggerated hopes to applications of linguistical methods to non-linguistic, though human, phenomena. As is usually the case, the ontological language is preferred to a methodological one; adversaries of the Lévi-Strauss programme make a point first of all of the qualitative peculiarity of the non-linguistic cultural realms, which allegedly thwart any attempt at extrapolating structuralist methodology to the general cultural analysis.

Two issues happen to be confused in most of the criticism. The first is whether the non-linguistic realms of human culture are constructed in the same way the language is; and so we proceed properly when trying to distinguish in them the same type of units and relationships which were discovered by de Saussure, Jakobson, Hjelmslev and others in language. And the second, whether all human culture, including language, stems from the same universal human effort to decipher the natural order of the world and to impose an artificial one on it, and whether in doing this all fields of culture are submitted to the same logical principles which have evolved to suit the properties of the universe; and so whether we are justified in applying to the socio-cultural analysis the general methodological principles, which have achieved the highest level of elaboration and sophistication in structural linguistics. It goes without saying that a negative answer to the first question does not necessarily presuppose rejecting the second proposition. Unfortunately, to many a critic it does.

There have so far been only few cases of defending the scientific relevance of the first issue. One of the most influential has been that of Kenneth L. Pike,[42] whose contribution has been briefly discussed already. Pike is concerned with exactly the opposite problem to that of the students of the second issue: not with what is signified by cultural items, how cultural items, how cultural phenomena organize and order the cognitive and operational field of human behaviour etc., but with proving that – regardless of their semiotic function – there are, in all institutionalized human behaviour, elementary units analogous to those of language. Pike's contention is that all culture is language in the formal meaning of the word.

The trouble with Pike's argument is that, although language is a part of culture (specialized in conveying information alone), culture is not a language; if not for other reasons, at least because cultural phenomena perform many other functions besides informing somebody about something. What follows is that it would be very odd indeed were the culture built according to constructive principles made to the measure of the communicative function alone. It is true that human beings, whatever they do, always build plenty of different things out of a limited amount of basic materials (the endless variety of each national cuisine, for instance, is achieved usually with the help of relatively few basic ingredients). But stating this fact would not bring us any closer to the understanding of human culture. The one possible result is likely to be a new version of the spurious classification-comparison feats of butterfly collectors: the 'knowledge' that, say, the 'cuisine language' is built of salt, sugar and pepper 'phonemes', while the 'language of gestures' is constructed of raising hands and lowering heads. It is doubtful whether moving along this way we can achieve something other than discrediting the very idea of the linguistic analogy. The fate of this analogy does not depend, furthermore, on whether Pike will succeed in discriminating 'emic units' everywhere, or whether Charles F. Hockett is right when declaring that 'it can be demonstrated very easily that not all cultural behaviour consists of arrangements of discrete units of the kind that we find in language when we analyse speech into arrangements of discrete phonemes'.[43]

What seems to be really important and fruitful is the second issue of the two mentioned above. Norman A. McQuown probably had this issue in mind when stating that[44]

the general principles which I cite are of such generality that they are probably attributes of the universe and not of human beings in particular, or human culture in particular, or of the structure of language in particular. . . . After all, all things have structure of some kind, and the elements within that structure contrast or complement each other, or are in free variation with each other, or show pattern congruence, or look elegant when we find out what the thing is like overall.

The chance offered by the structural principles discovered by linguists consists, briefly, of this: in search of the necessary general laws governing human culture we can now descend to the unconscious system which precedes and conditions all specific empirically approachable, socio-culture choices. Thus we can grasp the necessary relations where they really are. The only alternative available is the programme typified by Margaret Mead's statement: 'More widespread similarities in cultural behaviour which occur in different parts of the world, at different levels of cultural development' should be made understandable by assuming hypothetically a possibly biological organization which no cultural imagination may overstep or ignore.[45] What has been proposed here is to relate the *ex-post-facto* similarities, located on the level of cultural usages and performances, directly to the pre-human, universal biological nature; a procedure which can result only in Murdock's conviction of the biological foundation of the apparently universal human interest in sun, moon, rain and thunder. Instead of trying to discover the general cultural laws in the sphere of necessary, endemic and generative relations, we have been asked to locate them in the field of the accidental and external.

The direct application of the findings of structuralist linguistics to culture at large is inevitably limited by important differences between nonlinguistic and linguistic sub-systems of the human culture.

(1) It is generally assumed that the linguistical process is a 'pure communication'; the only reason why people use linguistical devices at all is that they wish to transmit to each other some information they consider useful or important. The more radical version of the above opinion says simply that each speech event has no other function but transmitting a message, thus it is a highly specialized activity and everything it consists of can be interpreted in the light of intended communication or intention to elicit a specific response.

Not all linguists and psycho-linguists are prepared to sign this statement. To give an example of rather forceful objections raised against the radically 'communicative' image of language we can quote A. T. Dittman and L. C. Wynne's list of omnipresent attributes of speech events which however cannot be considered as parts of the language system *sensu stricto*.[46] The authors distinguish, among others: vocal characterizers (voice breaking, laughing background etc.), segregates (sounds which are not words), qualifiers (crescendo or piano etc.), voice quality (tempo, rhythm, precision of articulation etc.), voice set (fatigue etc.). All these phenomena cannot be treated as parts of the language proper (we can add) because of their defectiveness: instead of being arbitrary signs, reserving their meaning to their relations with other signs, they are much closer to what was meant by Charles Peirce when he spoke of 'indices'; they can be read by the receiver, if he is acquainted with some kind of psychological and physiological knowledge, as information on the sender's state; but the knowledge of language would hardly help in their decoding. We would say with Karl Buhler,[47] that though they possess the *Ausdruck* quality (*fonction émotive*, according to Giulio C. Lepschy),[48] they have not been endowed with either connotative or denotative *intentions*, as have linguistical signs. But they do participate in each act of speech and thus make it much less homogeneous than it would seem at first sight. Another departure of natural languages from the purely communicative model has been pointed to by a distinguished Soviet linguist, S. K. Shaumian: 'We would not expect to arrive at the causes of linguistical change through immanent exploration alone. The structulal language is acted upon by psycho-physical and social factors, which are from its point of view external; their influence cannot be taken into account because as far as the linguistical structure is concerned – it is accidental.'[49]

If even the linguistical process cannot be looked upon as 'pure communication' it is doubly so in the non-linguistic fields of culture. With few exceptions (like the language of gestures and etiquette – it is not by accident that the word 'language' has been spontaneously applied to these phenomena) the non-linguistic culture operates with material which by itself is directly related to non-informative, in some way 'energetic', needs. Although we can justly consider non-linguistic cultural events as information-transmitting, the ratio information/energy is in their case much less favourable to information than in the case of purely linguistic acts. Which means that the role of thc non-informative elements in these events is much greater than in speech-acts, and so, almost by definition, much more influential in shaping the events themselves. First, the 'energetic needs' set the limits of freedom in adjusting the uses of a given material to semiotic purposes. Secondly, in the case of clash or friction between the informative and energetic functions it is not always the informative one which gains the upper hand.

At least in one of his more recent papers[50] Edmund Leach (though one can find contrary statements in his other works) seems to imply that a direct extrapolation from structural linguistics to the analysis of human culture in its entirety is warranted by the fact that 'the patterned conventions of culture which make it possible for human beings to live together in society have the specifically human quality that they are structured "like" human language and that the structure of human language and the structure of human culture are in some sense homologous' (although it can always be asked what the quotation marks on the word 'like' mean and what the sense is of 'in some sense'). Leach's analysis avoids crucially important distinctive features of non-verbal, though semiotical, sub-systems of culture – that, to use Roland Barthes' words, 'have a substance of expression whose essence is not to signify'; Barthes proposes to call 'sign functions' those semiotical signs whose origin is utilitarian and functional.[51]

The most important point is that the non-linguistic branches of culture cannot be exhausted by any description or modelling organized around the informative function alone. Two autonomous functions interfere constantly with each other and no cultural phenomenon is reducible entirely to one function only. Each cultural system, through the choices it makes, orders the world in which members of the respective community live; performs a clearly informative function, e.g. reduces incertitude of the situation, reflects and/or moulds the structure of action through signalling/creating the relevant portion of the web of the human interdependences called 'social structure'. But it also shapes the world of *concrete beings*, who, to survive, must satisfy their irreducible individual needs. This double aspect is clearly discernible in shelter, dress, cuisine, drinking, means of transport, leisure patterns, etc. We will try to elaborate this point later.

One more remark, however, is in place in this context. It is quite possible that the basic materials which serve as the object of human ordering activity have been in the first place pulled into the orbit of the human universe in virtue of their 'energetic' applications. But the variety of forms they subsequently acquire, the lavish abundance of sophisticated and elaborate usages which cluster around them, have little in common with their primary uses. We can risk a hypothesis that although the fact that artefacts of some kind are being produced by human beings at all is likely to be accountable for by basically non-informative human needs, the differentiation of their form and most of the intricacies of their genealogical tree must be referred, to be explicable at all, to the semiotic function they perform in relation to the social structure (i.e. in relation to the task of ordering the human environment). The most recent illustration has been supplied by the wild and technologically (energetically) wasteful and senseless outburst of imagination of the car producers. Were there no stratifying function attached to the cars in their role of signs, we would hardly be able to understand the fact that sophisticated products of modern industry become worn out after two years of use.

To sum up: contrary to the case of language, in analysing the non-linguistical sub-systems of culture we have to apply two complementary though independent analytical frames of reference. No single and qualitatively homogeneous model can account for all the empirical phenomena of culture.

(2) The second limitation concerns the 'law of parsimony'. It is frequently assumed that in the historical development of natural languages the most active factors are those of increasing economy; not only do the distinctions not backed by isomorphic discriminations of meaning tend to shrink and gradually disappear, but alternative types of expressive oppositions tend to congeal, thus diminishing the total number of oppositional patterns. Louis Hjelmslev has even defined language in opposition to all other cultural phenomena except a few (like art or games), 'comme une structure où les elements de chaque catégorie commutent les uns avec les autres'.[52] The central term 'commutation' means a correspondence between distinctions appearing on the level of 'expression' and those discernible on the level of 'content'. It is Hjelmslev's contention that expressive oppositions not backed by isomorphic differentiations of meaning and vice versa are simply 'extra-model' and phenomena and are not linguistic facts proper.

Even in natural languages the amount of this type of redundancy (which should not be mixed up with another, eufunctional type of redundancy safeguarding the proper deciphering of messages) seems however to be quite impressive. B. Trnka, one of the founders of the famous Prague School, points out that there are in each language plenty of phonemes which 'are in complementary distribution with each other and there is no environment in which both of them occur'. This means that 'their ever-present and potential capacity for differentiating words remains unutilized'. Trnka goes so far as to conclude that 'strictly speaking, the true function of phonemes is not keeping the meaning of words from each other, but only distinguishing phonemes between each other'.[53] Much of the phonemes' potential distinguishing power remains unused in every living language; which means that, whenever facing an opposition on the level of expression, we are entitled to suspect a 'commuting' opposition on the level of content, but we cannot be certain that there is one. Harry Hoijer has attacked the same issue from the point of view of relics and archaisms abundant in every language:[54]

> There are structural patterns like that which, in many Indo-European languages divides nouns into three great classes: masculine, feminine, and neuter. This structural pattern has no discernible semantic correlate. . . . Whatever the semantic implications of this structural pattern may have been in origin, and this remains undetermined, it is now quite apparent that the pattern survives only as a grammatical device, important in that function but lacking in semantic value.

Whatever can be said in this connection in relation to language, the exemptions from the 'law of parsimony' are much ampler in the case of non-linguistic cultural sub-systems. The discriminating capacity of the cultural items available at any given time to any given community outgrows as a rule their actual use. The empirical reality of each culture can be said to be full of 'floating' signs, waiting for meanings to be attached to them. This is, at least partly, determined by the particular situation of non-linguistic codes: while every geographically condensed community uses basically one language only, it is exposed to many criss-crossing cultural codes, institutionally separated but employed by the same people, though in different role contexts. The signs float freely over institutional boundaries, but when cut off from their intra-institutional systematic context they lose the 'commuting' bond with their original meanings.[55] The only set available as a common semantic frame of reference for all sub-codes used by the members of a given community is the social structure of the community as a whole. It is true that some signs meaningful inside specialized 'institutional' sub-codes acquire also an additional discriminating quality in the communal 'over-code' (as happens, for instance, to the signs originating in the framework of 'professional' sub-codes, usually indicative also of the position occupied in the overall societal stratification), but it is by no means a general rule. On the other hand, though human creativity is to a very great extent inspired by the demand for new signs to replace the older ones, worn out because of their frequency, it could not be reduced to this cause alone. Owing to its, at least in part, spontaneous and unmotivated character, human creativity produces cultural items in numbers exceeding the actual semiotic demand. These are 'would-be' signs, potential signs, which for the time being do not 'commute' with any real distinctions in the structure of human reality. Thirdly, there is also the tremendous role played by tradition – by the delays in cultural 'forgetting'. The development of any culture consists as much in inventing new items as in the selective forgetting of the older: of those which in the course of time have grown out of their meaning, and not having found any new semiotic function linger on as in explicable and meaningless relics of the past. Some of the items however refuse to disappear long after they have been shorn of their meaning. Surviving sometimes only because of de-synchrony between a system's change and the socializing institutions, they defy the functionalists' belief in the universal utility of everything real and feed the Durkheimian myth of the collective soul.

In short, not all elements in a cultural empirical reality are explicable by referring to their semiotic role. Once again, what may be said on a culture from the point of view of its actual semiotic function does not exhaust the richness of its empirical existence.

(3) One further conclusion from the communicative nature of language is that speech acts can be defined as events arising from an *intention* to convey a message. The French team of linguists led by André Martinet went far enough to define language as one of the 'very wide, and so far not very well delimited, kind of social phenomena which define themselves through intention to communicate, which can be checked with behavioural criteria'. Though the above sentence suggests that according to the authors' opinion the intention to communicate does not discriminate language alone, another sentence testifies to the contrary: 'Before it will be decided that the art is a language, it is reasonable to investigate carefully whether the artist has in the first place sought to communicate, or only to express himself.'[56] The idea of intention to communicate as the defining feature of linguistic phenomena has been so deeply entrenched in scholars' minds that Lévi-Strauss, when trying originally to expose the linguistic nature of the kinship system, seemed to assume that what this system is an attempt, in its own symbolic way, to achieve, is transmitting women or exchanging them with men.[57]

Now it seems doubtful whether the communicative function is indeed the most general one, to which all more specific functions pursuable in human society remain in the relation of subordination and particularity. It might be, but only if we had defined communication more in the spirit of modern system theory than in the 'exchange' tradition of 'passing something to somebody through somebody'. The modern system theory relates the notion of 'communication' to the concepts of 'dependence', 'orderliness', 'organization'. These concepts in their turn have been defined as some kind of limitations imposed on the otherwise unlimited (e.g. unorganized, chaotic) space of events.[58] Two elements are members of the same system (= they communicate with each other) if not all states of the first are possible while the second remains in a given state. In more descriptive language we can say that one element 'influences' the values the second may assume.

In short, we speak of communication whenever there are some limits imposed on what is possible or what can happen and what the probability of its occurrence is. We speak of communication whenever a set of events is ordered, which means to some extent predictable. If we now go from the sociological perspective to structural linguistics and not the other way round, we look at the totality of human activity as an endeavour to order, to organize, to make predictable and manageable the living space of human beings, and the language discloses itself to us as one of the devices developed to serve this over-all aim: a device cut to the measure of communication in the narrower sense. Instead of all the culture being a set of particularizations of the communicative function embodied in language, the language turns into one of the many instruments of the generalized effort of ordering, laboured on by the culture as a whole. This sociological approach to language and its functions is not alien to the original intentions of de Saussure himself, at least according to some of his followers, A. Meillet[59] in the first place.

It seems that to avoid misunderstandings caused by the equivocality of the term 'communication' it is better to speak of 'ordering' as the superior function of the culture as a whole. The direct effect of a linguistic act is to order in a way the cognitive field of the recipient of the message; as a result some other behavioural acts can follow, which organize the action space itself – but these acts, though consequences of speech, do not belong with the sphere of the language proper. On the other hand, the cultural events in the broader sense (of which purely linguistical acts can be a part) are accomplished only when the particular ordering has been achieved. The culturally institutionalized ceremony of addressing and greeting organizes the behavioural space for the interaction which follows – through signalling what patterns of behaviour are appropriate, and stimulating the participants to choose these patterns instead of others. Each participant is aware of the fact that particular patterns are likely to be chosen by his partner, and this knowledge enables him to plan his own actions and to manipulate the global situation in the framework of the options which are open to him.

The specific socio-cultural way of ordering-through-limitation is intimately correlated[60] with one paramount characteristic of the human condition: the link between an individual's position inside the group and his biological, 'natural' equipment is mediated. Which means that the 'social' status of any individual is not determined unambiguously, if at all, by his natural attributes in general, and his physical power and prowess in particular. Which means in turn that the inherited or developed, but in both cases biological, indices of an individual's quality in the framework of *Nature* become *socially* irrelevant if not misguiding. Impressive muscles in a docker would surely guarantee him a most respected status were he a member of a herd of deer or of a birds' pecking order. They are, however, utterly misleading as signs of his position in a human society.

The mediation began with the production of tools. Ever since, human beings have surrounded themselves with artefacts not to be found in natural conditions, products of their modelling activity. Once created and appropriated, these artefacts destroyed the previous homology between the natural and the social order by changing entirely the action-capacity of individuals and so creating a new arrangement of environmental opportunities and probabilities. Thus a decisive adaptive value was conferred on the ordering of, and orienting in, the web of specifically social (which in this context means primarily 'non-natural') relations.[61]

These two requirements of the specifically human condition – ordering and orientation – are as a rule subsumed under two separate headings: social structure and culture.[62] A historical study of circumstances which led to the petrification of the two inseparable faces of one coin into two, for a long time unconnected, conceptual frameworks, remains to be written. Whatever the reasons, however, a disproportionately time-consuming effort has been invested by scholars into solving what under closer scrutiny appears to be a sham and artificial problem. In keeping with the notorious human tendency to hypostasize purely epistemological distinctions, the two analytical concepts coined to 'describe' the two indivisible aspects of the human ordering activity have been taken for two ontologically distinct beings.

The primary fact we proposed to start from is that substituting an artificial environment for the natural one means that an artificial (not natural, not created independently of human activity) order is substituted for the natural one. 'Order' is a graded notion: the level or orderliness is measured by the degree of predictability, e.g. by the discrepancy between the probability indices of the events admitted by the system and those which the system is an attempt at eliminating. In other words, ordering means dividing the universe of abstractly possible events into two sub-sets of – respectively – events whose occurrence is highly probable and those which hardly can be expected at all. Ordering dissipates a certain incertitude as to the expected course of events, which existed heretofore. It cannot be accomplished except through selecting, choosing a limited amount of 'legalized' options from an unlimited multitude of sequences. This understanding of the way the orderliness of a system is achieved stands behind Boas' classic, though forgotten, remarks on the intimate link between statistical and moral meanings of the 'norm' in the order-generating and order-maintaining process:[63]

> The simple fact that these habits are customary, while others are not, is sufficient reason for eliminating those acts that are not customary. . . . The idea of propriety simply arises from the continuity and automatic repetition of these acts, which brings about the notion that manners contrary to custom are unusual, and therefore not the proper manners. It may be observed in this connection that bad manners are always accompanied by rather intense feelings of displeasure, the psychological reason for which can be found in the fact that the actions in question are contrary to those which have become habitual.

Let us turn our attention to the fact that Boas does not distinguish between the order-establishing and orientating-in-order faculties, probably assuming tacitly that we somehow like and evaluate favourably the habitual and expectable while disliking and rejecting the unusual and sudden (a conjecture which was granted full corroboration by psychologists); and that this single human capacity accounts for both the need for order and the efficiency of the culture's guiding function. A single vehicle is enough to achieve both aims, as (1) ordering (structuring) means making the ordered sector *meaningful*, e.g. arriving at a situation in which some concrete events usually follow a particular condition, and (2) some beings to *whom* the sector is meaningful know that these events do follow it indeed. In other words, the sector is meaningful to those to whom it is if and only if they possess some information on its dynamic tendencies. The divergence between the information actually needed to determine the sector completely and the amount of information which would be necessary were the sector entirely 'unorganized' measures the degree of its 'meaningfulness'.

We have arrived this far without having distinguished conceptually the two aspects of the human ordering effort: introducing meaning into the otherwise meaningless universe and supplying it with indices able to signal and reveal this meaning to those who can read. Both sides of the two-pronged endeavour, it seems, can be described and understood in a single analytical framework. The question arises, whether any other frame of reference or conceptual set, besides the one necessary to analyse the ordering activity itself, ought to be brought in to explain the social structure-culture relationship. The orderliness of the world they live in is so vitally important to human beings that it seems entirely justified to ascribe to it an autotelic value. It is hardly necessary, if not redundant, to seek a further explanation to the above need by pointing to a purpose which 'making the world meaningful' allegedly serves.

Consequently, it seems that the logic of culture is the logic of the self-regulating system rather than the logic of the code or of the generative grammar of language – this latter being a peculiar case of the former rather than the other way round. The most important conclusion which follows is the following: we are justified in extrapolating (to the non-linguistic spheres of culture) only the most general features of language; exactly those features, which characterize the linguistic interaction in its capacity as a case of a more inclusive class of self-regulating systems. Therefore we had better turn for inspiration directly to the system theory. That does not necessarily mean, however, that borrowing from the impressive achievements of the linguistical analysis of the nature of signifying should stop. What it does mean is that while allowing ourselves to be inspired by the achievements of linguistics we ought to be aware that they have no more proving power than analogies usually do possess.

(4) In its everyday use the term 'sign' means simply *aliquid stat pro aliquo* and the attention of the students of 'meaning' was traditionally turned to conditions on which a something 'stands' for something else. Closing – in the light of the theory of learning – the long line of development of the behaviouristic interpretations of sign, which began with Watson and passed through the classic works of C. K. Ogden and I. A. Richards and Charles Morris, Charles E. Osgood in 1952 defined the sign as something which 'evolves in an organism a mediating reaction, this (*a*) being some fractional part of the total behaviour elicited by the object and (*b*) producing distinctive self-stimulation that mediates responses which would not occur without the previous association of non-object and object patterns of stimulation'.[64] Thus from the behaviouristic perspective to solve the problem of meaning is to show that a 'non-object' through its association with 'the object' evokes responses akin to those stimulated by the object. For a psychologist whom a behaviourist would call 'mentalist', 'standing for' means 'sending to', which differs substantially from the behaviouristic definition in the terms it employs, but remains very well within the framework of the only question any

psychologist bothers himself with: just what a sign is to somebody to whom it is already or becomes a sign. As we have seen before, for a sociologist or 'culturologist' the main question is different: how it comes, that a 'something' acquires a non-natural, non-intrinsic power to stand for something else and so serve in the role of a sign. That is why – technically – the problem of socio- and culturo-logists is much closer to that dealt with by structural linguists who try to solve exactly the question of the conditions which have to be met by a 'non-object', not to evoke responses 'natural' for a concrete 'object', but to be able to evoke any responses at all.

Some linguists went so far as to distinguish between two entirely different types of information which allegedly lie behind the two questions. Thus according to Berzil Malmberg a message[65] may be said to contain information in a twofold way. It has its 'meaning', which is the traditional popular interpretation of the concept. The message 'gives us information about something'. But information also may imply what we can call here the *distinctive information*; that is to say the distinctive characteristics which make it possible for the receiver to identify the signs – or more exactly their expression level, for this information does not necessarily imply understanding of the message. The secret of signifying, conveying information and so on, lies in the first place in relationships between sign-bodies themselves (syntactic relations, according to the classic threefold classification by Charles Morris). V. A. Zvegintsev thinks it proper even to define the language, the most developed and specialized natural sign-system, by the qualities of peculiar intersign relations. It is due to these relations that the language plays the role of an 'instrument of discreteness, a classification system which emerges in the course of human speech activity. . . . Dissecting the perceived and sensed continuum of the world into discrete units, the language supplies men with means enabling them to communicate through speech'.[66]

Here we come across the first important feature of signs: they are discrete, separate, *different* from each other, and their being different is the very condition of playing the role of signs, of being perceived as signs, of 'standing for' or 'sending to'. It becomes clear at this moment how misleading it can be to confine discussion of signs to their relation to the signified object. Nothing can be learnt of the nature of signs from studying a relation between a single sign and a single signified object. Certainly discreteness and differentiation of signs, which appears to be their first defining feature, cannot be discovered in the frame of a 'single sign – single object' correspondence. In order for this correspondence to be possible at all, the signs must therefore enter beforehand some determined relations between themselves.

Roman Jakobson asserts repeatedly that it was Charles S. Peirce who discovered these initial conditions of any signifying, e.g. meaningful phenomena. It was he who decided that 'pour être compris, le signe – et en particulier le signe linguistique – exige non seulement que deux protagonistes participent a l'acte de parole, mais il a besoin, en outre, d'un *interprétant*. . . . La fonction de cet interprétant est remplie par un autre signe, ou un ensemble de signes, qui sont donnés concurremment au signe en question, ou qui pourraient lui être substitués'.[67] Typical of the more recent statements of the problem is the rather blunt formulation of A. J. Greimas: 'La signification présuppose l'existence de la relation: c'est apparition de la relation entre les termes qui est la condition nécessaire de la signification. . . . C'est au niveau des structures qu'il faut chercher les unités significatives élémentaires, et non au niveau des éléments.'[68] André Martinet and his disciples are even more explicit and definite: 'L'information n'est pas donnée par le message lui-même, mais par sa relation avec les messages auxquels il s'oppose.'[69]

The perceptive conjectures of Peirce were in the course of time reinforced and corroborated by the modern theory of information and have turned into unshakeable foundations of the contemporary understanding of signs and signifying function. One sign taken by itself has no meaning at all; what has meaning is a difference between signs which could be alternatively used in the same place. What follows is that any information is and can be conveyed by the presence or absence of a particular sign, not by the immanent qualities of the sign itself. Which means in turn that the most important, defining attributes of a sign are exactly those which discriminate it from alternative signs, and this discriminating capacity is the only thing which matters in conveying information, e.g. in turning a chaos into a meaningful system, or, in more general terms, in reducing the level of incertitude.

Now if human culture is a meaningful system (and it must be, if ordering human environment and patterning human relations is one of its universally admitted functions) what was said heretofore on the nature of signifying is entirely relevant in its context. Which means that trying to establish the meaning of a cultural item by analysing this item apart from others, in itself, is sometimes totally irrelevant and always inexhaustive and partial. But that is exactly what functionalists from Malinowski on usually do. They either try, as Malinowski himself did, to explain cultural phenomena through relating them to the individual needs they allegedly satisfy (to this habit George Balandier rightly retorted, that 'la place que Malinowski accorde aux besoins, dits "fondamentaux", peut inciter à trouver l'explication des phenomènes sociaux par un procédé (très aléatoire et très suspect du point de vue scientifique) de réduction de l'ordre socio-culturel à l'ordre psycho-physiologique',[70] – which it surely does) or – this time faithfully to the Durkheimian tradition – they mould an anthropomorphic concept of the 'need of the system' to allege a reasonable function for every single cultural pattern. Both approaches quite obviously contradict the methodological imperative to relate meanings to oppositions between signs and not to each sign taken in isolation. The meaning of a sign becomes transparent not in the context of some non-semiotic entities, but in the context of other signs to which the sign under analysis is systematically related.

Having focused our attention on differences between cultural items and patterns in their semiotic (information-conveying) role, we should not however conclude that every difference in physical shape of the items is necessarily meaning-loaded. Significant are only those differences which exist between alternative items, e.g. items which can substitute for each other in the same situation, in the same place of the string of human interaction. To this semi-otically important category belong different behavioural patterns employed by two persons in addressing each other, evening and casual dresses, mini- and 'simple' skirts, doors with and without a 'No entry' label, or two sides of the same door with the 'No entry' label on one side only. These are 'paradig-matically opposed' items, e.g. items mutually replaceable in the same section of the behavioural string. Whenever two cultural items are paradigmatically opposed, we can, conversely, suspect that they convey information on some non-semiotic reality. Before any of the paradigmatically opposed items or pat-terns was employed, the situation had been uncertain as each of the items was to some extent likely to appear; after one of the items did appear instead of the others, the uncertainty was reduced and so an order was achieved.

According to the well-known typology of N. S. Trubetzkoy,[71] the two mem-bers of a meaningful opposition may differ from each other in three alternative ways: each member may possess, apart from the part common to both, also an element which does not appear in the other; these are 'äquipol-lente Oppositionen'. Or every member possesses the same quality but in different degree; these are 'Graduelle Oppositionen'. And there is also a third category called 'privative': 'Oppositionen sind solche, bei denen das eine Oppositionsglied durch das Vorhendensein, das andere durch das Nichtvorhendensein eines Markmales gekennzeichnet wird.' This type of opposition, in which members are correspondingly 'merkmaltragend' and 'merkmallos' (Trubetzkoy), 'marked' and 'unmarked' ('Le langage peut se contenter de l'opposition de quelque chose avec rien' – Jakobson),[72] 'inten-sive' and 'extensive' (L. Hjelmslev), though statistically less frequent than equipollent opposition, is endowed with some particular features which should focus the attention of any student of culture. The most important feature consists in a 'double meaning' of the unmarked member: it 'repre-sents' either the entire category, or one part of it – the one left after the marked member had 'cut off' the other. Thus the unmarked member is indicative of a certain category of entities, but says nothing about the presence or absence of a certain feature whose appearance is signified by the marked member (is neutral toward this feature). Joseph H. Greenberg is fascinated by the 'pervasive nature in human thinking of this tendency to take one of the members of an oppositional category as unmarked so that it represents either the entire category or *par excellence* the opposite member to the marked cat-egory'[73] to the point of declaring the privative opposition one of the most pertinent 'language universals'.

There are reasons to assume that the 'unmarked-marked' opposition, being much more a general form of human ordering activity than a specific lin-guistic device, plays a crucial role in the functioning of culture in general and in its dynamics in particular. It seems, by the way, that this peculiar type of opposition caused generations of anthropologists to overlook distinctive functions of cultural entities and induced them to concentrate on analysing separate items. It happened this way, because by its very nature – the unmarked category discloses its 'unmarkedness' only when confronted deliberately with a marked one. Usually however we do not perceive it in terms of distinguishing; it denotes to us a 'normal', universal state of things, a 'norm' in the statistical sense whose very prevalence inspires a tacit assumption that there must be some 'general human needs' which make the particular unmarked category required and inevitable. The unmarked is a background rather than a distinctive feature. We had a special name for 'mini-dresses', but had no name for the rest of 'just-so-dresses'; we were ready to admit that the mini-dresses somehow distinguish their wearers, that they convey a specific message, are loaded with a particular symbolic value etc. – but at the same time it would hardly occur to most that since 'mini-dresses' have appeared the same can be said of 'just-so-dresses'; as to the latter, we have remained convinced that they perform some purely physiological function (body temperature protection) and – maybe some vaguely moral one, too diffused and universal to arouse suspicion as to its sectarian-discriminating character. It took some time for the mini-dresses to become so widespread and 'normal' as to turn into a new semiotically neutral background and by their very frequency, bordering on 'normalcy', to seem to be stripped of any distinguishing capacity. Thus the ground was prepared for the triumphant appearance of the 'maxi'.

In an extremely stimulating treatise by Victor Martynov[74] we find the following hypothesis. If the nuclear structure of a semiotically relevant sentence is SAO (Subject-Action-Object), then we can pass from one sentence V' to another V'' through modifying one of the three members of the structure. 'Modifiers' are those new signs which are added to one of the polar members; 'Actualizers' are signs added to the central element. Let us notice that both modified and actualized members are related to their previous versions as 'marked' signs to 'unmarked': S'' is the marked member of the opposition S'' – S' etc. This is actually the only way of creating new meanings; it always leads through cutting off some part of a formerly undiscriminated category, through extracting a specified feature of a particular subset of a larger set. Sometimes the older signs absorb their modifiers or actualizers (when they are frequently used together) while transforming their own shape; this process was called by A. V. Isatchenko[75] 'semantic condensation' and it seems to be responsible, at least in part, for the difficulties which any attempt to trace back the common roots of diversified signs regularly encounters. Still one is inclined to suspect that 'adding marks' (modifiers or actualizers) to already existing signs (= introducing finer, more subtle and more discriminating distinctions into a previously undivided category) provides the main, if not the only, road to ramification and enrichment of any semiotic code. It was noticed also by Martynov that the marks can be characterized by their peculiar 'wandering capacity' inside the nuclear structure: modifiers can turn into actualizers and vice versa (Man in office should respect his elders – man should respect his elders in office – man should respect in office his elders), which means that the same or kindred 'marked' meaning of the relation *in toto* can be expressed interchangeably through marking the subject of action, its object or the action pattern itself.

Now there is a striking homology between the nuclear structure of a sentence, analysed by Martynov, and the nuclear structure of social relation (= relation between socially institutionalized roles), as analysed, say, by S. F. Nadel.[76] Behavioural pattern and a corresponding social role are not only intrinsically interconnected; they are, as a matter of fact, two complementary ways of conceptualizing the same repetitive and recurrent process of interacting. The changing relation between two individuals (or, more properly, two categories of individuals) comes into relief through changing the social definition of role and changing the ascribed behavioural pattern at the same time. Practically – we can hypothesize – the appearance of a marked, discriminate sub-pattern of behaviour leads consequently to the distinguishing, inside the broader role, of a new, marked and narrower sub-category. New roles in a ramifying social structure appear to be categorized institutionalizations of a new, more specialized and specific function. The basic device operative in the process leading from the nuclear structure $R'_1A'R'_2$ to the more specific nuclear structure $R'_1A''R''_2$ are once again 'modifiers' and 'actualizers' – in short, markers and marking.

(5) Now, one of the basic axioms of structural linguistics is that the form of expression is basically arbitrary toward the content denoted. In the terms proposed by de Saussure, the 'signifiant' is 'unmotivated' by the 'signifié'. Not all linguists of stature would agree with this contention. One of the first to protest against the extremity of de Saussure's attitude has been Emile Benveniste: 'Entre le signifiant et signifié, le lien n'est pas arbitraire; au contraire, il est *nécessaire*. . . . Ensemble les deux ont été imprimés dans mon esprit; ensemble ils s'évoquent en toute circonstance.'[77] Today the same arguments are being exposed by Roman Jakobson. The essence of the argument is the intimate tie between a 'thought' or an 'idea' on the one hand, and the cluster of phonemes through which this idea is expressed and conveyed, on the other. The uttering of particular sounds evokes, if deciphered rightly, a particular idea; and this idea cannot exist but in its accepted expressive form; its existence is mediated and accomplished by the 'signifiant'.

However controversial the issue has been in the field of linguistics, there is no doubt that in socio-cultural phenomena the 'cultural signs' and the corresponding social relations are in most cases reciprocally motivated and *not arbitrary* towards each other. Their mutual relations can of course assume all shades of the spectrum from entirely accidental genetically to interwoven to the point of identity. But the frequency of relations close to the second pole of the continuum caused innumerable trespassings of analytical borders between sociology and 'culturology' (whatever its institutionalized name), and – worst of all – plenty of efforts wasted on phony problems of whether the 'ultimate essence' of the society is cultural or social. As a matter of fact all phenomena of human life seem to be socio-cultural in Benveniste's or Jakobson's sense: the web of social dependencies called 'social structure' is unimaginable in any form but cultural, while most of the empirical reality of culture signals and brings into existence the social order accomplished by the established limitations. Ungeheuer's famed principle 'In "Kanal" fliessen nur

Zeichenkörper'[78] is obviously irrelevant in the case of communication in the broader sense, which accounts for the overwhelming majority of socio-cultural phenomena. While choosing a particular cultural pattern we create in the sector of a given social action the web of dependencies which can be generalized into a total model of the social structure. And we cannot arrive at anything generalizable into this concept in any way but the one made possible by the available resources of cultural patterns. The social structure exists through the ever-continuing process of the social praxis; and this particular kind of existence is rendered possible by the fact that the praxis is patterned by a limited amount of cultural models.

If asked to express the 'structuralist programme' in one brief sentence, I would point to the intention of overcoming the notorious duality of sociological analysis while avoiding simultaneously the temptation to slip into one of its two extremist alternatives. There were recently attempts to adapt the structuralist method to traditional spiritualist idioms through a single device of postulating the realm of mentalistically interpreted 'meaning' as the semantic field of cultural signs. It is my conviction that the structuralist promise can be transferred from possibility into reality only if it is understood that the role played in linguistical analysis by the semiotic field is assumed, in the world of human relations, by social structure.

## Notes

1 Cf. P. Chambadal, *Évolution et applications du concept d'entropie*, Paris, Dunod, 1963, para. 20.

2 Cf. *Zur Verteidigung der organischen Methode in der Soziologie*, Berlin, 1898.

3 'What is information?', in *Communication and Culture*, ed. Alfred G. Smith, New York, Holt, 1966, p. 51.

4 *Sociology and Modern Systems Theory*, Englewood Cliffs, Prentice-Hall, 1967, p. 14.

5 *Całość i rozwój w swietle cybernetyki*, Warsaw, PWN, 1963, pp. 12; 19, 26.

6 Cf. 'The principles of self-organization', in *Principles of Self-Organization*, ed. Heinz von Foerster and George W. Zopf Jr., Oxford, Pergamon Press, 1962.

7 'Genèse et structure en psycho-physique', in *Entretiens sur les notions de genèse et de structure*, ed. Maurice de Gandillac, Lucien Goldmann and Jean Piaget, The Hague, Mouton, 1965, p. 127.

8 Cf. *The Mathematical Theory of Communications*, University of Illinois Press, 1949.

9 The idea has been elaborated particularly by a Polish cybernetician Henryk Greniewski. Cf. *Cybernetyka niematematyczna*, Warsaw, PWN, 1969, pp. 203–50.

10 Francis Macdonald Cornford's commentary in *Plato's Theory* of *Knowledge*, London, Routledge & Kegan Paul, 1970 (originally 1935), p.230.

11 *Sophist*, 246 A, B.

12 Cornford, op. cit., pp. 6, 244.

13 Ibid., pp. 3, 2.

14 *The Essential Descartes*, ed. Margaret D. Wilson, New York, New American Library, 1969, pp. 80, 82, 83,168.

15 Cf. *Structural Anthropology*, English trans. by Claire Jacobson and Brooke Grundfest Schoepf, New York, Doubleday, 1967, p. 275.

16 Quentin Lauer, *Phenomenology, Its Genesis and Prospects*, New York, Harper & Row, 1965 (originally 1958), p. 9.

17 Edmund Husserl, *The Paris Lectures*, The Hague, Nijhoff, 1967 (originally 1907), p. 9.

18 Edmund Husserl, *The Idea of Phenomenology*, The Hague, Nijhoff, 1968 (originally 1919), p. 41.

19 *Literature, Psychology, and the Social Sciences*, The Hague, Nijhoff, 1962, p. 157.

20 *Le Hasard et la nécessité, essai sur la philosophie naturelle de la biologie moderne*, Paris, Éditions du Seuil, 1970, pp. 116,117.

21 Ibid., p. 119.

22 *Structural Anthropology*, trans. by Claire Jacobson and Brooke Grundfest Schoepf, New York, Doubleday, 1967, p. 225.

23 Claude Lévi-Strauss, *Du miel aux cendres*, Paris, Plon, 1966, p. 330.

24 *Problems of Knowledge and Freedom* (Russell Lectures), London, Fontana, 1972, pp. 33, 41–2.

25 David MacLellan, *Marx's Grundrisse*, London, Macmillan, 1971, p.133.

26 *Writings of the Young Marx on Philosophy and Society*, ed. L. Easton and K. Guddat, New York, Anchor, 1967, p. 413.

27 Cf. *Système, structure, et contradiction dans le Capital, Les Temps Modernes*, 1966, p. 864.

28 Cf. 'The sociology of ethics and the ethics of sociologists', in *The Phenomenon of Sociology*, ed. Edward A. Tiryakian, New York, Appleton-Century-Crofts, 1971, pp. 259–76.

29 *Moral Education*, English trans. by Everett K. Wilson and Hermann Schnurer, New York, Free Press, 1961, p. 76.

30 *The Sociological Tradition*, London, Heinemann, 1967, p. 53.

31 Roland Barthes, *Elements of Semiology*, English trans. by Annette Lavers and Colin Smith, London, Jonathan Cape, 1969 (originally 1964), p. 56.

32 Cf. 'distinktive' und 'delimitative' Funktionen in N. S. Trubetzkoy, *Grundzuge der Phonologie*, Göttingen, Vanderhoeuk und Ruprecht, 1967, p. 241.

33 A. J. Greimas, *Sémantigue structurale*, Paris, Larousse, 1966, pp. 19, 20.

34 *Messages et signaux*, Paris, Presses Universitaires de France, 1966, p. 17.

35 The distinction goes back to the 'semainon' and 'semainenon' of the ancient Stoics; cf. Roman Jakobson, 'A la recherche de l'essence du langage', *Diogène,* 1965, vol. 51, p. 22.

36 Cf. Z. Bauman, 'Marxism and the contemporary theory of culture', in *Marx and Contemporary Scientific Thought*, The Hague, Mouton, 1969, pp. 483–97.

37 Joseph H. Greenberg, 'Language universals', in *Current Trends in Linguistics*, ed. Thomas A. Sebeok, vol. III, The Hague, Mouton, 1966, p. 61.

38 Cf. Lucien Goldmann, 'Introduction générale', in Gandillac, Goldmann and Piaget, op. cit., p. 12.

39 Cf. Z. Bauman, 'Semiotics and the function of culture', *Social Science Information*, 1968, 5, pp. 69–80.

40 Trubetzkoy, op. cit., p. 67.

41 V. V. Martynov, *Kibernetika, Semiotika, Lingvistika*, Minsk, Nauka i Technika, 1966, pp. 118 ff.

42 The fullest version of his theory is contained in the three volumes of his *Language in Relation to a Unified Theory of the Structure of Human Behaviour*, Summer Institute of Linguistics, Glendale, 1954–60. The quotations which follow have been taken from Pike's paper 'Towards a theory of the structure of human behaviour', in *Language in Culture and Society*, ed. Dell Hymes, New York, Harper & Row, 1964, pp. 54–62.

43 In *Language in Culture* (Conference in the Interrelations of Language and the other Aspects of Culture, 23–7 March 1953), ed. Harry Hoijer, Chicago University Press, 1960, p. 163.

44 Ibid., p. 162.

45 Cf. 'Anthropological data and the problem of instinct', in *Personality in Nature, Society and Culture,* ed. Clyde Kluckhohn and C. Murray, New York, Knopf, 1949, p. 111.

46 Cf. 'Linguistic techniques and the analysis of emotionality in interviews', *Journal of Abnormal Social Psychology*, 1961, vol. 54.

47 Karl Buhler, *Sprachtheorie*, Jena, 1934.

48 *La Linguistique structurale*, French trans. by Louis-Jean Calvet, Paris, Payot, 1968, p. 28.

49 *Strukturnaja lingvistika kak immanentnaja teoria jazyka*, Moscow, Nauka, 1958, p. 29.

50 In *Linguistics at Large*, ed. Noel Minnis, London, Gollancz, 1971, pp. 139–58.

51 Barthes, op. cit., p. 41.

52 *Le Langage*, French trans., Paris, Éditions de Minuit, 1966, p. 135, by Michel Olsen.

53 B. Trnka *et al.*, 'Prague structural linguistics', in *Classics in Linguistics*, ed. Donald E. Hayden *et al.*, New York, Philosophical Library, 1967, p. 327.

54 'The Sapir-Whorf Hypothesis', in *Culture, Language and Personality*, University of California Press, pp. 97–8.

55 Cf. the significant discussion of the 'fission' phenomenon by Umberto Eco, 'Lowbrow highbrow, highbrow lowbrow', *Times Literary Supplement*, 1971, p. 1210.

56 *La linguistique*, sous la direction d'André Martinet, Paris, Denoel, 1969, p. 165.

57 Cf. Jacobson and Schoepf, op. cit., pp. 44–5.

58 Cf. for instance W. R. Ashby, R. W. Sperry and G. W. Zopf in Foerster and Zopf (eds), *Principles of Self-Organization*, Oxford, Pergamon Press, 1962.

59 Cf. 'Le développement des langues', in *Linguistique historique et linguistique générale*, vol. II, Paris, Klincksieck, 1936, pp. 75 ff.

60 I wish to emphasize the use of the term 'correlated' instead of 'determining' and 'determined'. The relationship between the two factors reminds one much more of what has been named by cyberneticians 'positive feedback'.

61 Apart from the tight bond between tools and *emergence* of socio-cultural order, there is also an intimate link between the level of tools' development and the types of the socio-cultural regulating system. A good modern illustration has been pointed out by William G. Elliot Jr.: 'Without the motor vehicle, highway signs might well have remained primitive, local and highly *individualistic*. The motor vehicle that tremendously expanded the range of travel and brought an era of individual travel for masses also created new hazards and a need for vastly improved guidance for the strangers who were following new highways into distant places.' 'Symbology of the highways of the world', in *Symbology*, Art Directors Club of New York, 1960, p. 50.

62 What follows is one of the many manifestations of the traditional paradigm. T. O. Beidelman discusses 'the interplay between culture and society' as that 'between ideology (as exhibited in cosmology and moral norms) and social action (as exhibited both in adherence to and the divergence from such norms)'. 'Some sociological implications of culture', in *Theoretical Sociology*, ed. John C. McKinney and Edward A. Tiryakian, New York, Appleton-Century-Crofts, 1970, p. 500.

63 Introduction to *Handbook of American Indian Languages*, Smithsonian Institution, 1911; reprinted in D. E. Hayden *et al.* (eds), *Classics in Linguistics*, New York, Philosophical Library, 1967, p. 220.

64 Charles E. Osgood, 'On the nature of meaning', in *Current Perspectives in Social Psychology*, ed. E. P. Hollander and Raymond G. Hunt, New York, Oxford University Press, 1963.

65 Berzil Malmberg, *Structural Linguistics and Human Communication*, Heidelberg and Berlin, Springer Verlag, 1967, p. 31.

66 V. A. Zvegintsev, *Teoreticheskaya i prikladnaya lingvistika*, Moscow, Prosvjeschtchenie, 1967, p. 421.

67 Roman Jakobson, 'Le Langage commun des linguistes et des anthropologues', in *Essais de linguistique générale*, Paris, Éditions de Minuit, 1963, p. 40.

68 A. J. Greimas, op. cit., pp. 19, 20.

69 *La linguistique*, sous la direction d'André Martinet, Paris, Denoel, 1969, p. 155.

70 G. Balandier, 'L'Expérience de l'ethnologue et le problème de l'explication', *Cahiers internationaux de sociologie*, vol. 35, December 1956.

71 Trubetzkoy, op. cit., p. 67.

72 'Signe zéro', in *Mélanges de linguistique, offerts à Charles Bally*, Geneva, 1939, p. 144. Reprinted in E. P. Hemp, F. W. Householder and R. Austerlitz (eds), *Readings in Linguistics*, II, University of Chicago Press, 1966, p. 109.

73 In T. A. Sebeok (ed.) *Current Trends in Linguistics*, vol. III, The Hague, Mouton, 1966, p. 72.

74 V. V. Martynov, op. cit., p. 72.

75 A. V. Isatchenko, 'Kvoprosu o strukturnoy tipologii slovarnowvo sostava slavianskich jazykov', *Slavia*, 3,1958.

76 Cf. S. F. Nadel, *The Theory of Social Structure*, London, Routledge & Kegan Paul, 1957, especially pp. 22–6, 60.

77 'Nature de signe linguistique', *Acta Linguistica*, 1939. Reprinted in *Readings in Linguistics*, vol. II, ed. P. Hemp *et al.*, University of Chicago Press, 1966, pp. 105–6.

78 G. Ungeheuer, 'Einfuhrung in die Informations theorie unter Berucksichtigung phonetischer Probleme', *Phonetika*, vol. 4, 1959, pp. 95–106.

# 3
# CULTURE AS PRAXIS

The British anthropologists, for reasons described in the first chapter, have little use for the concept of culture; contrary to their American colleagues, who found it useful to describe what they *heard* in terms of culture, the generation of Radcliffe-Brown or Evans-Pritchard successfully accounted for what they saw in terms of social structure. The traditional British conceptual usage was aptly epitomized by Raymond Firth: social structure is that much of the social alignment, so much of the social relations, 'as seems to be of critical importance for the behaviour of members of the society, so that if such relations were not in operation, the society could not be said to exist in that form'.[1] Much can be told about the heuristic utility of such an obviously intuitive definition, in which crucial terms remain unspecified and the critical threshold undetermined; but the essential intention is clear enough, and the definition is indeed unambiguous if taken for what it is in fact, the signpost on the vital crossroads leading to a theory of social integration. The identity of a society is ultimately rooted in a more or less invariant network of social relations; the 'societal' nature of the society consists above all in a web of interdependences developed and sustained by and through human interaction. Social relations are themselves the 'hard core' of actual interaction (as social structure is a hard core of the social organization – of 'the way things get done over time in the community').[2] They are the lasting, time-spanning, little-changing skeleton of the societal practice. They are, indeed, patterns, the kernels of stability in the husk of floating events. Most British anthropologists seemed for a considerable time to be rather satisfied with this middle-of-the-way theoretical commitment; they rarely, if at all, asked how the patterns came about in the first place; or, for that matter, what the actual nature of the patterns is and what keeps them 'acting'. The notion of structure was, to be sure, close enough semantically to the intuition of cohesion and equiliblium. Evans-Pritchard made this association particularly explicit; for him, the very use of the word 'structure' 'implies that there is some kind of consistency between its parts, at any rate up to the point of open contradiction and conflict being avoided, and that it has greater durability than most of the fleeting things of human life'.[3] But again, little has been said about the origin of this consistency and the factors responsible for its perpetuation. Were the question asked in a systematic way, the answer would probably fall within a close distance of Durkheimian 'societal action', whether in the form of *mentalité collective*, or – less metaphysically – rites, usages, traditionalized socialization etc. The important point is that whatever factors would be pointed out, they would probably with no exception be carved in the 'material' flesh of empirically observable human interactions; the quest after causes and driving forces would hardly lead the explorers beyond the realm of institutions.

This 'beyond' has been however from the start the native territory of American anthropology. Even if American anthropologists discuss explicitly the concept of social structure (few of them do, in comparison with the British), they hasten to emphasize that they see it in a different light. To Redfield, social structure 'can be seen as an ethical system. It is an orderly arrangement of conceptions as to what good conduct is'. He would rather see social structure 'not so much as knots of people – connected by the cords of their social network – social relations – but as the characteristic and interrelated states of mind of the people with regard to the conduct of men to men'.[4] The social structure has been therefore reduced to a set of moral precepts, and the integration of norms and expectations has been substituted for the broader (or, perhaps, merely different?) question of the integration of the society as a whole. A. L. Kroeber has developed the depth-surface dichotomy of *ethos-eidos* as, in fact, the correspondent of Radcliffe-Brown's social structure-social organization relation: the *eidos*, we have been told, of a culture 'would be its appearance, its phenomena, all that about it which can be described explicitly'; while the hidden, deeper reality which provides the phenomenal surface with its consistency and regularity is *ethos*, 'the total quality' of culture, which simultaneously summarizes 'what would constitute disposition or character in an individual' and 'the system of ideals and values that dominate the culture and so tend to control the type of behaviour of its members'. In this somewhat ethereal, spirit-like existence *ethos* is the quality 'that pervades the whole culture – like a flavour – as contrasted with the aggregate of separable constituents that make up its formal appearance and are the *eidos*'.[5] The ultimate foundation of the world of the 'ises' is therefore moved into the universe of the 'oughts', and the mystery of the apparent cohesion of the observable, phenomenal plane finds its conclusive explanation in the field of norms and moral evaluations. The emergence and continuity of a social system becomes above all a problem of mental exchange, education, moral indoctrination, personality-formation.

The controversy between British and American anthropologists has a much wider bearing than the transient nature of the clash between the two accidentally disjoint genetic drifts would suggest. It reflects somehow and epitomizes a very long, and thus far inconclusive, argument about the nature of social integration, which leaves practically no major school in social science uninvolved. This argument, in its turn, seems to represent only one of the many facets of the dilemma deeply rooted in the most basic of human experiences and thus assiduously haunting the totality of human self-reflection, with sophisticated philosophical systems at the one pole and commonsensical apprehension of everyday life at the other. It seems, therefore, not very helpful to wrestle with the said controversy within the narrow confines of the original argument. For its full import to be grasped, it must be seen in a much wider perspective, founded in the last analysis on the essentially intuitive but persevering human perception of the life-process.

The irreducible duality of human existence is, perhaps, the most wide-spread, endlessly repeated experience of any individual – at any rate of any individual immersed in a pluralistic, heterogeneous social context, replete with clashes between desires and harsh reality. Most of the history of philosophy looks like a never conclusive, though often sanguine, effort to account for this duality, in most cases, by reducing them to a single (in a genetic or logical, epistemological or practical, sense) principle. This 'duality' is one of the percepts we 'receive' from the universe of reality; they seem to fall into two widely separated divisions, differing from each other in a number of vital dimensions. They seem to possess different 'substance', specific 'modes of existence'; they lend information about themselves, open themselves to human insight through different channels of perception; they seem, more important, to tolerate and admit different degrees of human manipulation, demonstrating various levels of malleability to the human will. The experience is in its essence intuitive, pre-theoretical, ineffable in an articulate discourse unless topped with a set of explanatory concepts. Since each set remains meaningful only within the semantic field of a chosen universe of discourse, and since no universe of discourse entails the totality of human experience, all known and all likely articulations of the basic experience are doomed to remain partial. Each articulation 'projects' the intuitively accessible certainty onto a separate plane of reference; because of the common root, all planes belong to one family – but they grow up fast into autonomous entities to the point of developing their own, allegedly unconnected logics of argument. We are faced, therefore, with apparently sovereign realms of philosophical or scientific argument, dubbed appropriately the issues of spirit and matter, mind and body, freedom and determination, norm and fact, the subjective and the objective. Whatever the level of sophistication and scholarly subtlety reached by the intricate definitions given to respective distinctions, they share a common pedigree going far back to a primeval, though in-itself-inarticulate, experience. It was William James, it seems, who came closest to grasping comprehensively the totality of the multi-faceted partition: we perceive ourselves as persons, he told us, as 'partly known and partly knower, partly object and partly subject'.[6] James's *Me* and *I* lie very much in the background of arguments as far removed as those manifested in the existentialist explorations of Jaspers, Heidegger or Sartre, the pseudo-phenomenologist inquiries into the nature of social life undertaken by Merleau-Ponty or Schutz, or the temerity of the behaviourist revolution in psychology, though only early existentialists were daring enough – with results not excessively encouraging – to forgo the effort to reduce the duality to a unifying common denominator. The thesis which I intend to develop in this chapter is that the culture-social structure controversy belongs organically with the family of issues stemming from the basic experience of the dual nature of the human existential status.

If we disregard the older philosophical manifestations of the existential duality, the modern philosophical treatment of the dilemma bearing relevance to the practical problems of the social sciences[7] goes back at least to late nineteenth-century German Neo-Kantianism. Windelband's distinction between the immanent and the transcendent played a crucial and fateful role here, containing *in nuce* the essential ideas of later *Verstehende Soziologie*, cultural anthropology and phenomenological philosophy. Transcendence has been defined by Windelband in its relation to the immediate experience, interpreted as a state of consciousness alone; thus the penumbra of 'transcendence' embraced the whole of the empirical world, and only the values, the 'oughts', the ideal shapes were left within the reach of the immanent accessibility. Windelband, however, was cautious not to step back onto the admittedly sterile ground of the metaphysical squabble between 'idealism' and 'materialism'. He picked up his problems where Descartes left the heritage of Plato. The very presence of the immanent beside the transcendent, the empirical, the physical, was to him the distinctive feature of the peculiarly human existence-in-the-world. It is, therefore, something by definition meaningful, e.g. cultural existence. Existing, unlike the physical phenomena, in the immanent, meaning-impregnated sense, human life may be grasped and assessed only if approached in a similar, immanent insight; methodology of the cognition of human affairs must, to be effective, reciprocate the immanent nature of these affairs. 'The special character of life is understood by means of categories which do not apply to our knowledge of physical reality. . . . Meaning, value, purpose, development, ideal, are such categories. . . . Meaning is the comprehensive category through which life becomes comprehensible.'[8] The totality of meanings constitutes the realm of the Spirit; this realm belongs neither to the world of phenomena nor to the universe of individual psychology, and cannot be exhausted by either. The Spirit is supra-individual; it makes the human individual, conjectural life-process possible precisely because this process partakes of the work of Spirit, is diving into the pool of meanings totalized in and by the Spirit. Contrary to many a sociologist's beliefs, the enigma of 'collective representations', far from having been invented by Durkheim, was a legitimate and important constituent of the European thought of the time. Our perception of its preposterous incongruence is, even if unconsciously, an after-effect of the positivist insistence on identifying admissible existence with event-like, empirical, sentient accessibility. The question, asked from this perspective about the existential modality of the Spirit, will however be hardly expressible, let alone self-evident, in the language of Windelband or Dilthey. The Spirit is, definitely, not a sum of individual consciousnesses, and the Meaning is not the opinion of the majority of people. Neither is it, nevertheless, a metaphysical figment – if the inexorable absence of evidence is the defining feature of metaphysical entities: it is, indeed, perfectly accessible to human knowledge and comprehension, though, as Rickert would say and Husserl elaborate, through the feeling of self-evidence rather than through sensory perception.

Not *Seele*, but *Geist* is, therefore, the real fulcrum of the understanding of life, and thus of the sheer capability of living. It is not the 'soul' of the other we comprehend when grasping the sense of a social event, since the soul of the other if treated as an empirical phenomenon is not qualitatively different from other empirical phenomena and thus must remain inaccessible to our understanding. It is only the component of the 'Spirit' penetrating the individual 'souls' which we do understand, since we ourselves equally participate in it, and since only the objective, the universal, the invariant, is amenable to understanding. Without forsaking its sovereignty, without being soluble in the multitude of individual 'souls', the 'Spirit' nevertheless underlies the existence of every 'soul'. To quote Dilthey again:

> Every single expression of life represents a common feature in the realm of this objective mind. Every word, every sentence, every gesture or polite formula, every work of art and every historical deed is intelligible because the people who express themselves through them and those who understand them have something in common.

And so[9]

> the fixed order of behaviour within a culture makes it possible for greetings or bows to signify by their nuances a certain mental attitude to other people and to be understood as doing so. . . . The expression of life which the individual grasps is, as a rule, not simply an isolated expression but filled with a knowledge of what is held in common and of a relation to the mental content.

The mental attitudes of individual persons, inter-communicable because of their bond with the shared territory of the Spirit, provide the mediating link between the realm of meanings and the actual human interaction, as well as its comprehension. The vocabulary may be different; the ideas, however, bear striking resemblance to Kroeber's ethos and, more generally, to the way in which the concept of culture is commonly approached in American anthropology.

Indeed, with or without the rather discomfiting idea of 'Spirit', the image of culture as an entity irreducible to psychological phenomena though rendering them possible in their intersubjective, communicative capacity, in short, the German concept of 'Geist' is widely and firmly entrenched in many traditions of social science. It was on its behalf that Kroeber fiercely opposed psychological reductionism in the science of culture, emphasizing repeatedly that 'a thousand individuals do not make society', and ridiculing contentions that 'civilization is only an aggregate of psychic activities and not also an entity beyond them' and that, consequently, 'the social can be wholly resolved into the mental'.[10] It was Kroeber who gave to the unrelenting efforts to disentangle the body of culture from its individual, psychical anchorage, the name of the 'superorganic' nature of culture. The programme was wholeheartedly seconded, together with many others, by Leslie A. White, in a statement apparently paraphrasing Durkheim's persevering motive: 'Culture may be considered, from the standpoint of a scientific analysis and interpretation, as a thing *sui generis*, as a class of events and processes that behaves in terms of its own principles and laws and which consequently can be explained only in terms of its own elements and processes.'[11] So culture is a reality in itself, different from both the 'hard', material constituents of the human world and its 'soft', mental, introspectional data. But what is the existential status of this peculiar reality, postulated by so many students of society? The answers given to this besetting question seem to fall into three broad categories.

The first is the much argued about Durkheimian *tour de force* aimed at unequivocal and exhaustive reduction of the cultural to the social. 'A society can neither create itself nor recreate itself without at the same time creating an ideal.' Far from being the ultimate source of cultural events, the human individual 'could not be a social being, that is to say, he could not be a man, if he had not acquired' this ideal.[12] Far from being novel, the idea goes back to Blaise Pascal and Jean-Jacques Rousseau; but it was Durkheim who dressed it in a quasi-empirical garb and thus paved the way for the essentially philosophical conjecture into the scholarly realms of sociology and anthropology. What has been subsequently discussed under the heading of culture was tackled by Durkheim as ideal, 'something added to and above the real', foisting itself upon human minds precisely by virtue of its intimate link with the very survival of society, i.e. with the human nature of man's existence. Through surrendering to the pressure of the *mentalité collective* and appropriating its precepts, human beings become and remain in and of the society. We may say that culture has been fully and successfully projected onto the societal plane only because society was crammed wholly into the semantic field of culture. In Durkheim, neither society nor culture is in fact 'primary' in either the historical or the logical sense. They merge into one, and are describable only in each other's terms.

The culture-and-personality theorists went the opposite way. They attempted to reduce the totality of culture to the totality of the human personality. The traditional concept of *ethos* was, for Kardiner, coextensive with the defining constituents of a 'basic personality structure'. This structure is constantly created and perpetuated by events of the sort akin to Durkheim's rituals and collective ceremonies; from the common class Kardiner, however, selected a somewhat different sub-set of items – those which Freud had credited with a particular relevance to the shaping of the human personality. Thus the attention is focused on processes of infantile training, ways of individual gratification, frustration creation and channelling. In cutting out the elements of their theoretical model of culture, the culture-and-personality theorists settled for what is essentially the psychologists' 'black box' – the directly inaccessible space between empirically tangible stimuli and responses. Culture, like personality, is the mechanism responsible for processing stimuli into appropriate behavioural patterns. Culture is *not* reduced to the plurality of individual psyches – Kardiner and his associates were careful to avoid what was defined by Kroeber as a mortal trap; again, neither culture nor personality is primary, historically or logically. They fuse into one and are intelligible solely in each other's terms.

The third is the explicitly methodological solution attempted originally by Max Weber. We can learn little from Weber's writings about the actual modality of culture's existence. *Geist* and kindred concepts smacking ominously of metaphysics would be at odds with Weber's intention to establish the scientific status of sociology. Still, with all the heavy emphasis laid on the 'interpretative understanding' as the major distinctive feature of scientific sociology, and meant as the distinctive object of sociological exploration, Weber dedicated his *opus magnum, Wirtschaft un Gesellschaft*, to 'drawing a sharp distinction', in opposition to Simmel, 'between subjectively intended and objectively valid meanings'.[13] His major departure from contemporary German philosophical trends, as represented by the Heidelberg school, consisted however in the total renunciation of all interest in the existential modality of the 'objectively valid meanings'. The distinction epitomized in the above quotation was not any more the opposition between mental experience and the Spirit, each granted an attribute of reality. Weber's dichotomy is kept consistently within the field of methodology. It has been generated by the interest in the objectivity of sociology as the 'understanding' science and Weber was determined to resolve the issues involved without committing himself to any specific ontological position. Still the quest for a superstructure of meanings, inexhaustible by any amount of singular, volatile and aleatory mental experiences, looms large and persistent in Weber's enquiry. Located in the methodological sphere, it leads now to a 'theoretically conceived pure type of subjective meaning attributed to the hypothetical actor or actors in a given type of action', as distinct from 'the actual existing meaning in the given concrete case of a particular actor'. 'The meaning appropriate to a scientifically formulated pure type of a common phenomenon' is different not only from actually intended 'private' meanings, but even from their statistically processed average, accessible through, say, sample surveys; there is, in fact, no way leading from the description of individual, subjective meanings to the construction of the 'ideal types', which represent objective meanings of given actions, and which serve the sociologists as types which have 'the merit of clear understandability and lack of ambiguity'. Pure types are objectively valid even if they have not 'actually been concretely part of the conscious "intention" of the actor'. The ideal type must be constructed 'before it is possible even to enquire how this action has come about and what motives determine it'. Priority and superiority of objective meaning over the subjective one became, therefore, of entirely methodological nature but it has still been priority and superiority all the same.

And so whatever solution to the vexing dilemma of the existential status of the 'superorganic' is sought and proposed, the idea of the autonomy of culture (as a concept, regardless of the term used to account for it) provides one of the few points of agreement between otherwise widely divergent theories. It is a total autonomy which is explicitly or tacitly assumed, toward both the experientially accessible worlds – the one of the material objects and the one of the subjective mentality. The second opposition is particularly strongly stressed by the classics of 'meaning-oriented' sociology, since the threat of dissolving the cultural in the psychological is in their case most salient. Florian Znaniecki, the one sociologist most keen on defining sociology as 'cultural science', was eager to dissociate himself from all specimens of psychological reductionism. With a determination seldom found in sociological literature

Znaniecki promulgated what amounts to a final indictment of subjective interpretations of meanings as the subject of sociological study: 'The episte-mological doctrine according to which an individual's consciousness of his own mental life is the foundation of all knowledge becomes conclusively dis-proved by the development of scientific research in the domain of culture – that very domain from which it draws most of its arguments.'[14] As far as the objects of the sociologist's study are concerned,

> it is utterly impossible to consider any such datum as contained in the minds of those individuals, for symbolic expressions and active performances of the latter furnish conclusive evidence that to each of them a cultural datum appeared as something which exists independently of his current experience of it, something that has been and can be experienced and used by others as well as by himself – whether it does or does not exist in the natural universe.

Lest some doubts will be left lurking in the minds of his readers, Znaniecki sums up his argument with an unequivocal proposition of the 'irreducibility of cultural data to either objective natural reality or subjective psychological phenomena'.[15] And Znaniecki has been the sociologist perhaps most fre-quently accused of subjectivist proclivity. Cultural data do enjoy existence in their own right, though of a different kind from the reality typical of the 'nat-ural universe'. Culture is not only intersubjective; it is indeed objective in its own specific sense.

We can now conclude our brief review of the basic ideas underlying the diverse usages of the term 'culture' or kindred terms. Though culture seems to belong with a large family of concepts descending from the 'inside' part of the universal experience of the world's duality, it is different from its kin in its attempts to transcend the opposition between the subjective and the objective (it shares this distinction with the concept of *Geist*). Its persistence in human thinking about the world is due to its roots going deeply into the primeval human experience of subjectivity; but it differs from the other offshoot of the same root in that it is grafted on the stem shooting from the opposite root, that of the experience of tough, unimpregnable and unflinching objectivity. However it is defined and described, the sphere of culture is always accom-modated between the two poles of the basic experience. It is, simultaneously, the objective foundation of the subjectively meaningful experience and the subjective 'appropriation' of the otherwise inhumanly alien world. Culture, as we see it universally, operates on the meeting ground of the human individual and the world he perceives as real. It resists stubbornly all attempts to asso-ciate it unilaterally with either one or the second pole of the experimental frame. The concept of culture is subjectivity objectified; it is an effort to understand how an individual action can possess a supra-individual validity; and how the tough and hard reality exists through a multitude of individual interactions. The concept of culture seems to be cast in the mould postulated by C. Wright Mills for the sociological enquiry focused on the link between individual biography and societal history. In short, the concept of culture, whatever its specific elaborations, belongs with the family of terms standing for the human praxis.

The concept of culture, therefore, transcends the immediate, naive datum of private experience – the all-inclusiveness and self-sustaining nature of subjectivity.[16] The level of sophistication to which it elevates the self-perception of the human condition is removed from the ground floor of commonsensical naivety by the qualitative difference between the individual and the human community; as I. Mészáros recently put it,[17]

> the most important difference is that while the individual is *inserted* into his ontological sphere and sets out from the *given* forms of human interchange which function as axiomatic premises of his end-positing activity, mankind as a whole – the 'self-transcending' and 'self-mediating being of nature' – is 'author' of its own sociological sphere. The temporal scales are, of course, also basically different. While the individual's actions are strictly circumscribed by his limited life-span – and furthermore by a host of other limiting factors of his cycle of life – mankind as a whole transcends such time-limitations. Consequently very different yardsticks and measures are adequate to the assessment of 'human potentiality' – a term applicable, strictly speaking, only to mankind as a whole and to the evaluation of the actions of the limited individual.

We would prefer the concept of community wherever Mészáros employs 'mankind', since the latter strongly implies the notion of the human being as a 'species specimen' rather than a member of a group welded together by a network of communication and exchange. The idea of creativity, of active assimilation of the universe, of imposing on the chaotic world the ordering structure of the human intelligent action – the idea built irremovably into the notion of praxis – is indeed comprehensible only if viewed as an attribute of community, capable of transcending the natural or 'naturalized' order and creating new and different orders. Furthermore, the idea of freedom, associated in turn with the notion of creativity, acquires an utterly different meaning when considered as a quality of a community, from when it is discussed in terms of a solitary human individual. In the first case it is the freedom to change the human condition; in the second, freedom from communal coercion and limitation. The first is a real, genuine modality of the human existence; the second often happens to emanate from a misplaced nostalgia for a new, more suitable human-ordering-of-the-world, cast into the illusory realm of individualism by the obfuscating impact of an alienated, ossified, immobile society. The community rather than mankind, frequently identified with the human species, is therefore the medium and the bearer of praxis.

Contrary, however, to Durkheim's absolutization of the community, communal praxis would hardly be possible were not human beings, as members of the human species, capable of producing creatively potent communities. Marx was deeply conscious of this truth, however misleading the conclusions that may be drawn from his consistent emphasis on community as the ultimate locus of understanding of the human condition. That is why Marx included sociability among the most essential and inalienable attributes of human nature. Rather than proposing sociability as the alternative for universality, as was recently suggested by Richard Schacht,[18] Marx picked a number of universal, species-anchored features as the precondition of social praxis, with the

quality of sociability particularly conspicuous among them. At variance again
with Durkheim, to whom everything human is possible only as of societal
provenance, Marx saw society as a factor mediating between universal human
qualities and the empirical condition of a human individual. It may be shown
that all the rest of the significant differences between the Marxian minority
and the Durkheim-inspired majority of contemporary sociology are inexorably pre-determined by this seminal disagreement.

Each analysis of the phenomenon of culture must, it seems, take account of
this universal precondition of all empirically specific praxis. The qualities
which make social life possible must be, both logically and historically, pre-
social, as linguistic capacity is prior to linguistic competence. Since all
cultural praxis consists in imposing a new, artificial order on the natural one,
one has to look for the essential culture-generating faculties in the domain of
the seminal ordering rules built into the human mind. Since cultural ordering
is performed through the activity of signifying – splitting phenomena into
classes through marking them – semiotics, the general theory of signs, provides the focus for the study of the general methodology of cultural praxis.
The act of signifying is the act of the production of meaning. Meaning, in its
turn, far from being reducible to a mental, subjective state of a sort, is
brought into existence by *'an act of simultaneously cutting out* two amorphous masses'; meaning, in Barthes' words, is 'an order with chaos on each
side, but this order is essentially a *division*'; 'meaning is above all a cutting-out
of shapes'.[19] Meanings, Luis J. Prieto would say, emanate 'grâce aux corre-
spondances qu'il y a entre les divisions d'un univers du discours et celles de
l'autre', the universe of discourse being brought into existence by an act of
indication, which splits a domain into a class and its negative complement.[20]
Human praxis, viewed in its most universal and general features, consists in
turning chaos into order, or substituting one order for another – order being
synonymous with the intelligible and meaningful. In semiological perspective,
'meaning' means order and order alone. It is detached from the performance
of an individual or even collective actor, whether interpreted mentalistically
or seen, as by behaviourists, as reactive mechanisms. It does not depend any
more on giving rise to an idea associated with the sign, as it was for C. K.
Ogden and I. A. Richards; neither is it a pattern of stimulation which evokes
reactions on the part of an organism, as it was for Charles E. Osgood or
Charles Morris. It is rather a cultural organization of the human universe,
which makes both these after-effects possible.

In this sense the immense, voluminous creation of Claude Lévi-Strauss
may be viewed as a tortuous quest for the generative rules of order. The controversial issue of the existential status of these rules – however significant it
may be philosophically – seems largely irrelevant to the study of the methodology of human praxis, just as the existential nature of a language as a system
is irrelevant to the study of its structure. Lest barren ontological squabbles
take the better part of our efforts to understand the mechanism of human cultural praxis, we would be well advised to treat lightly or metaphorically the
continuous references to 'l'esprit' or 'inconscient' in Lévi-Strauss's writings;

with the ontological question suspended, a virtually unlimited perspective on human praxis is opened by the seminal statement, that 'entre toutes formes' of culture, 'il y a différence de degré, non de nature, de généralité, et non d'espèce. Pour comprendre leur base commune, il faut s'adresser à certaines structures fondamentales de l'esprit humain, plutôt qu'à telle ou telle région privilégiée du monde ou période de l'histoire de la civilisation' [21]

### The cultural and the natural

It was this search for universality which perhaps guided Lévi-Strauss into starting his anthropological exploration with the prohibition of incest. Not so much because this prohibition belongs to the most obvious examples of 'universals' in Murdock's sense, in virtue of its presence in all known cultural communities; but because it constitutes the most elementary act of the culture's independence of Nature, the most fateful step from the universe ruled only by natural laws to the human realm in which a new, hitherto absent, order is imposed on the previous monopoly of the natural one. [22]

> Envisagée du point de vue le plus général, la prohibition de l'inceste exprime le passage du fait naturel de la consanguinité au fait culturel de l'alliance. . . . Considérée comme interdiction, la prohibition de l'inceste se borne à affirmer, dans un domaine essentiel à la survie du groupe, la prééminence du social sur le naturel, du collectif sur l'individuel, de l'organisation sur l'arbitraire.

The prohibition of incest offers a most conspicuous meeting-point between nature and culture: nature imposes the necessity of alliance, without defining its exact shape; culture determines its modality. *Dasein* is natural, *Sosein* is cultural; this seems to be a universal pattern for the links binding cultural phenomena to their natural foundation, but hardly ever is the pattern as transparent as in the domain explored in *Les Structures élémentaires*.

The contribution of nature boils down, in the case under analysis, to, essentially, two things: (*a*) The 'survival' necessity (which may be interpreted either functionally or logically) of creating some, loosely delimited, pattern; (*b*) The material (e.g. consanguinity) of which the pattern-forming signs may be constructed. The rest belongs to cultural praxis. 'Les structures mentales', which Lévi-Strauss picks as underlying all cultural ordering and thus constituting the true universals of culture, are three: (*a*) requirement of a rule; (*b*) reciprocity, as the most immediate form in which the opposition between me and the other may be overcome; and (*c*) the synthetic character of the Gift – the fact that transferring a value from one individual to another transforms the two persons involved into partners and adds a new quality to the object transferred. These three principles are sufficient to explain and comprehend the order-creating capacity of the prohibition of incest. Indeed, the prohibition of incest may be described in positive instead of negative terms, as a reciprocal offer of 'gift' – sisters – which transforms the offering brothers into allies, and the exchanged women into the bond of alliance. Lévi-Strauss seems to believe that the three universals suffice to comprehend the totality of the cultural process – not only one, however fundamental, rule of incest, but the creating and maintaining of the social structure in all its aspects – though, to the best of my knowledge, he never employed them in analysing any other structures but kinship. Their sufficiency in a wider context remains to be proved. It seems that to secure their applicability to the structures of complex societies, removed a considerable distance from the immediacy of blood-and-affinity bonds, one has to distend drastically the meaning of both reciprocity and gift. Still, the issue presents innumerable difficulties and requires vast explorations which, unfortunately, cannot be undertaken in the framework of the present study. Of all the universals spelled out by Lévi-Strauss only one will be treated here at some length: the crucial requirement of a rule. It is above all the rule which cuts off a parcel of the natural universe and transforms it into the venue of cultural praxis.

In his remarkable analysis of universal features of ancient and modern cosmologies, Mircea Eliade finds a striking distinction between the cosmological status of the 'islands of order', subordinated to the man-created rules, and the rest of the perceived universe.

> The world that surrounds us . . . the world in which the presence and the work of man are felt – the mountains that he climbs, populated and cultivated regions, navigable rivers, cities, sanctuaries – all these have an extraterrestrial archetype, be it conceived as a plan, as a form, or purely and simply as a 'double' existing on a higher cosmic level. But everything in the world that surrounds us does not have a prototype of this kind. For example, desert regions inhabited by monsters, uncultivated lands, unknown seas on which no navigator has dared to venture, do not share with the city of Babylon, or the Egyptian nome, the privilege of a differential prototype. They correspond to a mythical model, but of another nature: all these wild, uncultivated regions and the like are assimilated to chaos; they still participate in the undifferentiated, formless modality of pre-creation.

What is true in the space dimension, applies as well to the time gaps dividing the 'islands of order':

> Enthronement of a 'carnival' king, 'humiliation' of the real sovereign, overturning of the entire social order . . . every feature suggests universal confusion, the abolition of order and hierarchy, 'orgy', chaos. We witness, one might say, a 'deluge' that annihilates all humanity in order to prepare the way for a new and regenerated human species.[23]

The first and the most fundamental distinction accomplished by the human-activity-in-the-world is the one between the realm shaped by human praxis and all the rest. Creation begins with praxis. The regions inaccessible to praxis, or those forcibly introduced in between praxis-regulated stretches to underline the frontiers of order, are left behind as domains of amorphism, vagueness, chaos.

When analysing 'alimentary language', Roland Barthes enumerates a number of functionally distinct rules which seem to possess a much wider bearing and to constitute the necessary generative components of any cultural system. In the first place Barthes names 'rules of exclusion' (in the case of the alimentary language, this role is played by food taboos); creating of a cultural order starts with the application of a rule that specifies the domain to which rules of the given universe of discourse apply – delineating simultaneously the unregulated pale of chaos. The remaining classes of rules hold for the quarter already scrupulously circumscribed. The ordained oppositions are meaningful only within the limits drawn by the rule of exclusion; more important, the rules of association retain their regulative power only when employed well inside the circumscribed area; and, finally, rules of ritual are useless in efficiently organizing the domain unless transgression of its boundaries is effectively barred. From whatever corner we start, we arrive inevitably at the same conclusion: the role of the rules of exclusion is crucial, indeed fundamental, pre-conditioning applicability of all other rules.

In a much too little referred to essay[24] Edmund Leach developed and refined the seminal idea of the intimate bond between the need for a clear, functional system of concepts and the need to fill up or to repress the 'boundary percepts'. Because of the character of the volume for which the essay was commissioned, the discussion was limited to the 'verbal' concepts; yet, indeed, nothing in the chain of reasoning Leach displayed was of a nature barring the extension of the basic findings to cover cultural phenomena in their entirety, in any case in their communicative, semiotic function. The same information – the same realization of a morsel of the social structure – can be created and passed over equally effectively with a meaningful phrase or meaningful behavioural sign-pattern, and we can hardly expect two qualitatively distinct sets of generative rules related to the two interchangeable codes; the standards of clarity at least stem from the superior need for order rather than from the specific structure of a single semiotic code. We may, therefore, pluck Leach's argument from its circumstantial linguistical garment, and apply it to cultural phenomena *tout court*.

Ordering involves transmuting what is fundamentally a continuous, shapeless stream of perception into a set of discrete entities. In this sense the world is not pre-humanly 'given' as ordered; the image and the following praxis of order are culturally imposed on it. 'Because my mother tongue is English,' says Leach, 'it seems self-evident that *bushes* and *trees* are different kinds of things. I would not think this unless I have been taught that it was the case.' The following statement seems, however, by far the most important, since it elucidates the role played by the rules of exclusion in creating and reinforcing any cultural order: 'If each individual has to learn to construct his own environment in this way, it is crucially important that the basic discriminations should be clear-cut and unambiguous. There must be absolutely no doubt about the difference between *me* and *it*, or between *we* and *they*.' One cannot rely on the endemic, inborn discreteness of the world which will eventually vindicate itself in case of semiotic confusion; no 'natural' relations between sign-patterns and parts of the world exist, and lucidity, unequivocality of the watersheds and dividing lines must be guarded by cultural means. Leach names taboo as such means: 'taboo inhibits the recognition of these parts of the continuum which separate' the 'named', or, more generally, the culturally marked categories.

In the last statement two analytically distinct, though kindred phenomena have been, however, put unjustly into one box. It is true that 'picking up', through naming and employing 'species-specific' and 'acquired' 'generalization gradients'[25] leaves substantial parts of the reality in its 'pristine', pre-cultural state, unnamed and culturally irrelevant and neglected. These parts, until processed by the semiotic procedure of cultural praxis, as good as do not exist for human beings; unnoticed, inaccessible to human praxis, these conceptual unbeings cannot possibly jeopardize the orderliness of the culturally tamed and assimilated part of the universe. There is no need to 'suppress' them, and no ground for taboo; indeed, suppressing of something which is, culturally, as good as non-existing, would present insuperable technical problems. 'Non-things' do not and cannot constitute the target of taboo. They supply, instead, the inexhaustibly vast virgin land for prospective cultural assimilation, preceded in most cases by scientific probing and fencing. Where the powerful weapon of taboo finds its mark indeed is not the area short of praxis-bestowed meaning, but on the contrary, the awe- and anxiety-inspiring regions overloaded with meanings, particularly logically contradictory meanings. The stubborn continuity of reality resists all attempts at splitting it into impeccably neat, clear-cut divisions; operations of inclusion inexorably produce overlapping categories. It is not so much the 'no man's land' as the 'too many men's land' that creates the mortal threat to the very survival of cultural praxis. Taboo is an attempt to dispose of redundant, confusing meanings, rather than to account for culturally translucent desert areas.

The notorious ambiguity of the attitudinal complex associated with taboo is a match for the equivocality of situations and objects to which the taboo provides the institutionalized or instinctual response. The complex unites attitudes otherwise incompatible: awe and repulsion, admiration and abhorrence, attachment and hatred, explorative curiosity and escape drive – 'abiance' and 'adiance', in Holt's terms.[26] The taboo attitudinal complex is strikingly reminiscent of what in sociological literature since Durkheim is named 'the sacred'; indeed, convincing discrimination between the two notions is not an easy matter. One wonders whether the persistent habit of discussing the two categories separately has much foundation apart from the concatenation of intellectual traditions. Rules of exclusion-inclusion, vitally significant in the maintaining of the intelligibility and meaningfulness of the human universe, most naturally supply the very focus for the sacred. This hypothesis of the sacred as originating in the act of tabooing, driven by the rules of exclusion-inclusion, seems to carry much more likelihood than the mythical Durkheimian society erecting hallowed redoubts to force its subjects into an inward loyalty.

The focusing of religious and magical beliefs on some chosen objects of peculiar character long ago drew the inquisitive attention of ethnographers and anthropologists. The conjecture that the ambiguity of the existential status serves as one of the main criteria in selecting the objects credited with the supernatural and mysterious power is by no means of recent origin. Lévy-Bruhl analysed the peculiar attitude of Maoris to menstrual blood (shared, as it were, with a multitude of other peoples) as descending to the eerie meaning of this blood as a human being unfinished and incomplete; it could turn into a person, but did not, thus destroying a life yet unborn; menstrual blood is therefore an exemplary manifestation of existential and conceptual ambiguity, as only the death of something which never lived can be.[27] As such it belongs to one category with such apparently far removed, but persevering phenomena as the refusal to treat domestic pets as meat, the cult of the human God-Mother, the suspicious anxiety aroused by the marginal people, the ominous 'ubi leones' on the maps of the ancient *oikoumene*, or tricephalous Cerberus who guarded the vulnerable frontier between 'this' and the 'other' world.

Though the taboo-prone objects obtrude wherever a meticulous, faithfully observed distinction is endowed with a particular significance in the course of historical praxis, some frontiers seem to be exceptionally amenable to tabooing procedures in a well-nigh universal fashion, independent of historical contingencies; they shape, perhaps, the supra-historical, invariant frame for the historically changeable human praxis. These frontiers are particularly obstinately present in human sacred practices, not because the reality itself around them is more fluid and less discrete than in other places, but because their unequivocality is somehow more passionately emphasized by most known human communities than other watersheds. Leach cogently discussed some of these vehemently and nearly universally defended frontiers:

> First, the exudations of the human body are universally the objects of intense taboo – in particular, feces, urine, semen, menstrual blood, hair clippings, nail parings, body dirt, spittle, mother's milk. This fits the theory. Such substances are ambiguous in the most fundamental way. . . . Feces, urine, semen, and so forth are both me and not me

– they are the detachable components of the fundamentally indivisible 'me'; when separated, they turn into the component of the outer world – they belong to both sides of the border, and this insurmountable duality saps the border's security.[28]

> At the opposite extreme, consider the case of the sanctity of supernatural beings. . . . The gap between the two logically distinct categories, this world/other world, is filled in with tabooed ambiguity. The gap is bridged by supernatural beings of a highly ambiguous kind – incarnate deities, virgin mothers, supernatural monsters which are half men/half beast. These marginal, ambiguous creatures are specifically credited with the power of mediating between gods and men. They are the object of the most intense taboos, more sacred than the gods themselves. In an objective sense, as distinct from theoretical theology, it is the Virgin Mary, human mother of God, who is the principal object of devotion in the Catholic church.

Well, Jesus Christ himself, whose cult throughout the Christian world certainly overshadows the cult of the God-Father, has the utterly ambiguous existential status of God's son born of an earthly mother; he himself used the unambivalent name of 'son of man'; the insertion of the fundamental ambiguity into the accepted definition coincided with the elevation of Christ to the very top of the sacred hierarchy.

The third frontier of apparently utmost importance is the one between 'we' and 'they'. Suppression of the intermediate, ambivalent cases is a necessary condition of group cohesion, e.g. of the application of syngenic behavioural types as distinct from biocenotic ones, which are apposite in relations with aliens.[29] The very existence of the border-cases in this paramount area creates an enormous tension between two incompatible sets of behavioural and attitudinal patterns – comparable to the stress which makes a stickleback bury his head in sand when, having approached the borderline of his nest territory, he is unable to choose between the pugnacious stance of the native, chasing the intruder off his homestead, and the defensive posture of a rambler in a land of inhospitable aliens. Let us notice in this context, that the objection raised by Leach against Lévi-Strauss's heavy emphasis on the in-built tendency of culture to 'either-or' divisions – 'it is not sufficient to have a discrimination me/it, we/they; we also need a graduated scale close/far, more like me/less like me'[30] – stands in an obvious contradiction to the main core of his own argument. The graduality, intermediacy of the existential status is the very cause of the conceptual-behavioural earthquake to which taboo and the sacred provide the adequate remedy. The semblance of a graduated scale comes from the possibility and, indeed, pronounced tendency of cultural conceptualization to arrange diverse frontiers into a sequence or rather into a series of concentric circumferences centred in the ego's eye: the frontier 'me/it' is in this sense 'closer' than the frontier 'we/they', which in its turn is 'closer' than the ultimate frontier 'this world/other world'. Many other frontiers besides will inevitably be left behind, not finding their place in this 'subjective-focused' continuum – as, for example, frontiers between different states and forms of matter, which made of their transgressors – alchemists, iron-smelters, smiths – semi-sacred, semi-outcast figures. Whatever the importance of the ego-centred mapping of the world divisions (elaborated on, among others, by Alfred Schutz in sociology and Kurt Lewin in psychology), the act and its product are brought into effect by employing a series of clear-cut, either-or oppositions, and these oppositions only constitute the foci of taboos and sacredness.

Indeed, a graduated nature of 'we-ness' and 'they-ness', if at all imaginable, would undermine the very foundation of the human-orientation-in-the-world. 'We' play with each other a non-zero-sum-game, or at least try or pretend to, while with 'them' the zero-sum-game is what is to be expected as well as desired. 'We' share the same fate, grow rich together or get destitute together, while 'they' prey on our calamities and are hurt by our success. 'We' are supposed to assist each other, while 'they' lie in wait for our lapse. 'We' understand each other, feel the same feelings and think the same thoughts, while 'they' remain impenetrable, incomprehensible, sinister aliens. The frontiers of the 'we-group' – the truth articulated at least since Sumner – delineate the border of our intellectual and emotional security and provide the frame on which to hinge our loyalties, rights and duties. Here, inside, the order is known, predictable and manageable. There, outside, all is darkness and uncertainty. Still, if only the frontiers between 'here' and 'there' are marked clearly and unmistakably, the 'we-group' can do reasonably well even in the close neighbourhood of 'them'. The group, in fact, would have invented 'them' had 'they' not been in existence before. Any 'we-group' needs its own 'them' as an indispensable complement and self-defining device. 'They' are in their peculiar way useful, functional, and therefore tolerable, if not desirable. One cannot however think of any beneficial use to which the 'we-group' can put its 'inside-outsiders', belonging neither here nor there the marginal men.

We are told by Ian Hogbin of a Busama storekeeper, Yakob, who fancied himself to be a respectable European-like businessman while remaining in his native village:[31]

> The people disapproved of him so strongly that they always scolded me for talking to him. They never were indignant if I spent an hour or two associating with animals, but they used to criticize me severely when I bought a tin of cigarettes from him. 'He's a black man who wants to behave as though he were white, and you oughtn't to encourage him,' they used to tell me.

In a totally different culture, that of America in the times of McCarthyism, a university professor, Morton Grodzins, spelled out the heinous vileness of political Yakobs, the disloyals:[32]

> Loyalties provide [the individual] with a portion of the framework upon which to organize his experience. In the absence of such a framework, he would establish no easy, habitual responses. He would be faced with the endless and hopelessly complicated task of making fresh decisions at each moment of life. He would soon degenerate into wild and random inconsistencies or into a brooding state of confusion and indecisiveness, conditions that merge into insanity.

The names given to marginals fluctuate from epoch to epoch, from society to society; the names reflect historically effectuated, unique selections of concepts and images, typical of a given cultural code in a given time. Sometimes the people pinpointed as ambiguous and therefore marginal are labelled witches or sorcerers: 'Witches and their accusers,' wrote Philip Mayer, 'are individuals who ought to like each other but in fact do not. . . . The witch is essentially a hidden enemy but an apparent friend.' Most important of all, 'witches turn against their own neighbours and kinsmen; they do not harm strangers or people far away,'[33] although, curiously enough, witches are believed to be filled with an evil power which emanates, as it were, all around, spontaneously and blindly. In the framework of the accepted cosmology, the 'victimage', which Kenneth Burke thinks to be the indispensable concomitant of social cohesion,[34] materialized in the image of witches. The cosmology supplied however the verbal vehicles only for the operation of a rule transcending all specific ideologies. As Aldous Huxley put it,[35]

> In medieval and early modern Christendom the situation of sorcerers and their clients was almost precisely analogous to that of Jews under Hitler, capitalists under Stalin, Communists and fellow travellers in the United States. They were regarded as the agents of a Foreign Power, unpatriotic at the best, and, at the worst, traitors, heretics, enemies of the people. Death was the penalty meted out to these metaphysical Quislings of the past and, in most parts of the contemporary world, death is the penalty which awaits the political and secular devil-worshippers known here as Reds, there as Reactionaries. . . . Such behaviour-patterns antedate and

outlive the beliefs which, at any given moment, seem to motivate them. Few people now believe in the devil; but very many enjoy behaving as their ancestors behaved when the Fiend was a reality as unquestionable as his Opposite number.

The real target of these 'very many' is the portentous, ghoulish area in which 'here' meets 'there', 'in' meets 'out', and 'right' meets 'wrong'. The Marginals are alternately hated and granted superhuman powers because they embody this perennial fount of the most intense and gripping of all human fears.

The concept of marginality has already a long and impressive intellectual history. In the Anglo-Saxon form it is probably a direct descendant of 'der Fremde', the concept to which two great scholars, whose own life may offer a pattern-case for the students of marginality and its socio-cultural role, allotted a prominent place in their entire system of social science (Georg Simmel in *Soziologie*, 1908; Robert Michels in *Der Patriotismus*, 1929). To both 'der Fremde' (the Stranger, not the Foreigner nor the Alien – it was the 'inmate alien', the 'inside outsider', that fascinated them as a paramount sociological topic) was one of the 'zeitlose soziale Formen'. To Michels in 1929, in a remarkable foreknowledge of the much later discoveries of the 1960s, the grave significance of the Stranger consisted in his being 'der Repräsentant des Unbekannten. Das Unbekannte bedeutet Absenz von Assoziation und flösst bis zur Antipathie gehende Scheu ein. Ein Holländisches Sprichwort sagt: onbekend maakt enbemind. Fremdenfeinschaft entsteht aus Fremdgefühl, das heisst Beziehunglosigkeit zwischen zwei Umwelten.'[36] To both Simmel and Michels the problem of the Stranger meant in the first place his vulnerability, the precarious feebleness of his community status, as well as the impact of his weakness on the attitudes and the Stranger-oriented behaviour of the group responsible for casting the Stranger into his peculiar niche. But simultaneously the iconoclastic, sacrilegious role of the Stranger had been increasingly emphasized. The stranger, Alfred Schutz would say, commits the unforgivable sin of sapping under Scheler's *relativ natürliche Weltanschauung*, the one which 'takes on for the members of the in-group the appearance of a *sufficient* coherence, clarity, and consistency to give anybody a reasonable chance of understanding and of being understood'. The Stranger's offence consists in the fact that he 'does not share . . . basic assumptions [and] has to place in question nearly everything that seems to be unquestionable to the members of the approached group'.[37] The ultimate root of the Stranger's threat is therefore somewhat shifted; it is now in his penchant for bizarre questions which would not occur to a 'normal' person, for contesting the very distinctions which for 'ordinary' people are attributes of the universe itself rather than their views of the world. It is not only that the sheer existence of the Stranger blurs the coveted clarity of the we-they division; the Stranger, as if the first crime were not enough, becomes willy-nilly the epicentre of a total earthquake, since he tends to challenge not just one but all the distinctions which make up the intelligible world. The term 'strangers' turns into a name of a type of behaviour rather than a kind of existential status. A person, to whom the *relativ natürliche Weltanschauung* of the group to which he physically (but not necessarily mentally) belongs is 'not a shelter but a field of adventure',[38] bears a genuinely striking resemblance to the Mannheimian free-floating intellectual *franc-tireur*, that insidious and remorseless 'unmasker, penetrator of lies and ideologies, relativizer and devaluator of immanent thought, disintegrator of *Weltanschauungen*'.[39] The victimage, guarding the community's cohesion and always hanging over treacherous frontierlands, is seen here as focused around a much wider phenomenon than existentially ambiguous border groups; it falls on everybody who dares to question the 'natural', supra-human, once-and-for-ever character of the order imposed on and by the common praxis.

It is worth noting that the scholars who deal with the phenomenon of marginality all too often fall into the trap of popular prejudices; the deeply rooted popular belief that trespassing in existentially separate realms testifies to a superhuman power in the trespasser; the act of striding over the borders, entering the territories one does not belong in – modelled perhaps in the commonsensical, but archetypal image on the sexual violation of the primordial opposition between male and female is seen as the ultimate measure of the transgressor's acumen, dexterity and dynamic potency. The scientists, being anything but immune to the well-nigh archetypal mandalas, rarely succeed in shaking off the vestiges of the superstitious respect for the homeless cultural vagabonds. It was the great Gilbert Murray who ascribed the miraculous eruption of Hellenic creativity to the endemic marginality of the Nordic conquerors of the Aegean.[40] Sociologists of the Chicago school used to be almost thrilled by their own design of the 'marginal personality type'. The marginal man – went the story told by Robert Park – 'lives in two worlds, in both of which he is more or less of a stranger'. For this reason his personality is conducive to 'spiritual instability, intensified self-consciousness, restlessness, and malaise'. Thus far we move within the limits of empirical discourse. But suddenly we are asked to jump to a rather unexpected conclusion: 'It is in the mind of the marginal man . . . that we can best study the processes of civilization and progress.'[41] Following this recipe, Peter Gay recently ascribed the meteoric flare-up of cultural creativity in the Weimar Republic to the restlessness of some outsiders who happened to find themselves indoors.[42] It is hard to overlook, indeed, the striking affinity between the persistent belief in the artistic potency of cultural hybrids and the equally persistent faith in the unsurpassable sexual prowess of the *American* Negro; or, for that matter, in the supra-natural astuteness of the perennial marginals, Jews, and the magical knowledge of Gypsies.

In the most comprehensive study of the marginals published to date Everett V. Stonequist expresses compassion and pity for the 'racial hybrids' only. Concurrently, he respectfully acknowledges the key role allegedly played by the 'cultural hybrids' in pushing forward the progress of mankind:[43]

Because of his in-between situation the marginal man may become an accurate and able critic of the dominant group and its culture. This is because he combines the knowledge and insight of the insider with the critical attitude of the outsider. . . . He is skilful in noting the contradictions and 'hypocrisis' in the dominant culture. The gap between its moral pretensions and its actual achievements jumps to his eye.

The stone catapulted against 'rootless intellectuals' to kill and destroy had been caught, remoulded and transmuted into the sceptre of unique, salutary power. The self-congratulating mood, being the exact reverse of the popular fear, found its ultimate and fullest expression in Karl Mannheim's idiom of the 'privileged cognitive perspective'. Intellectuals should be proud of their being free from *groepsbewussyn*, the Afrikaaner's defining feature of a human being; it is precisely because of this alleged handicap that they can disregard the parochial loyalties of nations, communities, classes, races. And whoever is potent enough to step over the earthly frontiers, is surely able to converse with the Absolute.

What it is in fact to be a marginal we are told, for example, by Kathleen Tamagawa:[44]

> The facts were these – in America I was Japanese. In Japan I was an American. I had an Oriental father who wished to live like an Occidental and an Irish mother who wished to live like Japanese. . . . I began to see that people thought in groups, in societies, in nations and in whole races, and that they all thought differently. The unaccepted, the unexpected like myself, must remain forever outside of it all. . . . Was I a Japanese doll, or a menace ?

Behind the chilling story of the split and tormented self lurks the tabooing ritual of communities eager to guard their boundaries against intruders who recklessly pitch their tents between the border stones. Ruled by the ubiquitous law of least effort,[45] human minds tend to submit their praxis to simple, straightforward either-or precepts. But successful dichotomization implies suppression of the centre. A group of American social scientists listed in 1954[46] several devices applied by closed groups to maintain their boundaries:

> Ritual initiations into the in-group; cleansing ceremonies to reintroduce an in-group member to his society after an absence; secret activities for in-group members only; localizing ceremonies in the homeland; the cultivation of self-defining concepts, such as ethnocentrism or racism; the posting of territory or the lowering of isolationist 'curtains'; the designation of contact agents or aliens 'handlers'; high evaluation of the group's language or dialect; the erection of legal barriers.

On the other hand, Florian Znaniecki in his study of the sociology of education, pointed out the many precautions and expedients with which any group warrants its decision to award 'full membership' to a newcomer – and particularly the elaborate rituals of the transitional period, in which the 'candidate' is kept at a safe distance and, simultaneously, under close surveillance.[47] Obviously there is a common denominator to all this ingenious variety of ways and means: the group's tendency to divide the world neatly and clearly into two parts and two only, in a manner which yields no intermediate situation, confusion and contentious interpretation. A few simple examples may show what this tendency may be like when in action.

The Nuer, as we were told by Evans-Pritchard, had decided that their animal-like monster-children were hippopotamuses who were misplaced in a human womb; the decision enabled the Nuer to put bizarre-looking babies into the nearest river, where their real kin, hippopotamuses, lived. The tradition-abiding Jews, keen on keeping their group well-defined and clean, eliminate the very danger of the half-Jew monsters – having resolved that the offspring of Gentile fathers are still Jews, if only born of a Jewish mother, but the descendants of a Gentile mother are unequivocally Gentiles whoever their father happened to be. Explaining why this legacy of the ghetto should be taken over and solidified by state law, the Prime Minister of Israel stated flatly, that 'permission for mixed marriages will not be given from this country.' Thirty-five years earlier, on 15 September 1935, the authorities of a highly civilized central-European country decided, for ideologically opposite, though structurally identical reasons, that 'any marriages between Jews and citizens of German or kindred blood are herewith forbidden. Marriages entered into despite this law are invalid, even if they are arranged abroad as a means of circumventing this law.'[48]

The way of resolving the noxious problem of marginals is hardly limited to a specific cultural tradition or historical epoch. In Europe, its diverse versions can easily be found in virtually all periods of history. It was an unshakable article of faith, for example, in the Middle Ages, that 'although in an ideal Aristotelian sense each form might be thought of as striving to perfect itself, the process of perfection if indeed it involved motion or change in any mundane sense, took place solely within the conceptual boundaries of each category of the scale, not from category to category.' As it were, 'the vertical transmission of traits over "tracts" of time, the maintenance of tradition with its end product, temporal cultural uniformity, was regarded universally as good. . . . On the other hand, diffusion proper, or the lateral, horizontal, and overland transmission of culture was regarded as bad.'[49] This shapely, cohesive view of the world had its counterpart in the praxis, in shapely, cohesive corporations, in which reciprocally contrasting qualities were hermetically sealed without the slightest tendency to osmosis. Insofar as everybody held willingly to his own place, nobody was likely to feel particularly perturbed by the others' oddity. The result of the nearly perfect cohesion of praxis was the peculiar cultural blindness for which the Middle Ages are famous, the mysterious immunity which caused the pilgrims to the Holy Sepulchre to overlook the strangeness of the ways of life they came across while travelling through alien lands; which made Europe look with bovine equanimity on the strange creatures Columbus brought from the other shore of the Atlantic; which, finally, inspired the intellectual elite of the time to condemn excessive sensitivity to alien ways as *turpis curiositas*.

With the advent of the constantly changing, highly unstable modern world the perpetual stability of types could not be taken for granted any more; neither was it enough to wave away the few deviations with the aid of curt moral precepts. The orderliness of the human world, far from being automatically assured, now became a matter of continuous and active concern. The physical proximity of others now acquired menacing qualities when combined with cultural osmosis and the new, uneasy consciousness of the mutability and transmutational potency of forms. Much as the Jews were feared and despised in the Middle Ages (there was always an in-built marginality in being a Jew in the Christian world: infidels, who are the authors of at least half of Holy Scripture; the relatives and the killers of God; parents of the Holy, rejecting and rejected by their offspring), it was only the decay of the mediaeval order which turned the *Judengasse*, the symbol of privilege and corporative autonomy, desired above all by the Jews themselves and granted on their request, into the compulsory confinement of a walled ghetto, initiated by Pope Paul IV in Rome in 1555.[50] Raymond Aron expressed the opinion that antisemitism – a modern phenomenon *sensu stricto* – emerged in connection with the coincidence between the Jews leaving their isolation and the advent of modernity; everybody who had reasons to fear the change, and who felt threatened by the gradual nibbling away of what formerly used to be the trustworthy, majestically immutable Order, could easily forge his anxiety into the weapon aimed at the people who, by dint of their recent marginality, most fully reflected the advent of Chaos. The sudden spate of witchhunting, strangely out of place in the age of belligerent rationalism and the triumphant progress of empirical science (the apparent contradiction which Trevor-Roper recently so aptly brought to public attention), becomes easily intelligible if cast against the same background of total and intense anxiety rooted in the decay of the customary order. Similarly, the intrusion of Pakistanis and West Indians into the British Isles coincided with the disappearance of the imperial power which served many a Briton as the raw material from which to build up his feeling of secure order. One may be inclined therefore to focus on West Indians and Asians the frightful powers of the 'invisible enemy', who makes the danger to Britain's future greater today than 'in the years when Imperial Germany was building dreadnoughts, or Nazism rearming'.[51]

The nineteenth century witnessed numerous attempts to prevent the hybrid of Modernity from undermining the harmonious build-up of the human Universe. The real size and significance of the tendency become assessable only if we turn our eyes from the lamentably 'scientific' twaddle of a Gobineau or a Houston Chamberlain to the statements of the persons who set the pattern of the intellectual climate. Madison Grant, for example, when stating bluntly that 'the cross between a white man and an Indian is an Indian; the cross between a white man and a Hindu is a Hindu; and a cross between any of these European races and a Jew is a Jew',[52] was much more representative of the popular desire for the restoration of unequivocality than the excesses of the fathers of modern racialism. Indeed, Grant was entirely in line with the intellectual folklore of his epoch. The learned members of the Anthropological Society of London in a debate of 1865 acted on a couple of simple premises, which according to Fred Plog and Paul Bohannan ran as follows: 'If "natives" become "civilized", the fact may be attributable to "civilized" (perhaps illegitimate) ancestors'; or 'the change may be "nominal" or purely superficial'. Since the actual, genuine mixture of the 'native' and 'civilized' essences may produce only a monster, 'they seem to copy and keep all the vices of the white men and but few of their virtues. . . . In plain words, I found that every Christian negress was a prostitute, and that every Christian negro was a thief.'[53]

The most sinister and awe-inspiring of all ambiguities is, however, a hidden one – the one people may fail to locate in good time. That is what most worried a French anti-semitic crusader, Édouard Drumont: 'It is easy to appreciate that Jews who are not distinguished by their costumes are all the more effective because they are less visible. In the civil service, in diplomacy, in the offices of conservative newspapers, even in the priest's cassock, they live unsuspected.'[54] The most effective, though simplest, solution would be, of course, conspicuously marking the dangerous areas of ambiguity. It was proposed as early as 1815 by Christian Friedrich Rühs that 'solche Allerweltmenschen, die man . . . Juden nennt' (expression coined by Ernst Moritz Arnt) should wear a yellow patch on their dress.[55] The idea was to be made the best of by the Nazi law-makers, who decreed that the Jewish Star was to be placed both on the dress of Jews and on the entrances to their houses, and made compulsory the addition of Israel and Sarah to the names of Jewish males and females respectively.

The method looks like being foolproof, but not the most convenient and not always practicable. The alternative is a sort of 'psychological marking', which consists in cultivating deliberately – in fact whipping up to hysterical proportions – the instinctive fear of ambiguity. There is a proverb saying that fear has big eyes; the method consists in making them as big as possible. Much less harm can be done by ostracizing the unjustly suspected than by failure to recognize an enemy in disguise. If people cannot apply warning lights, they often settle for magnifying search beams.[56]

> The *nature* of a viper is to crawl, to have a scaly skin, hollow and moveable fangs which exude poisonous venom; and the nature of man is to be a cognitive, religious and sociable animal. All experience teaches us this; and, to my knowledge, nothing has contradicted this experience. If someone wants to prove that the nature of the viper is to have wings and a sweet voice, and that of a beaver to live alone at the top of the highest mountain, it is up to him to prove it.

Whoever lets this advice pass his ears and is left unconvinced of the overwhelming potency of the 'nature', which will eventually vindicate its rights, is told of the agonizing experience of a French duke who 'had married a Rothschild from Frankfurt in spite of his mother's tears. He called his little son, pulled a golden louis from his pocket and showed it to him. The child's eyes lit up. "You see," continued the duke, "the semitic instinct reveals itself right away."'[57] Moral-political norms ('one should stay with one's own kind'), the cognitive propensity to stereotype, and myths collaborate to keep vital frontiers of the human universe free from trespassers.

Miss Hazel E. Barnes, the American translator of *L'Être et le néant*, aptly chose the term 'slimy' as the English counterpart of the famous Sartrean 'le visqueux'.[58] The latest edition of Webster's *New International Dictionary* explains the term as 'viscous, glutinous', but spells out with that its other meanings: 'vile, offensive, vulgar'. One can hardly find another term in which the image of an amorphic, jelly-like, oozy substance fuses so exactly and consummately with the feeling of nauseating repulsion.

> If an object which I hold in my hands is solid, I can let go when I please; its inertia symbolizes for me my total power. . . . Yet here is the slimy reversing the terms; the

> For-itself is suddenly *compromised*, I open my hands, I want to let go of the slimy and it sticks to me, it draws me, it sucks at me . . . I am no longer the master in *arresting* the process of appropriation. It continues. In one sense it is like the supreme docility of the possessed, the fidelity of a dog who *gives himself* even when one does not want him any longer, and in another sense there is underneath this docility a surreptitious appropriation of the possessor by the possessed.

It is a 'poisonous possession'; 'the slime is like a liquid seen in a nightmare, where all its properties are animated by a sort of life and turn back against me.' It is a nightmare, because 'to touch the slimy is to risk being dissolved in sliminess.' The snare of the slimy lies in its fluidity; 'essentially ambiguous', 'aberrant' 'imitation of liquidity', to be sure. Its mode of being is treacherous, appropriating, greedy, and that is why 'so long as the contact with the slimy endures, everything takes place for us as if sliminess were the meaning of the entire world or the unique mode of being of being-in-itself.'

We have come a long way from Frazer's attempt to explain the primitive belief in the magical qualities of feces, menstrual blood or nail and hair clippings by referring them to the aberrant logic of magic which allegedly dominates the primitive mind until vanquished by triumphant modernity. What once seemed to us a deplorable deficiency of the immature mind, which will eventually recoil with little resistance before the cogency of modern reason, we see now as a case, conspicuous since strange, of a much more general rule of human praxis, whose domain extends far beyond the realm of 'primitive' culture. The point has been made lucidly and extensively by Mary Douglas:[59]

> When we honestly reflect of our busy scrubbings and cleanings – we know that we are not mainly trying to avoid disease. We are separating, placing boundaries, making visible statements about the home we are intending to create out of the material house. If we keep the bathroom cleaning materials away from the kitchen cleaning materials and send the men to the downstairs lavatory and the women upstairs, we are essentially doing the same thing as the Bushman wife when she arrives at a new camp. She chooses where she will place her fire and then sticks a rod in the ground. This orientates the fire and gives it a right and left side. Thus the home is divided between male and female quarters. . . . The difference between us is not that our behaviour is grounded on science and theirs on symbolism. Our behaviour also carries symbolic meaning. The real difference is that we do not bring forward from one context to the next the same set of ever more powerful symbols; our experience is fragmented. Our rituals create a lot of little sub-worlds, unrelated. Their rituals create one single, symbolically consistent universe.

The difference is between two types of social structures, not between two distinct structures of human praxis. In both there are the same endemic truculence against the slimy, the same thoroughness and consistency in imposing on the surrounding world whatever passes for the human order. Only in one case the 'surrounding world' is small and cosy enough to be embraced by a single set of ordering devices; in the other it consists of many intercrossing planes, each leading a partly autonomous life and offering partly autonomous semantic fields to anchor meanings. Multiplicity of symbolic codes in lieu of a coherent, unified code; but the procedure of signifying and deciphering signs remains much the same.

Mary Douglas is a staunch and faithful Durkheimian, at least as far as *Purity and Danger* goes; she firmly believes that *nihil est in sensu, quod non prius fuerit in* society. The odd persistence with which humans of all epochs fight disorder in their households and in the vulnerable areas adjacent to their bodies is accountable for, she postulates, by the perennial requisites of societal solidarity. It is 'society' that tries hard to survive, e.g. to keep its structure intact, or to force people to respect it in their behaviour, by bringing the message home through a series of symbolic, ritualistic battles against disorder as such. There is no reason why people should fear disorder if it were not a 'societal' disorder; indeed, they would hardly see an arrangement as 'disorderly' were it not a symbolic exercise in cleansing the only 'objective' disorder – a violation of the social structure. Nail-clipping is a threatening, fear-inspiring event only insofar as it symbolizes transgression of the group boundaries. We would say, there is a semiotic system which transforms defecating in private into a *signifiant* of the *signifié* of defending social stratification. 'We cannot possibly interpret rituals concerning excreta, breast milk, saliva, and the rest unless we are prepared to see in the body a symbol of society, and to see the powers and dangers credited to social structure reproduced in small on the human body.'[60] Mennenius Agrippa's ubiquitous metaphor is indeed immortal.

It would, however, be hard to imagine how society, or indeed any kind of ordered network of human relationships, would be possible in the first place, were there not a propensity to ordering praxis built into the human animals. One can trace a long and almost continuous line leading from the lower animals to Man and drawn by the changing nature of the organism-environment adaptive process. The line is paralleled on the level of mental qualities, i.e. intelligence: 'The more generalized functions of the organism,' says Piaget, 'organization, adaptation and assimilation – are all found once more when we turn to the cognitive domain, where all of them play the same essential part.'[61] The two structures – of bodily adaptation and intelligence operations – are indeed isomorphic, since the substance of intelligence, which entails both instinctual, hereditary repertory and input of learning, is nothing but the assimilatory-accommodating process of adaptation accomplished without 'material', irreversible changes in environment and without organic alteration of the body-in-adaptation. The broadening of the operative capacity of the organism in the process of evolution seemed to be accompanied by a consistent change in the composition of intelligence. The change has been taking place in two dimensions at least: (*a*) increase in the number of oppositions the organism is able to distinguish meaningfully, i.e. as releasers of distinctive modes of behaviour; (*b*) relative enhancement of the role played by behavioural discriminations learned through ontogenesis as compared to the instinctual repertory of the species. In both dimensions the process reached its peak in the human species. But the two trends of development, if combined, produce both necessity and capacity of supplementing (or, indeed, replacing) the natural order with an artificial one.

The more oppositions an organism is capable of distinguishing meaningfully, the 'richer' becomes its assimilated environment, the more involved the corresponding structure of internal organization; but the less tolerant is the organism of even subtle vacillations of environmental state. Worms, which distinguish very few and very generalized oppositions like dry-moist, bright-dark, may indeed survive a fairly wide range of environmental revolutions without noticeable alteration of their own structure; in a way, they are, species-wise, 'perfectly adapted' to a practically unlimited spectrum of widely differing conditions. This cosy and inherently stable situation, however, changes dramatically with the gradual increase in the number of cognitively accessible oppositions reciprocated by diversified behavioural patterns. The organism becomes inevitably more selective toward the range of available environments, and successively less tolerant toward their fluctuations; a deepened dependence on the unstable environment goes together with the gained flexibility of behaviour. The more 'specific' biologically is the species' adaptation, the less likely is the opposite evolutionary response to a new set of environmental demands. In short, the cognitively and behaviourally richer organism has in fact a diminished survival capacity. There is only one way of offsetting this paradoxical handicap: through shifting the brunt of adaptation from the species to the individual, from instinct to learning. But even the powerful instrument of learning (i.e. becoming sensitive to new semiotic oppositions and making them meaningful, i.e. attaching to them the correspondingly opposed patterns of response) would have only limited adaptive value, still being confined to a single, however widely conceived, type of environment to which the species is sensorily and effector-wise adjusted. The genuine 'increase in the possibilities acquired by the organism in the course of evolution', in which Piaget, following Rensch, sees the best measure of evolutionary progress,[62] becomes possible only if the ability to learn is supplemented by the growing capacity of the species to keep the environment (now incomparably richer in its meaning, and thus unlikely to remain 'stable' on its own) within the parameters delineating the frontiers of the species' evolutionary adaptation. Optimalization of the living conditions in a highly sensitive, semiotically rich, behaviourally diversified species may be accomplished, if at all, only through the active creation of an artificially (i.e. with the species' activity) stabilized environment. In other words, it requires the ordering praxis. Human praxis, with all its functionally inevitable generative rules, seems to be a prerequisite of human society, rather than its symbolically motivated artefact.

Feces and menstrual blood, nail and hair clippings need not symbolize street riots or *coups d'état* to be disgusting, mysterious, or even horrifying. They are what they are – almost instinctively – to us because of their 'slimy' semiotical status. They belong neither here nor there; they trespass the boundary whose unambiguity is the very foundation of order. They share this treacherous quality with foxes or mice, who belong to the 'wilderness' but foist their commensality upon us; or with strangers, who try to reconcile the irreconcilable: to be aliens and natives at the same time. Their 'sliminess' has little to do with their substance; it is, unlike the 'natural' slime, the product of human praxis. The quality of 'sliminess' fills the overlapping areas of the man-created distinctions, though, probably, to a varying degree. In this, genetic-semiotic sense rather than as symbols, the slime traces its location to the activity of the society. Or, more precisely, to the human ordering praxis.

An illuminating example of the endemic slime-generating quality of human praxis has been analysed at length by Leach in his classical study of *Magical Hair*. If a peculiar hairdress is chosen to signify a social status of the individual (as a sign discriminating between this and all other parts of the social structure), then a person *with* the hairdress belongs to a different category (defined by a distinct set of rights and duties) from that of a person without. But then the procedure of creating the hairdress, which involves the clipping of hair, is a potent creative act of bestowing on the person his new defining quality. And so the hair clippings, in addition to their 'natural' sliminess acquire a new, praxis-generated one, and their magic powers are intensified and magnified. They straddle not only the well-nigh pre-cultural boundary between 'me' and 'not-me'; they are on the two sides of an insurmountable wall meant to keep apart two distinct social positions. 'The act of separation . . . not only creates two categories of persons, it also creates a third entity, the thing which is ritually separated.'[63] We could say that its status is as unbearable as that of menstrual blood, though the pattern has been reversed: had not the blood been discharged, a new human being would have been born; had not the hair been clipped, the person would have remained in his previous status. Menstrual blood means death of the unborn; ritual hair-clipping means re-birth of the dead. The magic of the hair-clippings falls into one category with the mystique of the 'honour of uniform', disdain for the 'nouveau riche' and the fear-ridden admiration for double agents.

Prior to the human perception of sliminess there is, therefore, praxis. The relation of the two offers a wide, multi-dimensional programme of what seems to promise to be a fruitful research, rich in significant findings. The perspective we advocate suggests partly, a re-arrangement of numerous findings acquired within other analytical frameworks; partly, however, it does require research of an entirely new design. In both cases the task exceeds the limited volume of this study. What is to be done may be sketched here only in very broad and general outlines.

(1) The first dimension of the sought-for relation may be epitomized in the notion of 'cultural density'. As we know well, each culture is relatively rich in fine and subtle distinctions in one part of its cognitive field, while relatively poor in its remaining parts. The areas of particular concentration of meaningful oppositions, in which even the slightest hues are noted and marked, constitute probably a central core of the given type of praxis. Some of these areas are easily traceable to the technology of biological survival; the more so, it seems, the closer to the level of bare subsistence the society in question is. In societies with primitive technology, in which the most precarious sector of praxis is the one which bears direct relevance to the Man-Nature relation, the tabooed areas of sliminess tend to be focused around natural phenomena. In societies which, like early Western European feudalism, seem to be organized

mainly around the praxis of keeping a number of stomachs full amid a predominantly undernourished majority, the cultural repertoire is particularly
ingenious in multiplying fine social distinctions and tabooing social mobility
(we can see a not too different picture in our modern era, if we consider
mankind as a global society). It may be that with class differences somewhat
losing their former importance in conditions of relative abundance, and with
breathtakingly swift changes offering the hardest resistance to meaningful
assimilation, the focus of cultural density shifts into the inter-generational
areas, to which hypothesis the current contagious mystique of the 'slimy'
adolescent generation bears eloquent testimony. All these are, of course,
broad types of density foci, which do not exclude – in fact, imply – an exu-
berant diversity of more specific choices actually made within the type.
Neither do we wish to suggest, at this incipient stage of research, any kind of
technological or socio-structural determination of cultural phenomena; nothing is more alien to our intention, since the assumption, which has been
repeatedly emphasized in this study, is that all these facets of human existence
stem from the same root of human praxis. When analysing praxis, one would
do better to defy and abandon the pervasive tendency to split the analytically
distinguishable facets of the process into causes and effects. If one neglects or
fails to do it, the unavoidable penalty is another round of the sterile argument
between two equally well-founded but equally one-sided positions.

It is well known, for example, that the frequency and sophistication of Van
Gennep's *rites de passage*, or, as Raymond Firth has it, telectic rites ('putting
off the old and putting on the new')[64] shrink drastically with the advent of the
modern, complex and highly mobile society. The phenomenon has been
commented upon by a number of anthropologists. In this celebrated theory of
ceremonies, Max Gluckman rightly traced the sudden disappearance of once
ubiquitous rites back to the fact that the passage to a new role is in our society associated in most cases with a change of the set of interacting persons;
the new and the old groups alike know the individual in question in one role
only, so the public announcement of a new social quality of the individual
(which is the essence of *rites de passage*) will be superfluous. The underlying
ratiocination is, probably, the following: the omnipresence and high frequency
of the rites are called for by the requirements of a small, self-sustained society, in which individuals cumulate multiple roles, each being performed in a
functionally separate context of interaction, but in the same group, meeting
constantly, though on diversified planes; in a modern, complex society, the
spectators, addressees and partners of each role an individual may play
change together with the role played at the moment; the said rites, therefore,
not only lose their function and become redundant, but are meaningless to
the audience unaware of their structural context. The rites cease to be, in consequence, 'determined' by the structure of the society; and so they gradually
wither away.

Convincing and acceptable as it may seem, the above explanation – for all
the subtlety and refinement of the notion of determination it employs – would
not stand the test of the methodology of praxis. True, the context of a small-

scale, self-sustained, multi-tier network of intense social interaction 'presses' toward conspicuousness and clear visibility of the signs which signal behavioural crossroads. Still, the ease and versatility with which individuals pass from one role to another, sure that the adequate response from their companions will follow, constitute an achievement for which precisely the *rites de passage* must be held largely responsible. The type of society under discussion is created and perpetuated, among other things, by the praxis of *les rites*. This apparent reciprocity of influences is often handled with a logic-defying concept of the 'interaction of cause and effect' which, obviously, ridicule rather than rescues the conventional determinism. The whole idea of cause in relation to effect assumes the existence of the cause independent of the occurrence or non-occurrence of the effect; but this is precisely not the case in the analysed example as it is not, for that matter, in any other field of praxis.

The relationship we try to comprehend similarly resists treatment in conventional functional terms. The project of functionalism as explanatory methodology aims at a self-defeating target. It would not content itself with modelling the network of communications between the units of an empirically accessible or logically imaginable system; it wishes to account for the occurrence of some of these units in terms of 'requirements', 'prerequisites', or, simply, determination by other units or the 'system' as a whole, as a supra-entity. I. C. Jarvie rightly remarked that in selecting the system as the ultimate frame of reference the functionalist project can hardly live up to its own pretensions, 'it does not go beyond the facts it intends to explain',[65] and so what it offers is not what we are accustomed to mean by 'explanation' (reduction to a rule more general than the case explained). Important as the point is, the reasons for the endemic unsuitability of the functional project for the treatment of human praxis go much deeper than the still arguable awkwardness of functionalism in face of the task of deducing 'functions' from 'prerequisites' (rather than postulating 'prerequisites' from the presence of 'functions', which – in opposition to its explicit programme – functionalism in fact does). They go as deep as the very pivot of the functionalist methodology, the classification of the analytical units into dependent and independent, which is the legacy of the deterministic methodology absorbed and assimilated by functionalism; as Ernest Nagel would have it – into G's ('goals') and SC's ('state coordinates') of the system.[66] The G's have been specified in many different ways; among the most popular substitutions we can name the survival of a particular network of social relations, stability of a central value cluster, maintenance of a specific body politic. In each case the methodological position is much the same: some repeatable patterns of human praxis are 'explained' by pointing out the role played by them in the service of a 'G'. In this sense the essential logical frame of reasoning bears a striking resemblance to the one hallowed by the deterministic tradition: in a couple of events under scrutiny, one is endowed with a superior, the second with a subordinate or derivative role. The one difference between the two explanatory projects consists in determinism aiming at *deducing* the second event *from* the first, with functionalism practising rather a *reduction* from the second to the first. When, however, confronted with the dialectical methodology of praxis, this difference, whatever the intellectual passions it has aroused, bears only minor importance. The methodology of praxis radically opposes preferential treatment of any analytically separable aspect of the social process: from its perspective, the 'social structure' and the 'cultural' (in the ideational sense of the distinction) facets of the process are as inseparable and resistant to all 'hierarchization' as are *signifiant* and *signifié* in a sign-event.

The differentiation of the culturally distinct communities from the point of view of their focus of 'cultural density' (the point on which the most intense anti-sliminess activities are concentrated) can be best accounted for if dealt with from the perspective of the methodology of praxis. The rules of the praxis themselves, which transcend the boundaries of any single cultural community, may be 'explained', in a deterministic manner, by referring to their biological-species-evolutionary roots or biological-neurophysiological substratum; or in functional terms, when their correspondence to the pre-human nature of the universe, and, consequently, their adaptive value, are put to the fore. But neither the deterministic nor the functionalist project can provide an explanation of the specific use these rules are put to by specific cultures, an explanation immune to the indictment of inconclusiveness and one-sidedness. One would be well-advised to hold in memory Boas' recently unfashionable warnings against the neglect of history, without necessarily going all the way with this most influential adversary of cultural universals. What defies all attempts to apply consistently either deterministic or functionalist approaches to the historical praxis is its essential unpredictability, not necessarily at odds with 'inevitability' (as in the case of biological evolution or, for that matter, the development of intelligence the particular junction which was called by Piaget, following Lalande, 'vection').[67] Whatever happened, was 'determined' by virtue of the sheer logic of the deterministic analytical framework; but nothing which has not yet occurred, nothing still unaccomplished can be deduced unequivocally from what has already been petrified into a fact, since previous events constrain rather than determine their sequences in processes like biological evolution, growth of knowledge or the totality of human history. Nothing but the formal universals of praxis, its 'generative rules', constitutes the tough, invariant core of human history; and perhaps even this can be reasonably claimed only insofar as we deliberately confine our vision to the life-span of our species, which is, in itself, a historical event in a wider context.

(2) The second dimension of variation in reactions to sliminess is related to the stuff of which the warning signs 'Beware, the road is slimy' are made. This is a specific case of a much larger issue, of the diversity of substance of which the cultural item-signs are manufactured, and the relation of this medium to the socio-cultural distinctions these items mark and produce. We have dealt with this more generally phrased problem in the second chapter; we pointed out then, that whatever is the position in language, the non-linguistical cultural signs do not stand the test of arbitrariness of the *significant* in relation to *signifié*'. Most cultural items, whether artefacts of praxis or its patterns, are

related in more than just one, semiotical, way to the human life-process. In the present context the important thing is that the relative weight assigned to specific ways may change, depending on the shifts in the focus of the cultural density.

In their comprehensive survey of recent studies of aggressive behaviour[68] R. Charles Boelkin and Jon F. Heiser mention the threat to status as one of the major stimuli of an aggressive response. The established position of an individual is perpetuated and fortified by a plethora of signs, mostly patterned in the ritual of interaction:

> Between two men with different rank in the same organization the lower-ranking man usually will defer to his superior by opening doors; by following rather than leading through narrow passageways; by conceding first chance at the water cooler, or the bar, or the hors d'oeuvres; by offering to get coffee; by speaking less and listening more; and in many other ways too numerous to mention.

Boelkin and Heiser concentrate in the above description on signs meant to warrant the status of an individual directly, i.e. via the conduct of others addressed and oriented to him. But these signs belong semiotically in one category with all other ordering, frontier drawing-and-guarding signs, responsible for the continuation of the meaningful, predictable, and thus secure arrangement of events. What has been threatened by withdrawal of the signs of the 'individual' status deference is the feeling of certainty and manageability of the situation. But the same feeling, crucial to interaction, is in jeopardy if any other 'gate' mounted in any of the 'boundary zones' (Kurt Lewin's terms)[69] and governed either by 'impersonal', i.e. dispersed, rules, or by specific personalized 'gatekeepers', may go out of control. We can, therefore, postulate a similar extension of the scope of 'boundary violation' to which the following summary of Boelkin and Heiser applies:

> A superior will first detect the elements of a challenge when a closely ranked inferior ceases acting deferentially and assumes behaviour patterns consistent with those occurring between rank-equals [i.e. engenders a typically 'slimy' situation]. Recognizing a threat to his status [or, more generally, violation of order founded on unequivocality of discriminations], the threatened [in his cognitive-emotional security] individual may initiate a variety of repressive measures designed to 'put the upstart in his place'.

Predisposition to aggressive responses is aroused and prompted by a variety of events which hardly share a common feature except the incidence of 'frontier trespassing'. With remarkable insight Thelma Veness[70] accounts for the common aggression arising from an infringement on 'personal space' in overcrowded conditions by postulating an endemic fear of the loss of identity. Everything entering the 'personal space' becomes automatically slimy and releases the impulse of tabooing. Now, we should beware of taking the notion of 'personal space' too literally; the tendency of many psychologists, the ethologists in particular, to define the concept in its immediate, topographical sense of 'physical proximity' is well understandable in view of their interest in widely based behavioural propensities, which humans share with other animals; but the space in which human beings live is largely symbolic, and the proclivity to discriminate, which in the case of animals may materialize only in the media supplied by Nature, is set by humans upon a symbolic canvas, which often resists any attempt to map it in 'physical' space or time. Thus, the 'personal space' stands for security of status as well as the security of the body; 'life space', for the safety of the group boundaries as well as the inviolability of the grazing or hunting territory; while a large area of conceptual borders is unthinkable outside a symbolic universe and so has at best only a slight relation to the animal world.

Again, the problem which of many symbolically marked frontiers is perceived as particularly vulnerable and, therefore, most slime-generating depends ultimately on human praxis, as, inversely, does toleration of frontier-crossing and the illicit use of unbecoming, inappropriate and thus confusing signs. The material on which the signs are embossed is, above all, a technical matter. But for a few perennial stuffs supplied universally by Nature (hair, facial adornment, arms and bust shaping etc.),[71] which are the obvious first choice in most circumstances, almost all the materials vary, depending on the kind of substance processed in the course of praxis. The important point is that not all 'natural' differences are necessarily and in all circumstances perceived as frontier posts; they become such only if granted a social meaning by the communal praxis. Not very long ago the dress of the young was the ordinary 'adult dress' cut to a smaller measure, precisely as the young were socially defined as 'grown-ups' in miniature and measured by their growing proximity to the established adult standards. Sartorial standards have undergone the drastic change they did ensuing the abandonment of the old 'apprenticeship' concept and the congestion of significant social distinctions around the inter-generational frontiers. Similarly, there is ample evidence that skin colour went unnoticed in the ancient Mediterranean and was hardly thought important enough to be put on record; in the racial farrago of the Roman Empire social differences did not overlap with the 'natural' divisions, and the 'natural' distinctions between men were, purely and simply, not perceived, much less paid heed to. It takes, says Roland Barthes, a myth to 'transform history into nature',[72] to believe that the product of human praxis is an unencroachable law of Nature. One can hardly think of any exception to this rule, even in the case of such 'obviously natural', because well-nigh universal and pan-historical, differences as the one between man and woman. Modern praxis gnaws vigorously at our seemingly unshakeable trust in the irrevocability of this solidly established distinction by challenging the sanctified sexual oppositions in dress, courtship and intercourse roles, social habits, deference hierarchy etc. It is not that the frontier signs suddenly became illegible or lost their attraction with a recent swing in fashion: what did happen in this case, as in all similar cases of specific signs losing their signifying power, is the pushing away of the frontier itself; the signs, without ceasing to exist in the physical sense, are not border stones any more, and their unordered staggering does not lead to the 'slimying' of the invaded areas.

(3) The last dimension we wish to comment on briefly is that of the differentiation between individuals and groups within the whole which can be

reasonably considered a single culture. There is no uniformity in the degree of tolerance of the culturally defined sliminess. The problem of the response to sliminess is coextensive with the issues variously named as responses to uncertainty or to the feeling of insecurity, such as action under stress or the impact of frustrated expectations etc. Much has been written on all these topics and there is a rather broad agreement between psychologists that individual (personal biography with particular emphasis on childhood and pre-natal experience, as well as individual variations of genotype) and group-based (frequency and quality of interaction, information accessibility, dominance relations etc.) variables modify human behaviour in the above respects, though much less agreement has been reached as to the volume, much less the mechanism, of the intervention. It is, however, broadly agreed that tolerance of ambiguous situations is inversely related to personal and group insecurity; though equally ample evidence may easily be amassed to bear out the thesis of an intimate relation between insecurity and creativity, which obviously presages a lack of respect for the traditionally sanctified divisions. I doubt whether the progress of our reliable knowledge of the problem since 1954 has already outdated the conclusion reached then by Gordon W. Allport, that in the case of any particular condensation of intolerance of ambiguity 'maximum understanding of the problem can be gained only by knowing the historical context of each single case'[73] – which means, by appealing to praxis. In view of the notorious inconclusiveness of psychological findings, whatever follows must be treated as tentative probing of the field rather than articulate hypothesis.

It may be that the lack of success in arriving at a universally supported view on the subject under discussion is due to an unnoticed confusion present in some studies of the response to ambiguity. Since, for obvious reasons, the vision of any given researcher is narrowed to one, however generalized, kind of ambiguity, what is taken for a tolerant attitude to ambiguity as such may testify only to a 'thematic shift' in sensitivity to the slimy. It may be, that for some reason the whole universe-ordering effort of an individual or a group, in defiance of the attitude typical of their wider social neighbourhood, is condensed in one or a handful of distinctions; and for good reason, to be sure, since the preservation of these distinctions, and these distinctions alone, may decide the whole outcome of the group praxis – may, for example, secure for the group the sought for locus in the social structure which provides the focal point of the total world-view. One doubts whether groups, or categories of individuals, can be classified at all according to their global intensity of resentment of all kinds of equivocality alike. It is rather that (owing to the peculiarities of the group praxis or to individual idiosyncrasies) the foci of ambiguity most intensely resented or the types of sliminess most obsessively feared are differently located.

The perception of the particularly vehement intolerance displayed by radical movements may be founded, at least in part, on an optical illusion of a sort. Since the totality of the social existence of the group depends on the promotion of group ends which have not yet won the day, and since these ends exist solely as a project little warranted by commonsensical reality (unlike their better-established adversaries, who are accepted by popular 'reason'), a unique emotional intensity must be focused on the single task, and unusual care must be taken to guard the purity of the group and the clarity of its frontiers. The totality of the group praxis is indeed congested around the 'we-they' frontier line (at the expense of the other otherwise vulnerable and sensitive borders: hence the notorious dissolving of the individual in his group in most radical movements), with one 'we' only chosen to the detriment of all others, which are so varied in 'usual' circumstances. It may be that the logic of the peculiar praxis rather than self-selection of peculiar individuals accounts intelligibly for the odd conduct of radical groups. There is, indeed, little room left by the predicament of a group in a radical war with society for a liberal attitude, which was aptly defined by Barthes as 'a sort of intellectual equilibrium based on recognized places'.[74] The praxis of a radical movement is precisely about 'de-recognizing' the recognized places; and, above all, not only the places, but the projected totality within which the radical movement may be placed, are far from being recognized. The widely accepted opinion of the intense intolerance of the radicals and the radical groups toward ambiguity can hardly be squared with the notorious readiness of many radical movements to defy and trespass all other sacred divisions; the whole of their alleged intolerance is, in fact, discharged in the vigilance expressed in the famous formula 'whoever is not with us, is against us', meant to sweep clean of sliminess a single but vital frontier.

At this point we have come across an important distinction, which, *malgré tout*, has to be drawn inside the 'radical camp'. As popular wisdom, exacerbated by many a liberal-minded scholar, has it – *les extrêmes se touchent*, and the radicalisms of right and left dissolve in an all-embracing image of pugnacious, militant intolerance. They meet indeed – but only from the perspective of liberalism, which is the *Weltanschauung* of a secure and well-established world, in which everybody keeps to his recognized place; the tolerance is extended willingly, since it is hardly necessary. When the perspective of tolerance (toward established order, or rather toward everybody, since everybody acknowledges it) versus intolerance (toward established order, or rather toward the majority, since the majority acknowledges it) is applied, the right and left radicalisms indeed steer suspiciously close to each other. Within this perspective the effort to draw a clear line between the two is truly frustrating. In a sense the final failure is built into the original sin of selecting a cognitive perspective uncongenial to the task. Contrary to the opinion which is rather gaining ground in academic science, it seems that there are reasonably clear criteria to warrant the traditional distinction between radicalisms of the left and of the right, (though not necessarily between organizations claiming this label) whatever the number of Mussolinis and Doriots that can be brought out as a misleadingly persuasive proof to the contrary.

We wish to propose tentatively the following distinctions: the distinguishing feature of right-wing radicalism is a widely diffused, unspecified and amorphic, dispersed intolerance. Its sensitivity to the threat of sliminess does not arise from the project it tries to foist upon the world but finds as yet at variance with reality; on the contrary, it selects the securely habitual reality, spreading all around, well founded, mirrored in scores of reciprocally reinforcing events, predictable and unobtrusively obvious, as the only tolerable (or, indeed, the only habitable) universe. It is endemically short of any project sidetracking from the well-trodden routes; it is, in fact, motivated in its radicalism by its intrinsic fear of the unusual, the strange, the not-yet-materialized, the unknown; fear of the idea as set against the reality. Right-wing radicalism cannot transcend the vantage point of the real; that is why it is terrified by an idea which questions the unchallengeable monopoly and wisdom of the real and thus calls for scrutiny of the obvious, i.e. of the inscrutable. The intolerance of the right-wing is, therefore, as unfocused, as the reality itself which it defends. It lies in wait instead in scores of ambushes laid wherever the reality meets its own future.

There is a social type (rather than class) whose status predestines it to the role of the chief purveyor of right-wing radicalism. Since Marx, the type has been called petit-bourgeois. To quote Roland Barthes again, 'the petit-bourgeois is a man unable to imagine the Other. If he comes face to face with him, he blinds himself, ignores and denies him, or else transforms him into himself. . . . This is because the Other is a scandal which threatens his essence.'[75] There is no room for the Other in the petit-bourgeois finite universe of meaning, since the essence of the petit-bourgeois is the universal, endlessly and monotonously repeated mirroring of one and the same existential pattern; the Average elevated to the absolute heights of Universality. The mode of being of the Average is that of the slimy; indeed, the prototype of sliminess. The Average ruminates on everything it comes across. It devours, digests and transmogrifies everything it happens to lay its teeth on. Like an Alpine meadow eaten away by a flock of voracious sheep, the world smoothed down by the Average turns into a uniformly dull and dreary heath. Everything imprudently splashed on the treacherously smooth and peaceful surface of the Average disappears never to return; the Average gets its strength, indeed perpetuates its own existence, by disintegrating everything around and turning it into its own body, ever growing, never reaching its limits. The Average is not the only covetous and expansive entity; its distinctive feature, however, consists in gluttony being the only mode of survival open to it. It can either swallow and assimilate everything it comes in touch with, or die. For the Average, all the rest of the world divides neatly into the substance about to be swallowed and the enemy to be fought unremittingly and mercilessly. There is no room for fine distinctions and contemplating the hues and nuances of the canvas. Consisting himself of pure, shapeless generality, the petit-bourgeois cannot help but see his Enemy only as the Arch-Enemy, an omnipotent Satanic power, a generalized concentration of all his genuine and make-believe threats. It was the petit-bourgeois who clutched greedily at Dan Smoot's simple (since generalized) formula of the complexities of world politics: 'I equate the growth of the welfare state with Socialism and Socialism with Communism.'[76] Or read keenly the statistics of the John Birch Society's

*Bulletin*, which rated communist control over the U.S. as 20–40 per cent in 1958, 30–50 per cent in 1959 and 40–60 per cent in 1960 (the corresponding estimate for Britain in 1960 having been 50–70 per cent).[77] Or imbibe avidly the thrilling news of the all-in concentrate of the Enemy, in which religious rebels, West Indian streetsweepers, Harold Wilson, newspapermen, university teachers, civil rights enthusiasts, adversaries of the South African cricket team and student trouble-makers expediently lumped together and melted into one infernal substance.

The summary blending of everything bizarre and out-of-Average into one compound, easy to grasp, easy to spot, and powerful enough to keep high the necessary vigilance, results in a 'hysterical belief', defined by Neil J. Smelser as 'a belief empowering an ambiguous element in the environment with a gen-eralized power to threaten and destroy'.[78] It may seem that the stirring up of hysterical paroxysms would hardly serve as a healing device were the deep anxiety the malaise one sought to cure; rather than setting horror-stricken minds at rest, it would push the fear to well-nigh unbearable limits by inflat-ing the real or illusory danger. In fact hysteria is a medicine, and a very effective one at that. It mollifies illness in two ways. First, to quote Smelser again, by establishing some level of 'stability':

> Hysterical belief eliminates the ambiguity which gives rise to anxiety by positing a threat that is generalized and absolute. Thus the threat, originally only ambiguous and precarious, becomes certain to harm and destroy. In this way a hysterical belief structures the situation and makes it more predictable, even though the structuring process results in deep pessimism or terrible fears. In an ambiguous setting, a per-son is anxious because he does not know what to fear; holding a hysterical belief, a person at least believes he knows what he fears.

The phenomenon is much more general than the petit-bourgeois propensity to generalize his scare of the out-of-average, since, as the hero of *Darkness at Noon* has painfully learned, 'every *known* physical pain was bearable; if one knew beforehand exactly what was going to happen to one, one stood it as a surgical operation – for instance, the extraction of a tooth. Really bad was only the unknown.' Besides, however, hysteria is foolproof in coming to grips with the kind of anxiety which emanates from the presence of the slimy: by lumping it together with an overt, undisguised, allegedly well-known enemy, the hysterical belief deprives the slimy of its most venomous fang, the treach-erous lack of a distinctive shape, and so restores everything to its 'right' place, the integrity of the threatened ego included. In short, as Clyde Kluckhohn postulated in the case of one of these generalized, all-explaining enemies, 'one of the manifest "functions" of belief in witchcraft is that such belief supplies answers to questions which would otherwise be perplexing – and because perplexing, disturbing.'[79]

When discussing the right-wing social movements, 'which are premised on the assumption that humanity is being conquered by a powerful, pervasive conspiracy', Hans Toch shows that to the man in the street, who 'on occasion shows a distinct predilection for theories entailing plots',[80]

> in addition to providing a concrete target for tensions, conspiracies can simplify the

believer's system of reasoning and his conception of social causation. . . . In a conspiracy, causation becomes centralized (in that all events can be blamed on one group of plotters), and it is also integrated (because the plotters presumably *know* what they are doing and *intend* the consequences of their action).

The conspiracy theory meets the condition of generalization, which arises from the existential mode of the petit-bourgeois; the frequently stressed intimate link between the petit-bourgeois and right-wing radicalism is by no means coincidental. Orrin E. Klapp, however, draws our attention to alternative valves used to discharge the same excessive petit-bourgeois anxiety without calling upon a ruthless and omnipotent plot. People who 'do not really know what is wrong, especially when there is physical prosperity yet a sense of being cheated', may seek rescue from their deep-seated, yet indeterminate, anxiety in '"ego-screaming", concern with costume and self-ornamentation, style rebellion, concern with emotional gestures rather than practical effects, adulation of heroes, cultism, and the like'.[81] There is an evident difference in emphasis between the first and second solution; the first is outward-, the second is inward-oriented. The petit-bourgeois may try to bring into relief the alienness of the Other; he may as well set himself to work at the other end, attempt to bring out his own identity by reinforcing it with abundantly redundant warning signs. Whatever way is chosen, both intentions and results are strikingly similar: a neat and clear-cut demarcation of the 'we-they' watershed, enhancing the postulated and visible opposition between 'we', the universal, and 'they', the odd, the repellent, the unassimilable.

We have dealt so far with defensive mechanisms aimed at restoring or reinforcing the weakened or undermined barriers or identities, which is a typically right-wing praxis; or with devices meant to safeguard a brittle, inchoate identity of a new, unusual project, which is a distinctive feature of left-wing praxis. A new tendency however, one associated often with the concept of modernity, is gaining momentum in the Western world. In virtue of the natural propensity to classify everything bizarre into already meaningful divisions, this tendency is frequently described as a new specimen of the category already well assimilated in our world-image, either as a 'new left' or as 'neo-fascism'. In fact, the tendency in question hardly falls into either class. The reason why any attempt to identify it with one extreme of the spectrum is so easily challenged, and why counter-arguments can so swiftly be piled up against any offer of an unequivocal classification, is the fact that the features which mark off the discussed tendency are simply not located on the left-right axis. The tendency of modernity runs counter to both, and renders both their controversy and their joint argument with the supine, light-hearted leniency of liberalism rather obsolete. The tendency in question is not discriminated by the site on which it proposes to elevate the anti-sliminess redoubts and turrets; it denies the very need of the struggle. In fact, it denies the sliminess of the slimy; it is for bridging the unbridgeable, transcending the impassable, welding the unmixable. The project of the founding fathers of Surrealism, the pioneering movement of modernism, as it was described recently by Alfred Willener, may serve as a fairly typical pattern:[82]

To establish *contacts* between spheres that were hitherto regarded as foreign to one another, in order to create, from the resultant shock, the *overthrow* of sensibility. . . . There are no walls between different fields, or at least those separations that still survive can be knocked down and the work of knocking them down must be started.

One has, probably, to distinguish carefully the incisive formulations of the *avant-garde*, directed openly and unashamedly 'against thc totality of a well-functioning, prosperous society', against all hitherto sanctified principles of meaningful order (and so alienating the *avant-garde* from the masses and limiting the pool of its potential militants to 'active minorities, mainly among the young middle-class intelligentsia')[83] and the perhaps less spectacular and obtrusive, but deeper penetrating change gnawing at established popular habits. The 'active minority' *avant-garde* would go so far as to proclaim 'flip dismissal of linear time, of logic, of history itself' and to demand a 'new primitive life-style' which 'is surrender to a never-ending game: a game which must break even the rule that all rules must be broken'.[84] Granted the narcissistic lack of restraint of the *avant-garde* and the sadistic raptures it seems to find in putting the others' endurance to the test, the 'majority' is likely to be driven away into the self-delusion of the outdated, rusty protective armours; the over-zealous and uncompromising haste lavishly displayed by the *avant-garde* may, indeed, lead to the resurrection of the traditional petit-bourgeois responses to the situation of confusion and uncertainty, which will again render the genuine trends of modern society even less legible. Though understandable under the circumstances, to overlook the new patterns of praxis permeating modern life would be an unforgivable error of judgment. What seems to be emerging slowly and perhaps erratically is a new level of tolerance toward sliminess and, indeed, toward trespassing of vital frontiers of meaning. It is still far from clear whether only the specific, hitherto acknowledged and sanctified frontiers are the singled-out victims of the present semiotic upheaval; or whether the current turmoil presages a total revision of the past patterns of praxis. For the first time, however, there is at least a chance, however slim, that the principle 'la recherche de la paternité est interdite', proclaimed proudly by the Code Napoléon two centuries before its time, may turn into the new style of human thinking and action. It is still far too early to pass final judgment. If the chance materializes, human culture will face a revolution unmatched by the most drastic upheavals of the past, since the one aspect of it which has so far never been seriously challenged, and which has invariably emerged victorious and intact from the deep waters of revolutionary tumults and agitation, is the structure of human praxis.

### Culture and sociology

Culture has had an admittedly rough deal from sociology. When not whittled down to a 'branch-name' for what used to be traditionally considered the domain of the high-brow style (belles-lettres, refined music and arts, leisure activities) or stretched to embrace the totality of human and/or social existence, it is, at best, handled in a way which infallibly renders it redundant.

Brought into the realm of modern sociological discourse first and foremost via American cultural anthropology, the concept of culture had been adopted originally to express the theoretical-methodological premiss of the social systemic order as, above all, an accomplishment of internalized, shared, mutually congruent norms. The same routine monotonous, repeatable and predictable course of human interaction, with which the British anthropologists dealt successfully under the heading of the 'social structure', has been cognitively organized by their American colleagues on the plane of norms rather than actors. True, this fateful understanding of culture had been begotten in England. It was Sir Edward Tylor who invited social scientists to study the 'condition of culture', as 'a subject apt for the study of laws of human thought and action', which may account for 'the uniformity which so largely pervades civilization' as well as for its 'stages of development or evolution, each the outcome of previous history'.[85] But it had been mainly the half-century of the American experience and discussion which Kluckhohn and Kelly summed up in 1945, defining culture as 'an historically created system of explicit and implicit designs for living, which tends to be shared by all or specially designated members of a group at a specified point in time'.[86] It was by then a firmly established view among American anthropologists that culture 'exhibits regularities that permit its analysis by the methods of science',[87] i.e. it is an ordered, systematically behaving entity. Interpreted in the spirit of the already established American usage as 'mutuality of normative orientations', the notion of culture entered the Parsonian theory of action as, above all, the cultural *tradition*.[88] Whether as an object or as an element of the actor's orientation, culture is viewed here as a reality preceding the action, shaped and settled well before the actual action may indeed begin. Elaborating on the way in which the concept of culture is employed, Kluckhohn would describe it as 'a precipitate of history' and insist on its 'systemic character', resolutely observing that culture cannot 'be used as a conceptual instrument for prediction unless due account is taken of this systemic property'.[89] All along, the term 'culture', when used within the limits of thought drawn by Tylor's seminal ideas, conveys no information which the concept of the 'social system' as such would not contain. Like the notion of social system, the term 'culture' responds to the need to express the vague idea of the interlocking, dovetailing of elements of human life, of an intrinsic congruence of human individual biography as well as of consistency within the individuals' interaction; it stands for the hope of the essential predictability of the human responses to standard contingencies, the hope built on the assumption of the basically determined nature of human life activity.[90]

The veracity of the last statement is not immediately obvious. Is not the use of the term 'culture' indicative that man is being viewed as 'at one and the same time a slave to and the master of his own past creations'?[91] Are not the sociological addicts of culture only too keen on emphasizing the creative aspect of the cultural outfit? Has it not been commonly accepted that culture, as man's unique feature, stands in the first place for man's peculiar ability to create his own world? Is not the prominent place allotted to this ability considered the main and conscious advantage of the 'culturologist' approach over the inert mechanism of straightforward behaviouristic determinism?

On the second thoughts, however, the spuriousness of the element of activity, creativity, freedom, supposedly riveted onto the concept of culture, becomes transparent. The idea of creativity is habitually disposed of by a ritualized reference to the 'man-made' origin of everything cultural, as opposed to the 'natural'. Occasionally an additional circumstance is pointed out – the element of choice testified to by the apparent diversity of human ways and means. Neither reflection however adds much strength to the claim of the endemically 'activistic' nature of the culture concept. As far as the 'human origin' of culture is concerned, it supports human creativity as efficaciously as the fact of his fetters having been 'man-made' safeguards the freedom of the convict. Sir Peter Medawar had indeed captured the very gist of the 'manmade' argument in his announcement that the 'fundamental distinction between the Springs of Action in mice and men' (the one the concept of culture ordinarily stands for) is that 'mice have no traditions', which leads to the conclusion that only human evolution 'is mediated not by heredity' but by 'transfer of information through non-genetic channels from one generation to the next'.[92] The second reflection does not make much difference: human freedom of choice is duly acknowledged only in retrospect, when the decision has already been made and subsequently incorporated by the culture, i.e. when its consequences have begun to impress themselves on human behaviour with a potency reminiscent of that of nature. To be 'cultural' as distinct from idiosyncratic, aberrant, irregular and unfit for scientific treatment, an item must already be pinioned into some sort of orderly arrangement: it must exist as an element of *reality*, as conclusive accomplishment. Only such reality may be subjected to scientific scrutiny, and the scientific treatment of the phenomenon of culture has always been, and still remains, the unshakeable ambition of sociologists. In one of the most recent culturologists' professions of faith, David Kaplan and Robert Manners reluctantly admit that 'we must modify our desire for theoretical perfection and settle for something less than 100% certainty';[93] they cheerlessly agree with Anatol Rapoport that the social scientist's aim 'must be lower than that of the physicist';[94] but they would not budge if asked to accept that physics and sociology do not necessarily belong to one continuum, and that what separates them is of a more than quantitative nature. And they would violently object if someone attempted to question their certainty that physics supplied the unsurpassable ideal for all scholarly endeavours to emulate, if not in its methods and research strategy, then at least in the type of precision and power of prediction it had achieved and the capacity of control it armed men with.

Let us be clear as to the target of our attack. Much nonsense has been recently floating around about the philosophical status of modern science, thanks mainly to the zealous militancy of the converts to the specific, Schutzian version of 'phenomenology'. (It is seldom that these militants reach as deep as the works they pass judgment on with a naivety passing for self-assurance; their summary opinions on 'positivism' – and, one would suspect, their knowledge of it – are more and more often founded solely on quotations from Schutz and, by way of reciprocal reinforcement, from fellow-believers.[95] One cannot resist the temptation of a historical parallel. True, the precedents of similar behaviour are not particularly numerous in the history of science, but they are conspicuous in the history of churches, whether sacred or secular. Devoted Christians could learn the views of early critics of Christianity like Celsus only from the fragments quoted in the writings of the Fathers of the Church. As one of the Fathers, Tertullian, put it, 'After Jesus Christ we do not need curiosity, as after the Gospel we do not need inquiry'.) Neither Kaplan and Manners, nor the other authors whom we have quoted, represent some particular, narrowly circumscribed camp in modern science, which can be sensibly isolated from the rest of science by attaching to it a restrictive label, like, for instance, positivism. Their conduct, and the postulates these scholars put forth, are not only perfectly legitimate and typical of the modern science in its entirety, but they indeed constitute the only conduct and the only methodological programme admissible within the framework of science as it has emerged historically in the west. Modern science is the only heir and the only logical elaboration of the ancient Greek stance of Τέχνη, which assumed the objective, self-sustained existence of the cosmos to undergird the object-oriented manipulatory capacity and ambition of man. Francis Bacon's elaborate praise of the utility of science as the only secure fulcrum of technical knowledge, and Auguste Comte's celebrated stock phrase 'savoir pour prévoir, prévoir pour pouvoir', far from being just partisan pronunciamentos of a particular philosophical school, reflected faithfully the kind of attitude which stood at the cradle of science as such, and which still very much remains with us, permeating all scientific endeavour. Positive science in this sense, in the sense which had been given to the term by the author of the *Cours de philosophie positive* himself, is too wide and seminal a programme to be tapered to (or worse, mixed up with) the idiosyncratic and arbitrary banishment of the non-sentient entities by a Skinner. Its essential premises are still the cornerstones of science as a whole. The point should be accorded major importance, since it is not only the definitional subtlety which is at stake. The terminological fog generated partly by human forgetfulness, partly by the vicissitudes of the partisan struggle, has spread recently with a speed which outstrips any informed discussion.

The Baconian-Comtean programme of 'positive science' was meant, as has been aptly pointed out by Jürgen Habermas, as – above all – the 'release of knowledge from interest'.[96] This is not to say that the cognitive activity which ensued has been indeed detached from all human interests. The very idea of 'interest-free' (or, later, *wertfrei*) knowledge was inevitably predicated on the human utilitarian, practical intention. This knowledge was, from the very outset, a courageous *tour de force* aimed at discovering – inside the cosmic, self-sustained order – the guiding principles for successful human activity. Even when self-aware of its motivation, this knowledge must have hidden the actual impact of the motivating interest on the course of its enquiry, on the shape of the facts it recorded, on the structure of the theories it modelled; otherwise the purpose of the whole effort, and the authority of whatever came out of its pursuit, would have been killed in the cradle. Thus it had to turn a blind eye on its own work and tactfully, though steadfastly, refuse to focus its attention on the process of enquiry. It would have liked to have its looking glass (or at least to pretend to have it) thinned to the point of downright transparency; if possible, to dissolve it completely in the transcendental object, in which the sole authority and hope for secure and reliable knowledge are vested. It is not the human interest which is denied status in the realm of science: the interest can be, as it were, seen as the object of scientific enquiry – and in this case no objection would be raised as to its legitimacy. In both aspects in which values entered routine sociological investigation and discourse – as objects of action and as attitudes motivating this action[97] – they were, of course, permeated with human interest; but the interest they were imbued with was that of the human *objects* of enquiry. The scientific stance as such does not beg the question of the nature of the object under study, but it does resolve uncompromisingly the nature of the enquiring subject. It is the subject who must be *wertfrei* – the scientific ideal is there 'to provide the subject with an ecstatic purification from the passions'.[98] Nothing may stop the enquiring subject from resigning himself, obediently and willingly, to the unquestionable reality of the transcendental object.

One has to distinguish, therefore, between the adventitious features of this or another body of scientific practice or of this or another scientific philosophy on the one hand, and the necessary attributes of the scientific stance as such, universal enough to involve strategies as far apart as those of the empirical-analytic sciences and of hermeneutics on the other. Features like the inclusion or exclusion of the subjective experience of investigated human beings as admissible 'factual' evidence, circumscribing the body of percepts which are accorded the status of 'primary data', or the rules determining the way in which concepts must be linked to the primary data to be admitted to scientific discourse, belong to the first category; however radical and intransigent are the attitudes taken toward these matters, they still remain well within the vast territory of 'objective science' as delineated by the Baconian-Comtean seminal principles. Whereas the assumption of an unbridgeable abyss between 'abstract' Ought and 'real' Being, the acknowledgment of the unconditional supremacy of the Object in the process of cognition and verification, and the postulate of complete indifference, neutrality and dispassionateness on the part of the cognizing subject, constitute the second category; they are, indeed, indispensable constituents of the scientific attitude. The last postulate bears every sign of repressed self-awareness; but, as Habermas has rightly remarked, this false consciousness has an important protective function: remove the shield of self-deception, and nothing will be left to debunk and expose the incongruous absurdity of a 'Soviet' genetics or a 'Fascist' physics.[99] Positive science with all its assumptions – even with its obstinate and wilful self-blindness – is the only way in which the human interest in technical mastery may be gratified.

To accept this is not, however, to accept positivism, unless one defines positivism as the scientific attitude. Historically, positivism has been a once dominant school of philosophy asserting that science is the only knowledge worth our while, the only source of statements reliable enough to be worth human attention; that cognition is not a futile (or even deleterious) effort only if it is subordinated to the rules of positive science; and that there is nothing to be apprehended and cognitively appropriated apart from the kind of reality accessible via positive science and pivoted on its assumptions. Since the rule prohibiting the drawing of normative conclusions from assertions about reality has always been the cornerstone of positive science, there is an irreducible and inherent inconclusiveness in the positivist argument. Inevitably, positivism is a normative attitude; and this is the very kind of modality which it denigrates as cognitively superfluous and irrelevant. Disdainful of the means which could have supplied it with the kind of authority it arbitrarily granted to transcendental reality, positivism is doomed to carry on as an act of faith.

A strong case may be made for the supposition that positivism is the self-awareness of the alienated society. Indeed, one can see a striking congruence between the type of life generated by this society and the seminal positivist assumptions about the nature of the universe and the origin and function of knowledge.

The alienated society sharply distinguishes between the public and the private spheres of human life. But from this separation the private sphere emerges split into two parts, divided by a constantly widening, unbridgeable gap. The phenomenon called society is squeezed between the two halves, feeding on their breach, thriving on the incurability of the wound and foreclosing the meanings spontaneously generated in each half. The first half of the private sphere is the person's endowment with his unique work capacity; the second is the gratification of his unique needs. The natural link between the two having been irretrievably shattered, the only, inevitably vicarious, path leading from the first to the second runs now through the public sphere through the 'society'. The continuous and perennially inconclusive effort to plug the gap between the two and to restore their primeval unity may be seen as the inexhaustible fount of human concern with society and of the persistent tendency to hypostasize the social.

The separation of creation and control – the pith and marrow of alienation – lies at the basis of the reality of the society and of its mental image. The act of creation is the only way open to man to control his existence-in-the-world, to wit, to accomplish the double-pronged process of assimilation and accommodation.[100] With control plucked out from the act of creation and transplanted into the sphere of the transcendental, the truncated relic of human work presents itself to its subject as an act thoroughly emptied of its original and inborn meaning. The subjectivity itself becomes senseless and petty, since no obvious and self-imposing meaning is to be traced within the part of the life-process left as a private domain. The transcendental sphere of the public – 'the society' – becomes the sole abode of control. The only way in which a person may consummate his otherwise maimed, imperfect existence is to avail himself of the resources of control stocked in the sphere of the public. The subjective life-process of the person can be made complete only by turning the subject into the object of control; the person appropriates his illusory subjectivity only by acknowledging the unquestionable authority of the public.

The philosophy of positivism faithfully reflects this reality of the alienated world of humans. It makes a virtue of dissolving the cognizing subject in the transcendentality of the cognized object. It re-creates, in the idealized universe of Mind, what has been already accomplished in the reality of the human condition: the expedient of turning the better part of the subject into the object of authoritarian control and rendering the rest of it meaningless and irrelevant. The close harmony between the positivist view of the cognitive aspect of man's relation to his world and the alienated reality of its practical aspect constitutes probably the most important cause of the surprising vitality and impressive cogency of the positivist argument. It may be that the flourishing of *positive science* has its foundation (as Habermas would assert) in the immortality of human technical interest; the striking success of *positivism* as a world philosophy is certainly founded on the historical temporary suppression of subjective creativity expropriated from control, and on the reduction of creativity to the sheer technicality which has been the consequence of this suppression. The positivist ideas find indeed a warm and sympathetic response in the 'intuitive self-evidence', or whatever passes for it for a member of an alienated society; but this intuitive self-evidence does not emanate from a supra-temporal 'natural attitude' (or, rather, it seems only as if it does to the philosophical seekers of the Absolute); it 'simply means subjective certainty', as Piaget reminds us;[101] and subjective certainty, more often than not, may be traced back to the repetitiousness and coherence of commonsensical experience as illuminated and perceptively organized by commonsensical knowledge.

Positivism is, therefore, more than the philosophy of professional philosophers and the praxis of professional scientists. Its epistemological roots as well as axiological sprouts are intimately interwoven into the very texture of the human life-process in an alienated society. Just how pervasive are the basic tenets of positivism, owing to their firm roots in the alienated praxis, is amply demonstrated by the naive willingness with which many a critic of the positivist restrictive epistemology tacitly and docilely accepts the expedient of turning necessity into virtue: the way in which positivism reduces the subject's multi-faceted relation to his world (to his alienated world, I must constantly repeat) to its cognitive platform. The error, inspired by the restrictive practice of the positivist mind, consists in believing that the battle against positivism may be staged, fought and won on this plane only. The error is only too easily understandable in the circumstances when both positivism and its enemies wish to draw from and appeal to the same commonsense of the alienated society.

The tragedy of the anti-positivist departures, too half-hearted and diffident (regardless of the compensatory violence of their vocabulary) to debunk this error, consists in a dilemma of (*a*) either settling in the end for another science cut to the positivist measurements (with the supreme authority of the reality-object not questioned, and the cognitive foci only re-arranged); or (*b*) risking the dubious company of unsolicited and unwanted bedfellows, when going as far as rejecting not only positivist imperialism, but the idea of positive science itself. One can distinguish two essential categories in which to classify these ill-starred departures.

Both assume what a mind moulded by the alienated society and trained in the positivist commonsensical 'Self-obviousness' is expected to: that the relation between the individual and his world is – at least for the purpose of enquiry – an essentially cognitive one. To wit, it can be altered by an operation carried on entirely within the field of cognition. The struggle against positivism should be waged in terms of 'illusions', 'myths', 'hypostases', 'false consciousness' – and their repudiation. The frequency and intensity of anti-positivist broadsides are stimulated directly by dissatisfaction with the social reality itself rather than merely with its philosophical reflections; with the praxis of suppressed subjectivity and denigrated privacy rather than with the philosophers' epistemological neglect of the subject. But the triumph of positivist philosophy reaches its most spectacular heights in the efficiency with which this philosophy serves as a lightning-rod intercepting the thunderbolts aimed at the social world it has only described. With the missiles safely diverted from their intended trajectory, the main bulwarks of the alienated reality, the real foundation of the uncompromising supremacy of Being over Ought can and indeed does emerge unscathed.

Ardent as it is in challenging the specific make of positive social science which gained the ascendancy while elaborating on Durkheimian ideas, the 'epistemological person' stance stops short of questioning the actual seminal principles of positivism. The rejection of the positivist belief in the supremacy of Being over Ought is out of the question; so is any doubt as to the virtuousness of the investigator's value neutrality. Not only does the trend under discussion remain silent as to the virtues or vices of our, or any other, society, but it deprives itself of the intellectual means which would enable it to incorporate, as its legitimate component, any statement to this effect. Owing to the purely formal, substance-free nature of its basic categories, it can produce no fulcrum strong enough to carry an indictment of the shape historically assumed by any human society, and no yardstick one can wield to gauge a society's qualities. It is a revolution of thought the school is explicitly after. It is against fellow social scientists that the school releases its most passionate anger and most poisonous arrows. It is them that the school proposes to heal and reform. Otherwise it can hardly be seen how anything else may be re-shaped, even as the result of a completely successful and comprehensive thought-reform. As it is, the school does not propose to teach people how they *should* construct their society; its only aim is to discover how they in fact have done it since time immemorial, without any hope that the newly acquired self-awareness will make any difference to what is, allegedly, the epistemological, generic attribute of man-being-in-the-world. The only refreshing, albeit transient and ephemeral, impact of the intended thought-reform might have been another re-awakening of our already prolonged awareness of the alienated nature of the social world we live in; we are however invited to retreat to the pre-Marxian position, hopefully long since abandoned, from which the alienation, as well as its overpowering force, was seen, much in the style of *les philosophes*, as essentially a mental operation. It was to similar views propounded by Bruno Bauer and like-minded writers that Marx retorted: 'ideas never lead beyond the established situation, they only lead beyond the ideas of an established situation. Ideas can accomplish absolutely nothing. To become real, ideas require men who apply a practical force.'[102] And again:

> 'All forms and products of consciousness cannot be dissolved by mental criticism, by resolution into 'self-consciousness' or transformation into 'apparitions', 'spectres', 'fancies', etc., but only by the practical overthrow of the actual social relations which gave rise to this idealistic humbug; ... not criticism but revolution is the driving force of history, also of religion, of philosophy and all other types of theory.

This revolution Marx, in the course of the same argument, defined as 'the coincidence of the changing of circumstances and of human activity or self-changing'.[103]

The hope, if there is any in some militants of the school, of restoring the intimidated and mutilated subjectivity to its lost (or, for that matter, never appropriated) dignity by the means the school offers, is fatuous and futile. It was certainly not the philosophy of Comte or the methodological principles of Durkheim which subordinated the subjective world of the individual to the high-handed despotism of the 'objective' society. And the tyranny is not likely to vanish the moment Comte and Durkheim are publicly stigmatized and pilloried.

In one respect at least this anti-positivist departure seems to support the alienated world with more consequence and self-abandonment than its philosophical enemy. It shares with positivism the unremitting demand for neutrality and value-indifference in the cognizing mind. But it extends the field on which this rule is to hold to frontiers that the ordinary positivist, or rather the ordinary practitioner of positive science, would not dream of. The indifference of positive science is limited to abstemiousness toward values, ideals and everything else which the act of canonization of the transcendental reality has relegated to the extra-scientific wilderness of the Ought. But positive science will indignantly snub any advice to view with similar equanimity the problem of the true knowledge of 'reality' On the contrary, the entire project of positive science, and for that matter science as such, rests on an unshakeable belief in the essential possibility of selecting, from the multitude of contradictory accounts of reality, one account which is more truthful, adequate and trustworthy than all the others. The explorers of the 'epistemological person' would not settle for this. What has been revered as 'the social reality' by the positive social scientists is degraded to the status of a contingent, varying by-product of the 'typifying' work of the 'members'; but the most important point is that the attribute of reality is not predicated on this objective, palpable and perceptible, by-product (if it had been so, then the school under discussion would have been merely one of many current theories of societal process, hardly extraordinary in its rebelliousness); reality is the sole property of the views the members hold of the shared sphere of negotiation or 'ongoing accomplishment'. These views are, however, admittedly diverse; nothing is there in principle to stop them from being mutually contradictory. But nothing is there, either, to distinguish between a true and a false one; in fact, the school would be hard put to it to express the definition of truth in the language it considers legitimate. Not only the terms 'right' and 'wrong', but 'true' and 'false' as well are conspicuously out of place if squashed into its vocabulary. One cannot remain loyal to the school's axioms and make a statement that a specific 'definition of situation' is wrong; or, indeed, try even to pose a problem that a particular holder of a particular 'definition' has been cheated, hoodwinked, conned, double-crossed, duped, or – purely and simply – has revealed his gullibility or sheer stupidity. And so the school can offer little guidance to a person in quest of the lost purpose. When everything is equally valid, since 'experienced', nothing can be relied upon as the sure way out of the predicament.

The most intimate link between positivism and our alienated society has found its expression in the positivist profession of faith, that the only valid knowledge is the one void of interest and therefore *wertfrei*. To this complacent acquiescence to the human condition in which the control-stand of the life-process is beyond the reach of the person by whom this life is lived, the alleged challengers of positivism have subscribed in earnest. Their inroads against positivism have been misdirected to hit the positivist worship of objective truth – the only uncontroversial redoubt of the philosophy which supplied our civilization with its strongest asset – positive science. It seems as if recent challengers of positivism were set on leaching away the most valuable sediment of the positivist erosion of intellect, only to lay bare those seminal principles of the philosophy they supposedly condemn: those which owe both their origin and persistence to the reality of the alienated society.

No attack on these principles can be entirely successful if limited to philosophical criticism alone, if the positivist philosophy is singled out as the sole target, while the alienated society, to which it owes its buoyancy and its irresistible hold on common sense, is tacitly accepted as the unencroachable reality. Positivism stands and falls together with the society which lends cogency to its argument about the transcendental locus of all authority, whether practical or cognitive. The way toward dismantling the foundations of the positivist ascendancy does not lead through the questioning of the human right to fuse interest with knowledge, but through challenging the assumed monopoly of the 'real' as the source of valid knowledge. Which is not to say that the knowledge of the real is not valid; the 'natural' laws of political economy, Antonio Gramsci would say, hold well in so far as the human masses behave in the ordinary routine, monotonous, perfunctory way habitual in an alienated society; in so far as they do, one can easily rely on the apparent repetitiousness of the observed phenomena as the foundation of a trustworthy knowledge. But the allegedly secure basis goes topsy-turvy the very moment that the masses emerge from their comatose compliance and embark on an 'unusual', 'unlawful', 'improbable', 'unwarranted' adventure. Positive science may tell us little about these sudden spurts of mass creativity, much less 'predict' them the way it predicts the behaviour of a solution in a test-tube. Positive science is at its best when describing the real. It falls to its all-time low when asked to discuss the possible. Hopefully, positive science, with all its unquestionable accomplishments, is not the only knowledge human beings need and can create. It is here, we think, that the concept of culture comes in.

We started our present considerations with the complaint that the concept of culture as appropriated and employed by social science had been unduly tapered to cover only the predictable, routine, institutionalized aspect of human behaviour. This having been done, the phenomenon of culture has been successfully accommodated within the field of the 'transcendental reality', where it can be appropriately dealt with by positive science – and only by it. Positive science has found in the concept of culture a singularly agreeable relative, which looks like a condensed but wholesome epitome of the interest which – explicitly or implicitly – set the scientific project in motion. Kaplan and Manners, following the universally accepted usage, would describe culture as 'the primary mechanism through which man begins by adapting to and ends by controlling his environment'[104] – the well-nigh perfect statement of the utilitarian, submissive view of 'technical function' bred by the alienated society: you cannot achieve your ends unless you surrender to the authority of the real; then you will be able to control it, to wit, employ its rules to make whatever you think is best for you; to slice out, in other words, the fattest chunk for your personal use. Culture is an adaptation to the tough, inflexible reality which can be made usable only if adapted to. Repetitive declarations as to the 'creative' nature of this adaptation have a hollow ring insofar as the seminal paradigm of the transcendental, supreme and overpowering reality remains unchallenged. Creativity boils down to the sheer expediency, cleverness and dexterity which guileful humans display to turn an inhospitable environment to their advantage. The ingenuity of a stock dealer or an adroit merchant supplies the ready-made pattern for this specific kind of creativity which the harsh, cruel, gory alienated world makes the condition of human survival. But, as we wish to object together with Habermas,[105]

> society is not only a system of self-preservation. An enticing natural force, present in the individual as libido, has detached itself from the behavioural system of self-preservation and urges toward utopian fulfillment. . . . What may appear as naked survival is always in its roots a historical phenomenon. For it is subject to the criterion of what society intends for itself as *the good life*.

Human activity in the world transcends the sheer logic of survival in at least two important respects: the survival value of a project on which humans embark is ordinarily pushed well down the list of the criteria they apply to assess the project's desirability, and it is always an ideal state which *ought* to be achieved which makes them move, rather than the cognizance of what *can* be achieved.

This remarkable quality of the human species (and that is precisely the unique feature we wish to pinpoint when declaring that men are the only 'animals with culture') was long ago discussed at length by Marx.[106]

> It is true that the animal, too, produces. It builds itself a nest, a dwelling, like the bee, the beaver, the ant, etc. But it only produces what it needs immediately for itself or its offspring; it produces one-sidedly whereas man produces universally; it produces only under the pressure of immediate physical need, whereas man produces free from physical need and only truly produces when he is thus free; it produces only itself whereas man reproduces the whole of nature. Its product belongs immediately to its physical body whereas man can freely separate himself from his product. The animal only fashions things according to the standards and needs of the species it belongs to, whereas man knows how to produce according to the measure of every species and knows everywhere how to apply its inherent standard to the object: thus man also fashions things according to the laws of beauty.
>
> Thus it is in the working over of the objective world that man first really affirms himself as a species-being. This production is his active species-life. Through it nature appears as his work and his reality. The object of work is therefore the objectification of the species-life of man; for he duplicates himself not only intellectually, in his mind, but also actively in reality and thus can look at his image in a world he has created.

Human creativity is at its best when man is free – free of immediate necessity to secure the means of his survival, free of the poignant pressure of his physiological needs. The order of things is exactly the reverse of the one implied by the identification of culture and adaptive survival. It is not only untrue that man's creativity is solicited by the pressure of a hostile environment, but it is true that this creativity develops in full only when the pressure subsides or is done away with. The modern transformation of the same motif by Abraham H. Maslow comes immediately to mind: the distinction between 'deficiency needs', which humans share with other animals, and the 'needs of growth' ('Growth is seen not only as progressive gratification of basic needs to the point where they "disappear", but also in the form of specific growth motivations over and above these basic needs, e.g. talents, capacities, creative tendencies, constitutional potentialities'), which come to the fore only when deficiency motivations are disposed of. As long as the primary, animal, deficiency needs motivate man,[107]

> the primary aim of the organism is to get rid of the annoying need and thereby to achieve a cessation of tension, an equilibrium, a homeostasis, a quiescence, a state of rest, a lack of pain. . . . [On the contrary,] the appetite for growth is whetted rather than allayed by gratification. . . . Growth motives . . . maintain tension in the interest of distant and often unattainable goals. . . . The new experience validates *itself* rather than by any outside criterion. It is self-justifying, self-validating.

Only the growth motivations, like culture, are truly specifically human. The adaptive, survival-motivated, bustle of men is not-yet-fully-human; their banausic, enforced activities acquire human meaning only as clearing the ground for the genuine human way of being-in-the-world. Humanity is the only known project of rising above the level of mere existence, transcending the realm of determinism, subordinating the *is* to the *ought*. Human culture, far from being the art of adaptation, is the most audacious of all attempts to scrap the fetters of adaptation as the paramount hindrance to the full unfolding of human creativity. Culture, which is synonymous with the specifically human existence, is a daring dash for freedom *from* necessity and freedom *to* create. It is a blunt refusal to the offer of a secure animal life. It is – to paraphrase Santayana – a knife with its sharp edge pressed continuously against the future.

Culture stands, to put it in a somewhat different way, for what Erwin W. Strauss had in mind when he called man 'a questioning being', who 'breaks through the horizon of sensory phenomena' and 'transcends the immediate present'.[108] Or for what Maurice Merleau-Ponty meant by the 'ambiguous human dialectic': 'it is first manifested by the social or cultural structures, the appearance of which it brings about and in which it imprisons itself. But its use-objects and its cultural objects would not be what they are if the activity which brings about their appearance did not also have as its meanings to reject them and to surpass them.'[109] Culture constitutes the human experience in the sense that it constantly brings into relief the discord between the ideal and the real, that it makes reality meaningful by exposing its limitations and imperfections, that it invariantly melts and blends knowledge and interest; or, rather, culture is a mode of human praxis in which knowledge and interest are one. Contrary to the stance of positive science, culture stands and falls on the assumption that the real, tangible, sentient existence – the one already accomplished, sedimented, objectified – is neither the only nor the most authoritative; much less is it the only object of interested knowledge. The unfinishedness, incompleteness, imperfectness of the real, its infirmity and frailty, undergirds the status of culture in the same way as the unquestionable, supreme authority of the real buttresses positive science.

In an alienated society this inalienable nature of culture tends to be obliterated or concealed. With the centres of control removed safely far beyond a person's (*qua* person) reach, all protruding, unbridled, refractory postulates of culture present themselves as socially irrelevant, bizarre aberrations. As Herbert Marcuse put it,[110]

> the modes of thought and research which dominate in advanced industrial culture tend to identify the normative concepts with their prevailing social realization, or rather they take as norm the way in which society is translating these concepts into reality, at best trying to improve the translation; the untranslated residue is considered obsolete speculation.

The intellectual correlate of the tyranny of the transcendental reality in an alienated society is the fact that cultural postulates can retain their intellectual status and dignity only as alleged attributes or descriptions of reality. It is assumed that they are incorporated into the accomplished Being. Whatever stands out conspicuously enough to defy this assumption is banished into the realm of 'irreducible subjectivity', transformed into a purely personal, incommunicable affair, made into an eternal drama of solitary, tragic cravings of unfulfilled self, alleviated only by the consoling philosophy of the kind of freedom achievable apart from and in spite of societal realities; in this utterly personalized, implacably subjective garb it is chased away from the realm of culture as a collective project of humanity. It is deprived of the most important of all attributes of all culture: its critical capacity, based on its assumed and struggled-for supremacy over the real. Turning the unfulfilled content of culture onto the self-perfection and self-liberation of the subjective person means succumbing to the unswerving supremacy of the Real on the interhuman, societal plane. The positivist correlate of the alienated society, Marcuse would say,

> refers its concepts and methods to the restricted and repressed experience of people in the administered world and devalues non-behavioural concepts as metaphysical confusions. Thus the historical validity of ideas like Freedom, Equality, Justice, Individual was precisely in their yet unfulfilled content – in that they could not be referred to the established reality, which did not and could not validate them because they were denied by the functioning of the very institutions that were supposed to realize these ideas.

The historical role of culture lies in this denial and in the incessant effort to re-make these institutions. The culture may exist only as an intellectual and practical critique of the existing social reality.

Now sociology, as it emerged and took shape historically, is a positive science, eager to share all the hopes and anxieties of all other irreproachable academic disciplines. It accepts the universal validity of the criteria of science. It agrees with Weber that 'sociology is a matter of discovery, not of invention'.[111] It aims at the explanation of one kind of reality, whatever may be said about the distinctive features and uniqueness of this particular kind. Positivism has recently become a tag which it is fashionable and gratifying to attach to whatever one dislikes in the explicit or implicit methodological premisses of other sociologists; this circumstance should not, however, blunt our alertness to the truth that both genuine and imaginary positivists, as well as their *verstehende* adversaries, subscribe unreservedly to the founding principles of any positive science, such as value-neutrality or the causal nature of explanation (as Runciman aptly puts it, 'human action is not less explicable – indeed it is more so – when it follows from the self-conscious pursuit by the most effective means of a freely chosen end'[112]). Whether it is through the praiseworthy modesty of sociologists, or through their still unhealed inferiority complex, we usually tend to overlook and play down the vast amount of technically valuable knowledge that sociology has accumulated while remaining within the confines of positive science. Still, the more precise and technically adroit sociology becomes in its pursuit of factual record and scientific explanation, the more likely is the successive eruption of dissent, which always verges on not less than a total rejection of the sociological project. It seems as if an almost neurotic proclivity to self-abuse and self-intimidation has been riveted into the very structure of sociology as an intended science of human pursuit. It seems as if the development of sociology must be forever as devious and fraught with loops and retreats as it has been so far.

The strange and unique drama of the cyclical record of sociology is too trivial a fact to be dealt with at length. What, however, is less known, and understood still less clearly, is that most efforts to break loose from the wearisome revolutions of the treadmill in order to set sociology on straight tracks are inconclusive because they are, from the very outset, adulterated by a misunderstanding of the genuine nature of the sociological project. These efforts consist in endless re-locations of the reality-focus – from human situations to their definitions and back again. Whatever the current location of the focus, it is always put in front of the student as an accomplished, complete, intrinsically exhaustive reality, i.e. processed to the condition in which it can be handled by means of positive science. It always lays before the enquiring mind the task of grasping the human reality in its capacity (to paraphrase Hegel's notorious adage) as 'a corpse which was left behind by its living impulse'.[113]

The point is, however, that as far as human affairs are concerned, our belief that the cognitive horizon as circumscribed by this methodology is sufficient to embrace the totality of relevant topics can be upheld only on the assumption that the human world will indefinitely retain its 'natural' character, which is tantamount to the supposition that society will interminably remain alienated. Only then can the logic of human life continuously reinforce the plausibility of the supremacy of the Being over the Ought. Culture, as the critical rejection of reality, would then be reasonably seen not as an autonomous, well-founded and reliable brand of knowledge, but as – at the most – one of many objects of positive study. We would easily detect in this intellectual denigration of culture a mental reflection of its practical degrading. The disappearance of the sociological imagination, noted with sorrow and anxiety by Wright Mills, is but a necessary complement of a social reality which only too successfully defends its own structural principles. With control tools kept safely far beyond human reach, there is no difficulty in dissolving the cultural call for freedom, equality, vindication of subjectivity in a sanctification of alleged liberties, social equity and the spurious individualism of existing institutions. The same happens to the cultural stance as such, the future-oriented challenge of the present; outspoken praise of the future is whittled down to the acquisition of novelty – the future caught, materialized, encapsulated and riveted into the already-accomplished-and-finite present. The style of fleeting fads squeezed into the shallow immediacy of the present is substituted for the future-orientation of the dominating cultural norm. Some authors follow the ad-men in turning the hoax into public belief and calling 'future shock' what is merely the hollowness, tedium and amorphousness of a flattened present deserted and bereft of its meaning-bestowing culture. The result is 'the insecurity of modern progress which has strangely no past and no future and is thus obsessed with conformity'.[114]

Culture is the only facet of the human condition and of life in which knowledge of the human reality and the human interest in self-perfection and fulfilment merge into one. The cultural is the only knowledge unashamed of its partisanship and ensuing bias. It is the only knowledge, for that matter, which is bold enough to offer the world its meaning instead of gullibly believing (or pretending to believe) that the meaning lies over there, ready-made and complete, waiting to be discovered and learned. Culture is, therefore, the natural enemy of alienation. It constantly questions the self-appointed wisdom, serenity and authority of the Real.

It is our contention, therefore, that instead of considering the role of culture as one of the many categories – or, rather, objects – of sociological enquiry, we should rather fathom the vast cognitive space which the borrowing of the cultural stance by sociology may lay open. Assuming the cultural stance does not require rejection of the attitude which undergirds the project of positive science. But it does imply transcending the range of questions and methodological tools which this attitude condescends to legitimize. Without challenging the scientific pursuit of truth as a correspondence between knowledge and reality, the cultural stance refuses to acquiesce in the narrowing attitude of positive science and its claim that only the already-accomplished, sentient, 'empirical' reality, attainable in the way we appropriate the past, may be called in as the standard of valuable knowledge. While encompassing the future in its unique quality of irreducibility to the past, the cultural stance admits a multiplicity of realities. The set of universes it explores in the way the positive sciences investigate the real, contains also the possible, the potential, the desirable, the hankered after, even if as yet improbable worlds. This concept of sociology comes very close to the suggestion, rather hesitantly made seven years ago by Johan Galtung, of which, regretfully, our discipline seems to have taken little notice so far. It has been Galtung's idea that one of the sociologist's tasks[115]

> is not just to uncover mechanisms to account for the empirically existing, and to predict what will happen. It is also to escape from the straitjacket of the empirically existing and narrow range of the predictions – into the total range of the socially possible. That is, one assumes that the social order found empirically is only one among many orders possible, and even though it has been encountered, it should not be granted undue prominence. . . . There is no argument with the goal of prediction in science, but there should be, we feel, an argument with the kind of thinking that always asks: 'Given these conditions, what will happen?' and never asks 'What is the total range of possible variation, and what are the conditions for different states of the social system within this range to obtain?' Mechanisms must be uncovered, to explain and predict, and they are also indispensable in opening the range of possibilities for those who want to form a social order.

Culture is unique to man in the sense that only man of all living creatures is able to challenge his reality and to ask for a deeper meaning, justice, freedom, and good – whether individual or collective. Thus norms and ideals are not the remnants of metaphysical pre-rational thinking which blind man to the realities of his condition. On the contrary, they offer the only perspective from which this condition is seen as the human reality and acquires human dimensions. Only by adopting and appropriating this perspective can sociology ascend to the level of the humanities in addition to being a science; and resolve, therefore, the old and seemingly insoluble dilemma which haunts its history.

Then and only then can sociology come into direct touch with the human

praxis (the alternative, as Jules Henry put it, would be the following predicament: 'Everywhere the human disciplines run away from the humanity of
human beings. Obviously, then, human beings will turn away from the human
disciplines'). The praxis does not distinguish between the Is, which is 'over
there', powerful and unproblematic, and the Ought, which is 'inside here', feeble and doubtful. It does not distinguish, either, between knowledge, which is
reliable and praiseworthy, and interest, which is crippled and disgraceful.
Through culture man is in a state of constant revolt, in which, as Albert
Camus would say, he simultaneously fulfils and creates his own values, the
revolt being not an intellectual invention, but a human experience and
action.[116] In so far as the human praxis retains its nature of sacrilegious,
intractable revolt, the cassandric prophecies of a world deprived of meaning
can be, and indeed are, made light of and lose their sinister, paralysing
impact. The meaninglessness of the world is nothing but a twisted way of saying that the alienated society forced man into an obsequious surrender of the
right and ability to bestow meaning on the world – the faculties that only *he*
can entertain. A human knowledge, which limits its task and perspective to
those of positive science only, is guilty of supporting and reinforcing this de-
humanizing surrender.

As that maverick Marxist romantic, Anatol Lunacharsky, put it:[117]

> Marx could not possibly be a cosmocentric thinker, since the human practice was
> to him the only real world. . . . The only thing which is known indeed, is the human
> species – whose life, heartbeating, tensed energy we feel inside ourselves. That is for
> us the force which creates everything, the source of our encouragement, the living
> truth, beauty, good – and their root.

## Notes

1 *Elements of Social Organization*, London, 1951, p. 42.

2 Ibid., p. 211.

3 *Social Anthropology*, London, 1951, p. 20.

4 *The Little Community, Viewpoints for the Study of a Human Whole*, University of Chicago Press, 1955, p. 46.

5 *Anthropology*, New York, Harcourt, Brace, 1948, pp. 293–4.

6 *Psychology*, New York, World Publishing Co., 1948 (originally 1892), p. 176.

7 And thus we leave aside the initial statements of existentialism, particularly Kierkegaard's, which are, precisely, statements of irrelevance of the issue of 'subjective essences' to social sciences – which amounts to a declaration that a sociology which selects them as its methodological principle is not possible.

8 Wilhelm Dilthey, *Patterns and Meaning in History*, ed. H. P. Rickman, New York, Harper & Row, 1962, p. 105.

9 Ibid., pp. 123, 121.

10 The superorganic' (originally 1917), in *The Nature of Culture*, University of Chicago Press, 1952, p. 41.

11 *The Science of Culture*, New York, Farrar, 1948, p. xviii.

12 *The Elementary Forms of Religious Life*, English trans. by J. W. Swain, London, Allen & Unwin, 1968, pp. 422–3.

13 *Social and Economic Organization*, English trans. by A. M. Henderson and Talcott Parsons, New York, Free Press, 1969, pp. 88 ff.

14 *Cultural Sciences, Their Origin and Development*, University of Illinois Press, 1963, pp. 131–3.

15 Ibid., p. 134.

16 Cohabiting within the same, patently inconsistent, commonsense with another naive assumption of a self-sustained objectivity of the world.

17 Marx's *Theory of Alienation*, London, Merlin, 1970, p. 279.

18 Cf. *Alienation*, London, Allen & Unwin, 1971, p. 74.

19 *Elements of Semiology*, English trans. by Annette Lavers and Colin Smith, London, Jonathan Cape, 1969, pp. 56–7.

20 *Messages et signaux*, Paris, Presses Universitaires de France, 1966, pp. 20, 26.

21 *Les Structures élémentaires de la parenté*, Paris, Presses Universitaires de France, 1949, p. 96.

22 Ibid., pp. 36, 56.

23 *Cosmos and History*, New York, Harper, 1959, pp. 9, 57.

24 'Anthropological aspects of language: animal categories and verbal abuse', in *New Directions in the Study of Language*, ed. Eric H. Lenneberg, University of Chicago Press, 1964.

25 Cf. Nathan Stemmer, 'Some aspects of language acquisition', in *Properties of Natural Languages*, ed. Yehoshua Bar-Hillel, New York, Reidel, 1971, pp. 208 ff.

26 Innate approach and escape tendencies respectively, cf. *Animal Drive and the Learning Process*, 1930. Also John M. Butler and Laura N. Rice, 'Adiance, self-actualization and drive theory', in *Concepts of Personality*, ed. J. N. Wepman and R. W. Heine, London, 1964, pp. 81 ff.

27 Cf. Lucien Lévy-Bruhl, *La Mentalité primitive*, Paris, Presses Universitaires de France, 1947.

28 'Anthropological Aspects of Language' in Lenneberg (ed.), op. cit., pp. 38–9

29 More considerations relevant to this topic in Z. Bauman, *Kultura i Spoleczenstwo* (*Culture and Society*), Warsaw, Panstwowe Wydawnictwo Naukowe, 1966, chap. 3.

30 'Anthropological Aspects of Language', in Lenneberg (ed.), op. cit., p. 63.

31 *Social Change*, London, 1958, p. 108.

32 Morton Grodzins, *The Loyal and Disloyal, Social Boundaries of Patriotism and Freedom*, University of Chicago Press, 1956, p. 6.

33 Philip Mayer, 'Witches', in *Witchcraft and Sorcery*, ed. Max Marwick, Harmondsworth, Penguin, 1970, pp. 47, 55, 61.

34 Cf. 'On Human Behaviour considered "dramatistically"', in *Permanence and Change*, Los Altos, California, Hermes, 1954.

35 *The Devils of Loudun*, Harmondsworth, Penguin, 1971, pp. 124–5.

36 Robert Michels, *Der Patriotismus, Prolegomena zu seiner soziologischen Analyse*, Munich, Duncker und Humblot, 1929, p. 120.

37 'The stranger', in *Collected Papers*, vol. II: *Studies in Social Theory*, The Hague, Nijhoff, 1967, pp. 95–6.

38 Ibid., p. 104.

39 Maurice Natanson, 'Knowledge and alienation, some remarks on Mannheim's sociology of knowledge', in *Literature, Philosophy, and the Social Sciences*, The Hague, Nijhoff, 1962, p. 170.

40 Cf. *The Rise of the Greek Epic*, Oxford, 1907, pp. 78 ff.

41 'Human migration and the marginal man', *American Journal of Sociology*, vol. 33, 1928, pp. 881–93.

42 In a book under the title which itself tells the story: *Weimar Culture: The Outsider as Insider*, New York, Harper & Row, 1969.

43 *The Marginal Man: A Study in Personality and Culture Conflict*, New York, Scribner, 1969, pp. 154–5.

44 *Holy Prayers in a Horse's Ear*, Crown, 1952. Quoted from *Sociology through Literature*, ed. Lewis A. Coser, Englewood Cliffs, N.J., Prentice-Hall, 1963, pp. 319, 320, 323.

45 Cf. G. K. Zipf, *Human Behaviour and the Principle of Least Effort*, New York, Addison-Wesley, 1949.

46 Leonard Broom, Bernard J. Siegel, Evon Z. Vogt, James B. Watson, 'Acculturation: an exploratory formulation', *American Anthropologist*, vol. 56, 1954.

47 Cf. *Socjologia Wychowania* (*Sociology of Education*), vol. I: *Wychowujace spoleczen'stwo* (*The Educating Society*), Lwów, Książnica Atlas, 1928.

48 Quoted from Louis L. Snyder, *The Idea* of *Racialism*, Princeton, Van Nostrand, 1962, p. 164. The two cases do not obviously belong to the same functional category, since in the German context Jews themselves were slimy and since the intention of the Nürnberg rulings was to mark the marginals clearly rather than to prevent the situation of marginality from arising.

49 Margaret T. Hodgen, *Early Anthropology in the Sixteenth and Seventeenth Century*, Philadelphia, University of Pennsylvania Press, 1946, pp. 434, 257, 258.

50 There is a lucid account of what happened to the Jewish European communities with the advent of the modern era in: Howard Morley Sachar, *The Course of Modern Jewish History*, New York, Dell, 1958, chapter I: 'The Jew as Non-European'.

51 It is indeed illuminating how often politicians (particularly those of a rightist, petit-bourgeois flavour), perhaps sensing intuitively the resentment their clientele feels to the unorderly, make the point of the insidious vagueness and indefinability of 'the enemy'. La Rocque offered his leadership to the masses to combat not less than 'les grandes angôisses de l'univers contemporain' (*Le Flambeau*, September 1932). Drieu la Rochelle advertised the reassuring acumen of Doriot by emphasizing that he 'met la main' on 'grandes forces anonymes et aveugles' (*L'Emancipation nationale*, April 1937). Quoted from J. Plumyère et R. Lassierra, *Les Fascismes français* 1923–1963, Paris, Editions du Seuil, 1963.

52 In L. L. Snyder, op. cit., p. 76.

53 In *Beyond the Frontier, Social Process and Cultural Change*, ed. Paul Bohannan and Fred Plog, New York, Natural History Press, 1967, pp. 124, 134.

54 *La France juive*, English trans. by R. H. S. Philipson in *The French Right,* ed. J. S. McClelland, London, Jonathan Cape, 1970, p. 103.

55 Cf. Hans Kohn, *The Mind of Germany, The Education of a Nation*, New York, Harper & Row, 1965, pp. 77, 94.

56 Joseph de Maistre, in J. S. McClelland (ed.), op. cit., pp. 41–2.

57 Édouard Drumont, ibid., p. 88.

58 Cf. p. 695 of the French original; pp. 600 ff. of the English translation, *Being and Nothingness*, London, Methuen 1969.

59 *Purity and Danger*, London, Routledge & Kegan Paul, 1966, pp. 68–9.

60 Ibid., p. 115.

61 *Biology and Knowledge*, English trans. by Beatrix Walsh, Edinburgh University Press, 1971, p. 212.

62 Ibid., p.123.

63 'Magical hair', in *Myth and Cosmos, Readings in Mythology and Symbolism*, ed. John Middleton, New York, Natural History Press, 1967, p. 98.

64 'Verbal and bodily rituals of greeting and parting', in *The Interpretation of Ritual, Essays in honour of I. A. Richards*, ed. J. S. La Fontaine, London, Tavistock, 1972, p. 3.

65 'Limits to functionalism and alternatives to it', in *Theory in Anthropology*, ed. Robert A. Manners and David Kaplan, London, Routledge & Kegan Paul 1969, p. 199.

66 Cf. Francesca Cancian, 'Functional analysis of change', in *Theory in Anthropology*, pp. 204–12.

67 *Biology and Knowledge*, trans. by Beatrix Walsh, Edinburgh University Press, 1971, pp. 122–3.

68 'Biological bases of aggression', in *Violence and the Struggle for Existence*, ed. D. N. Daniels, M. F. Gilula, F. M. Ochberg, New York, Little, Brown, 1970, p. 43.

69 Cf. *Field Theory and Social Science*, New York, Harper, 1951, pp. 186, 57.

70 Cf. 'Introduction to hostility in small groups', in *The Natural History of Aggression*, ed. J. D. Carthy and F. J. Ebling, New York, Academia, 1964.

71 Cf. the remarkable comparative study by Irenäus Eibl-Eibesfeldt, *Love and Hate*, London, Methuen, 1971.

72 *Mythologies*, English trans. by Annette Lavers, London, Jonathan Cape, 1972, p. 129.

73 *The Nature of Prejudice*, New York, Doubleday, 1958, p. 249.

74 *Mythologies*, trans. by A. Lavers, p. 152.

75 Ibid., p. 151.

76 Quoted from Daniel Bell (ed.), *The Radical Right*, New York, Doubleday, 1964, pp. 15–16.

77 Quoted from Alan F. West, 'The John Birch Society', in *The Radical Right*, ed. Daniel Bell, p. 243.

78 *Theory of Collective Behavior*, New York, Free Press, 1963, p. 84.

79 *Navaho Witchcraft*, Kluckhohn, Bacon Press, 1962. Cf. Marwick (ed.), *Witchcraft and Sorcery*, New York, Penguin, 1970, p. 221.

80 The Social Psychology of Social Movements, London, Methuen, 1971, pp. 45, 51–2.

81 *Collective Search for Identity*, New York, Holt, Rinehart & Winston, 1969, p.vii.

82 *The Action-image of Society*, London, Tavistock, 1970, pp. 218–19.

83 Herbert Marcuse, *An Essay on Liberation*, Harmondsworth, Penguin, 1972, p. 57.

84 In *Bamn*, ed. P. Stansill and D. Z. Mairovitz, Harmondsworth, Penguin, 1971, p. 170.

85 Edward B. Tylor, *Primitive Culture*, vol. 1, London, Murray, 1891, p. 1.

86 Cf. 'The concept of culture', in *The Science of Man in the World Crisis*, ed. Ralph Linton, Columbia University Press, 1945, pp. 78–107.

87 Melville J. Herskovitz, *Man and His Works*, New York, Knopf, 1948, p. 625.

88 Cf. *Toward a General Theory of Action*, New York, Harper, 1962, pp. 7, 16.

89 Cf. 'The study of culture', in *The Policy Sciences*, ed. Daniel Lerner and Harold D. Lasswell, Stanford University Press, 1951.

90 There is, to be fair, one aspect in which the culture concept does add something to the notion of the 'social system': like many other 'residual concepts' of a similar kind, it serves a useful role whenever the need arises to account for the deviations or, merely, variability inexplicable within the framework of the chosen basic attributes of the system. For these 'irregularities', as seen from the 'social system' theoretical perspective, the cultural contingencies are usually – and conveniently – held responsible.

91 Lewis A. Coser and Bernard Rosenberg, *Sociological Theory*, New York, Macmillan, 1964, p. 17.

92 Cf. P. B. Medawar, *The Uniqueness of the Individual*, London, Methuen, 1957, pp. 141–2.

93 *Culture Theory*, Englewood Cliffs, N.J., Prentice-Hall, 1972, p. 15.

94 'Various meanings of theory', in *Politics and Social Life*, ed. N. W. Polsby, R. A. Dentler and P. A. Smith, Boston, Houghton Mifflin, 1963, p. 79.

95 One can find an almost laboratory-clean example of this hardly scholarly conduct in *New Directions in Sociological Theory*, by Paul Filmer, Michael Philipson, David Silverman and David Walsh, London, Collier-Macmillan, 1972.

96 *Knowledge and Human Interest*, Heinemann, 1972, p. 306. English trans. by Jeremy J. Shapiro.

97 Cf. e.g. William L. Kolb, 'The changing prominence of values in modern sociological theory', in *Modern Sociological Theory*, ed. Howard Becker and Alvin Boskoff, New York, Dryden Press, 1957, pp. 93–132.

98 *Knowledge and Human Interest*, p. 306.

99 Ibid., p. 315.

100 On the dialectics of the process, see Jean Piaget, *La Naissance de l'intelligence chez l'enfant*, Neuchâtel, Éditions Delachaux et Niestlé, 1959. Also published as *The Origin of Intelligence in the Child*, trans. M. Cook, London, Routledge & Kegan Paul, 1953.

101 *Insights and Illusions* of *Philosophy*, London, Routledge & Kegan Paul, 1972, p. 20. English trans. by Wolfe Mays.

102 K. Marx, F. Engels, *The Holy Family*, Moscow, 1956, p. 160.

103 K. Marx, F. Engels, *The German Ideology*, Moscow, 1968, pp. 51, 660.

104 *Culture Theory*, p. 77.

105 *Knowledge and Human Interest*, pp. 312–13.

106 *Early Texts*, ed. D. McLellan, Oxford University Press, 1971, pp. 139–40.

107 *Toward a Psychology of Being*, Princeton, Van Nostrand, 1962, pp. 24, 27–9, 43.

108 *Phenomenological Psychology*, London, Tavistock, 1966, p. 169. English trans. by Colin Smith.

109 *The Structure of Behaviour*, London, Methuen, 1963, p. 176. English trans. by Alden L. Fisher.

110 'A redefinition of culture', in *Science and Culture*, ed. Gerald Holton, Boston, Houghton Miffin, 1965, p. 225.

111 W. G. Runciman, *A Critique of Max Weber's Philosophy of Social Science*, Cambridge University Press, 1972, p. 16.

112 Ibid., p.17.

113 'A corpse which had left behind its living impulse', Hegel, *The Phenomenology of Mind*, London, Allen & Unwin, 1964, p. 69.

English trans. by J. B. Baillie.

114 *Sociology as a Skin Trade*, p. 19.

115 In *Sociological Theories in Progress*, vol. I, ed. Joseph Berger, Morris Zelditch Jr. and Bo Anderson, Boston, Houghton Mifflin, 1966, p. 179.

116 Cf. Thomas Hanna, *The Thought and Art of Albert Camus*, New York, Henry Regnery, 1958, p. 79.

117 *From Spinoza to Marx* (orig. 1925). Quoted from the Polish edition in *Pisma Wybrane*, vol. 1, Warsaw, Książka i Wiedza, 1963, p. 110.

# SUBJECT INDEX

# NAME INDEX